WMG WRIT

BUNDLE ON BUSINESS

A WMG WRITER'S GUIDE

KRISTINE KATHRYN RUSCH & DEAN WESLEY SMITH

WMG
PUBLISHING

CONTENTS

BUNDLE ON BUSINESS

USA TODAY BESTSELLING AUTHOR

DEAN WESLEY SMITH

HEINLEIN'S RULES

FIVE SIMPLE BUSINESS RULES FOR WRITING

A WMG WRITER'S GUIDE

For all the writers who dare to follow these business rules. Have fun.

INTRODUCTION

In almost 150 published novels (over one hundred with traditional publishers), I have always followed Heinlein's Business Rules. And in hundreds and hundreds of short stories, I have followed the five rules as well.

For well over thirty years now, actually, I have done my best to stay on Heinlein's Rules. I must admit, I slipped at times, but I'll explain why later on in the book. And how I climbed back on.

So how did I get to these rules? A little about my personal story first.

I started writing at the age of 24 in 1974.

I had hated writing up until that point, but I had to take some English credits to get my degree in architecture, so I took a poetry class for non-majors.

My poems were pretty much hated and the professor called them "commercial." At that point, I had no idea what she was talking about, but it sounded insulting and I was getting a "C" in the class.

Commercial seemed very, very bad.

Then as an assignment, she had her entire class mail a poem to a major national college poetry competition. One of my "commercial" poems won second place and paid me one hundred bucks. The professor had never had a student even get into the book, let alone win.

And I had just made more money than she had total with all of her poetry sales.

Oh, oh... To say I was not popular in the English Department would be an understatement.

But I found writing poems fun and started mailing them out and selling them to top literary journals around the country. Great fun. Seemed major literary magazines liked commercial.

Sold around fifty or so in one year.

And along the way, I thought it would be a lark to write a short story.

So on my trusty electric typewriter, I banged out a 1,000-word story, and didn't rewrite it, just sent it to a horror semi-pro magazine.

They bought it.

I did it again.

They bought the second one.

Spring of 1975 was when things went really wrong. I figured since I was having fun with writing stories, I should learn more about how to write stories, even though I had sold my first two.

So down I went into the myths of writing. (Add bubbling sounds of a person going underwater for the last time.)

I heard I needed to rewrite at least three or four times, so I did, even though I hated to type.

I heard I had to write slow to make it good, so I did, producing exactly two short stories a year for the next seven years.

And every story I thought was gold, a perfect masterpiece of fine art.

All of them were form rejected. And I made it worse by sending each story out only once or twice.

I was convinced the editors were too stupid to see my brilliance.

The two stories I had not touched or rewritten and wrote fast had sold, but the reality was I was too stupid to understand that. I believed in the myths and would defend them, by golly.

But after seven years, by the fall of 1981, I was very, very discouraged. I started looking around at how the writers I admired did what they did.

Bradbury, Silverberg, Ellison, all wrote fast, one draft, and never rewrote past a few minor corrections. And I studied the old pulp writers

I admired. Same thing. And I dug through the stories of the literary writers like Hemingway and others. Same thing.

Then by chance, I ran across an edition of *Of Worlds Beyond: The Science of Science Fiction Writing.*

Edited by Lloyd Arthur Eshbach, published in 1947, the book had articles in it by John Taine, Jack Williamson, A.E. van Vogt, L. Sprague de Camp, E. E. "Doc" Smith, John W. Campbell, Jr., and Robert A. Heinlein.

All of the articles are forgettable, sadly, including Heinlein's article, except for the last four paragraphs.

He starts the last four paragraphs with this:

"I'm told that these articles are supposed to be some use to the reader. I have a guilty feeling that all of the above may have been more for my amusement than for your edification. Therefore I shall chuck in as a bonus a group of practical, tested rules, which, if followed meticulously, will prove rewarding to any writer."

Then in one more paragraph he lists his "Business habits."

1. You must write.

2. You must finish what you start.

3. You must refrain from rewriting except to editorial order.

4. You must put it on the market.

5. You must keep it on the market until sold.

Then Heinlein said this:

"The above five rules really have more to do with how to write speculative fiction than anything said above them. But they are amazingly hard to follow—which is why there are so few professional writers and so many aspirants, and which is why I am not afraid to give away the racket! ..."

I finally understood completely what I had been doing wrong for seven long years. And why my first two stories had sold.

Duh.

So on January 1st, 1982, I made a resolution to write a story per week, following Heinlein's Rules, and mail the story and keep it in the mail.

I wrote 44 stories that first year and started selling regularly in early 1983 and have never looked back.

And stayed focused on those five rules to this day.

Why So Difficult?

The reason these rules are so hard is that they fly into the face, solidly, of what every English teacher on the planet teaches. And has taught from even before Heinlein wrote the rules down.

But remember, English teachers are there to do the almost impossible job of helping students gather knowledge about the language. **They are not there to help a student become a professional fiction writer.**

So these simple five business rules smash right into all that learning and teaching we all had as regular English students.

And with the modern world of computers, rewriting is easy, much easier, let me tell you, than it was on a typewriter. So not doing it is even more difficult.

Also, these five rules smash into so many writing myths, it will take most of this book to just detail out how each rule will cause many people to be uncomfortable.

Or even angry.

If one of these rules makes you angry, you need to check in with yourself. Your critical voice is really, really having issues and trying to stop you.

So over the course of this book, I'm going to work through each of the five rules, explaining why the rule is important to becoming a professional fiction writer, how missing a rule stops millions of writers, and how to use the rule in this modern world to access your creative voice and bring fun into your fiction writing.

One note: This is a book about fiction writing. This book is designed to help you on the road to being a professional fiction writer. This does not apply to nonfiction writers or writers of critical essays and the like.

Heinlein was talking about fiction writing. Please keep that clearly in mind.

In 1947, Robert A. Heinlein "...gave away the racket!"

But also, as he said, almost no one can follow these five business rules.

On the front the card was divided into six panels. Each panel showed this mouse sweating to push this huge elephant up a hill.

And with each panel the elephant got higher on the hill.

I opened the card and there, inside, was the elephant sitting at the top of the hill and the mouse looking down at a herd of elephants in valley below.

The caption on the card said, "**Congratulations! Now, do it again.**"

Exactly.

Now, almost thirty years later (I sold that first novel in May of 1987) I am still having a great time moving those elephants to the top of the hill, one right after another.

Writers are people who write.

I am a writer.

And thanks to Heinlein's Rules, especially Rule #1, I make my living writing fiction.

And I have since 1987.

CHAPTER THREE

Still working on rule number one.

Rule #1: You Must Write.

Back in 1982, when I climbed onto my challenge to use Heinlein's Rules and write a story per week and mail each story every week, I had one major issue that I fought.

Fear.

No idea what I was afraid of, but the fear was real.

On December 31st, 1981, my thinking was that every story had to be perfect, had to be worked over and over before I dared send it out. And it had to be written slowly and carefully to be good. I believed everything English teachers taught me.

Hook, line, and sinker.

One day later, January 1st, 1982, I went to Heinlein's Rules, not rewriting, writing a story and just mailing it after fixing typos.

Cold turkey.

So from that moment forward, I thought that every story I sent out was crap. Total crap.

I didn't just think that, I believed it completely.

I had no doubt. None.

I was still in the "must be perfect" mode (kidding myself that I knew what perfect even was, of course).

But I was going to give the Heinlein's Rules challenge a try because so many major writers wrote that way and I had had no luck at all the other way for seven years.

So week after week, I mailed off stories I thought sucked. Oh, I did my best on them, made sure they were as typo-free as possible, but I spent no time on them as I had with my precious two-stories-per-year gems that sat molding in files.

And fairly quickly the form rejections turned to personal letters and then to nice letters from editors. Shock!

Then early in the second year I started selling. I sold to *Writers of the Future, Oui Magazine, Gem Magazine*, and to a Damon Knight edited anthology. (You can still read my story in volume #1 of *Writers of the Future.*)

And the sales kept rolling in.

I still thought every story I wrote was crap.

Every one of them.

But I was starting to catch a clue that if I just let my subconscious tell the story and stay out of its way, my stories were pretty good.

Also, I kept learning and seeking out details of advice that made sense with my new way of approaching things.

What was also happening at writing a story per week was that I was practicing. I wrote more in the first fifteen weeks of 1982 than I did in the previous seven years.

Any wonder my stuff got better?

You Must Write.

I had figured out a way to do that.

Dare to be Bad

One fine day during that first year, I was complaining to the great fantasy writer Nina Kiriki Hoffman about how I felt I was mailing out crap every week. Sure, I was staring to get nice letters from editors, but I still couldn't get past the training of wanting to make every story "perfect."

And I felt like I often wrote stories too quickly, so they couldn't be good.

Yup, even six months or so into the challenge of following Heinlein's Rules, I was still lost in the myths. Completely.

Nina was living above my bookstore and she was doing the same challenge I was. We had bet each other to get a new story per week out.

Now I was in law school, had a job tending bar, and I owned and ran a bookstore. I was married and I had no time to write a story per week, but I was doing it.

Nina was still in college. She had no time either. But she was doing it also.

So in response that day to my complaining about how I felt I was mailing out crap, Nina basically said, "It takes more courage to try something and fail than to not try at all."

We talked about how true that was, and Nina coined the phrase "Darc to be bad."

It takes more courage to write and put the story out than it does to only talk about writing and not do it. You have to dare to fail sometimes.

So I took that saying and stenciled it in big letters and tacked it on the wall over my typewriter in my bookstore.

Dare to be bad.

What that saying did to help me seemed critical in one area. That saying got me past the fear of writing.

Rule #1: You Must Write.

What stops most people isn't lack of time, it's fear.

Committing words to paper means you might have to show them to someone. The words might fail; you might be found wanting.

So it is easier to let the fear stop you before you even get to Rule #1.

Most people who say they would like to write are just too afraid and don't know how to get past the fear.

The "Dare to be Bad" saying helped me jump past the fear.

And what that ultimately did was allow my subconscious to do the work.

My job became, fairly quickly, staying out of the way of my subconscious and just mailing the final product, no matter what my conscious brain thought of it.

That's right. I have trained my critical front brain to just stay out of the way of the storyteller that is my back brain.

Easier said than done, and still a constant fight.

To this day, when I hand a story or a novel to Kris, I believe it is crap. I have learned my critical judgment means nothing when it comes to my own work.

And when Kris hands me something she wrote and says it sucks, I know I am in for a real treat.

Why?

Because if Kris's critical brain is afraid of something she wrote, that means she took chances, went to places she had never been before, took risks with the story or the writing.

And she knows that even if she thinks the story sucks, she needs to release it to someone who has perspective.

Kris won a Hugo Award for her editing, and yet with her own work, she can't judge it.

No writer can.

So does that mean the fear isn't real that we all feel?

Nope. It's a real fear.

Trust me, I feel it with every story or novel I finish.

But the only repercussion on the negative side is that you allow the fear to win. If you release the story, you quickly come to see that the fear is baseless.

Doesn't make it feel any less real, however.

And it is this fear of some made-up repercussion that stops most of the 90% of writers who say they want to write and can't find the time.

Anyone can find the time to write a little every day.

But only about 1 in 10 can figure out a way, as I did, to climb past the fear, or just live with the fear of failure by writing.

It is better to write and fail then not write at all.

Rule #1. You must write.

Dare to be Bad.

You might discover along the way just how good a storyteller your subconscious really is.

I did.

CHAPTER FOUR

Moving now to the second rule.

Rule #2: You Must Finish What You Write.

Say 9 out of 10 people who claim they want to write are wiped out by Rule #1 because they "just can't find the time."

If that is the case, then my guess is that another half of the remaining writers are stopped cold by Rule #2.

Now, I have to be honest, I never had an issue with this rule, so I mostly just ignored it. I always finished what I wrote. Part of that was the early challenge to mail a story per week, but mostly I just hate leaving things unfinished.

So until Kris and I started teaching workshops, I had no idea how really deadly this not-finishing-projects was to many, many writers. I just had no idea, because it is not my problem.

So I talked with a lot of writers over the last fifteen years about various aspects of this problem of not finishing.

And I started watching all the excuses people give for not finishing, and it became clear how really deadly this rule is for many.

At first I thought it was a craft problem writers had. I thought maybe writers didn't understand the ending structure, or how to build to an end, or even how to see an ending.

Sure, there were minor aspects of that, but when that was scraped away, it boiled down to a few common problems I'll detail below.

How it Works

The feeling of this problem goes like this for many:

Step one: Excitement about a story or an idea.

Step two: Excitement carries the writer a distance into the story or novel or an outline.

Step three: Excitement wears off, critical voice plows in, story looks like crap and too much work to keep going.

Step four: Writer makes up some excuse to stop and go find a project that is exciting again.

Step five: Repeat the first four steps without ever finishing anything.

Outlines do not help this problem.

Finishing has been made into an "important event" and thus almost impossible to actually get to. Like that pot of gold at the end of a rainbow.

As long as you are working on something, you can call yourself a writer. But when you finish, you aren't writing, so it is better to stay a writer and just keep working on it.

You can't fail if you just keep working on a project.

Writers with this problem can't see not finishing as failure.

Two Major Areas

1. Fear

To put it simply, finishing something risks that what you finished will fail.

In my early days, failure was the story not selling to an editor. In this modern world, it can still be that, or it can be that you put it out indie and no one buys it.

If you keep working on something to make it better, rewriting it for the fifth time, reworking that plot you don't think works, and so on and so on, you won't risk the failure of no readers in the end.

To writers with this problem, a story must be some imaginary image of "perfect" before it can be released. And no story ever attains that.

For any of us, actually.

Kris did an entire book on this called "The Pursuit of Perfection." That book deals with this problem and so much more and worth your time and money if you have this problem.

Fear of failure is real and if it has become the dominating force in your writing, you need to go get professional help to get past the problem. It is that serious. Not kidding.

Rule #3 coming up also works into this rule.

Finishing a sloppy first draft that you must rewrite is not finishing. Sorry.

As long as you are working on a story in some fashion or another, it is not finished, and thus you don't have to risk the fear of failure.

And a small slice of writers have this issue because of fear of success. Not kidding here either. They don't finish because their ego tells them their work is so wonderful, it will be an instant bestseller and they don't want to be famous.

I have met a couple of these writers. I managed to not laugh until I walked out of the room.

Also, finishing brings in another fear.

Fear of mailing.

I have been an editor off and on for over thirty years. Not once do I remember a story that didn't work. Why?

Because editors don't read stories that don't work.

Duh.

I can't even remember the thousands of stories I have bought at various magazines over the years, let alone any story I didn't read.

Duh.

But yet the fear of mailing to an editor scares some writers beyond words. So they are better off not finishing than to have to face that fear.

And now the fear of learning how to indie publish scares writers, so better to not finish than have to learn all the new stuff.

Fear.

On and on.

Excuse after excuse.

. . .

2. Love of a Project

This is also fear-based, but in a different way. It goes like this:

"If I finish this project, what do I do next?"

This boils down to the early fear all writers have of not finding another idea. I do a six-week online workshop called "Ideas to Story" that helps writers fix that issue completely.

And as you write more and more, you quickly come to realize that ideas are everywhere and far too many for you to ever get to.

I used to write ideas down in notebooks because of this fear. But after a few years I stopped because if I couldn't remember the idea in a week, it wouldn't be worth my time to write it.

And now I never even come up with ideas.

I don't. Honest.

I write from triggers, an advanced way of telling stories, granted. But given enough time, every writer can get there.

But I do understand this excuse to not finish. I have a number of worlds I love to play inside. But I write and finish stories and novels inside the worlds. I never just work on one thing for years.

But I have seen more writers than I want to admit that are working on "their novel." When they say that, you know this is their problem and Rule #2 is going to kill them.

Writers like this will finish a draft, maybe, then go into major rewrites, even though they have no idea how to rewrite or how to tell a better story, they still need to stir the words around.

Then they give it to some "editor" that they pay a vast amount of money to (called a scam) and the editor has them work on it some more.

And on and on.

Never finishing.

Sadly, I have never seen a writer find a solution to this. They can't even admit the problem to themselves so they just cycle in the same world, same characters.

These writers will never finish because if they finished, all the people around them who had watched them work on "their novel" for years might actually have a chance to read it.

Far, far too dangerous to allow to happen.

You also see this with most of the sloppily drafted NaNoWriMo novels. They will never be fixed and no one will ever read them because it's too dangerous for the writer to let their supportive family who sacrificed time so they could write see how really bad the book might be.

If Writing Is Not Fun

Writers who can't seem to finish much, if anything, believe in the tortured "artist" myth, that writing must be hard and only years of working in the salt mines can make a novel brilliant.

Nope. That's a myth.

Thankfully.

So two major reasons why this simple Rule #2 stops so many writers.

1. Fear of failure.
2. Fear of moving on to something new.

Notice fear is the major word in both.

If a fear of any kind is crippling you and stopping you from finishing a novel or story, don't fight the story through. You won't beat the fear that way.

Step outside of that one novel, that one story, and deal with the fear outside of any one story.

What are you afraid will happen?

And is that worse than never finishing anything?

Heinlein's Rules are so simple. Remember, even he said that.

So let me lay out clearly what he meant with the first two rules in relationship to failure and fear of failure.

Think of the rules this way:

Rule #1... You Must Write. Not writing is failure.

Rule #2... You Must Finish What You Write. Not finishing is failure.

So if you are having fear issues, move the fear over to not writing and not finishing.

I can tell you this for a fact: The idea of not writing and not finishing what I write scares hell out of me.

Get help with your fears, move the fear to a fear of not writing.

And move the fear to a fear of not finishing.

Because not writing and not finishing are true failures.

I hate to tell you this folks: Every time you claim you want to write and then don't write or don't finish, everyone around you knows you are failing.

That should scare you more than anything.

CHAPTER FIVE

Moving now to the third rule.

Rule #3: You Must Refrain from Rewriting Unless to Editorial Order.

So, this is the rule that gets all the attention here in the modern world, even though it is the first two rules that stop most wannabe writers. And the fourth rule also stops writers who can finish something from becoming professional writers.

Everybody in this modern world looks for ways and reasons around this rule. That's how ingrained the modern myth of rewriting is in our culture.

One good thing right off about this rule: If you don't rewrite, just get it correct the first time through, you have more time to write new stories. And writers are always pressed for time.

Yet, time seems to make no difference to writers having trouble with this rule.

Rule #3 is actually an offshoot of Rule #2 failure.

Rule #2 is that you must finish what you write. If you are rewriting, you are not finishing.

And this rule plays right smack into every beginning writer's fear that what they wrote isn't good enough.

(Personally, I'm not sure where the thinking comes from that if they couldn't get it correct the first time, why looking at it and stirring the words around will make it better, but that is the myth.)

So there is a lot to this rule.

And people are always wondering what Heinlein really meant.

Well, he meant exactly what he wrote. You must refrain from rewriting unless to editorial order.

Period.

That simple.

So let me break the rule down into the three parts and try to show how some of these parts work and why they fit just fine in the modern world if you actually follow the rule as Heinlein intended.

Part One... You Must Refrain

Part Two... Rewriting

Part Three... Unless to Editorial Order

Part One of Rule #3... You Must Refrain

Heinlein, at the time he wrote this, was talking to beginning writers about what they were hearing about writing. At the time, in 1947, university programs were booming because of the GI Bill and so many WWII vets going back to school.

English teachers by this point in time had bought completely into the articles published in the late 1800s about how writing slowly would make better literature.

And at the same time writers such as Hemingway were tired of all the new-writer questions as being stupid. Everyone knew Hemingway was a reporter who wrote one-draft fast articles and books. He had made that clear.

Yet he still kept getting the same questions, as all experienced writers get, from wave after wave of new writers. So he started making stuff up about how he wrote, making it so outlandish that he was sure that writers would just laugh and realize they were being made fun of.

Of course, new writers have no sense of humor, so generations of new writers wrote standing up and did thirty or forty drafts because Hemingway told them to. It was a joke, folks.

So when Heinlein wrote his article and gave his five business rules, he was in a way trying to tell the truth to young writers to fight the idiocy coming out of Hemingway's jokes.

So the phrase "You must refrain…" means exactly that. Do not think about a second draft. Just flat don't do them.

Get it right the first time through. Just refrain from what some writers were saying in jokes and English teachers were spreading around to get writers to slow down so they didn't have to read as much.

Also, at the point Heinlein wrote this, the pulp magazines and digests were still going strong and building circulation again after the war. Writers wrote for 1 cent per word on typewriters. As one major pulp writer said when asked, "They don't pay me to rewrite."

Part Two of Rule #3… Rewriting

What is rewriting? Wow, can't tell you how often I get that question and writers want me to define it right down to how much they can and can't touch.

Well, first let me tell you what rewriting is not. Got that?

Rewriting is not:

—Fixing errors

—Fixing typos

—Fixing wrong details

If you want to know how Heinlein and other major one-draft writers used to do it, simply find online some of their pages of manuscripts. I am sure the pages put online will be the most marked up, but that's fine as well.

What those of us who started with typewriters knew was that you could fix mistakes on a page before mailing it. Up to ten mistakes before you had to retype the page. That's why the manuscript format is double spaced, so there is room between lines to add in words or even a sentence.

Most of Heinlein's manuscripts have a hand correction about every page of a detail fixed. At least the manuscripts I have seen.

I've also seen a lot of Harlan Ellison manuscripts. You know he wrote one draft on a typewriter in store windows and posted each page as he finished it. I was also his publisher for a time and his manuscripts are very clean, usually only one or two word corrections a page.

You get the story correct the first time, but you can fix typos, spelling, and wrong details.

That's what Heinlein meant.

That's what I mean.

It really is that simple.

Creative vs. Critical Voice

Over the years I have spent a lot of time talking about the difference between writing in creative voice and writing in critical voice.

Critical voice is that voice in your head that says everything is shit. That your story is bad, that you must fix it.

That's critical voice. Nothing good ever comes from critical voice. Critical voice wants to make your stuff the same and safe and dull.

Creative voice is that surprising place where nifty stuff just springs forth.

Professional writers have learned to leave that creative voice alone and let it work. We do everything in our power to stay out of its way and then not change what it has produced (other than fixing typos and small details.)

—Rewriting comes from the thought, "I need to fix that before it goes out."

That's critical voice and it is almost always wrong. When you hear that, just fix the typos and mail the story or publish it and move on.

—Rewriting is also caused by sloppy first drafts. Somewhere over the last twenty or thirty years, a deadly saying has cropped up. "Get it down, then fix it."

This makes writing from creative voice almost impossible.

Think of your creative voice as a two-year-old kid. If you tell that voice that it can do what it wants, but it won't matter, parents (critical voice) will just make it better later, the kid won't want to play at all.

But if you follow Heinlein's 3rd rule and promise your creative voice you won't touch what the creative voice comes up with, you will be amazed at how freeing that is and how much original and unique work comes out.

The idea of sloppy writing is just such a waste of time.

Basically, when Heinlein said, "You must refrain from rewriting..." he was telling new writers to work to get it right the first time through.

Yeah, yeah, I know, that's not what your English teacher told you.

That's not the myth.

So keep doing many, many drafts, maybe as many as Hemingway told you to do, and remain an aspirant as Heinlein said.

Also remember, if you are rewriting things all the time, you are not finishing anything and Rule #2 has got you in its grips.

Part Three of Rule #3... Unless to Editorial Order

This used to be such a forgotten part of this rule for decades. It was obvious.

If you mailed off your story or novel to a major editor and the editor asked for a rewrite to fix something to help the story fit their magazine or book line better, then you considered it.

You might do it, you might decline.

Harlan Ellison added to Heinlein's rule... "And then only if you agree."

All of that still applies.

But this new world has really confused things for this last little clause of rule #3.

First off, agents are not editors.

Duh.

Yet beginning writers will rewrite and rewrite and rewrite for agents who can't write a check or even have a clue what they are doing.

I'll be honest, and I have talked about it number of times on my blog, this practice is the stupidest thing I have ever seen in publishing.

Period.

If you are trapped in such stupidity, here is my suggestion:

Stop!!!

Withdraw the book and move on. Go back to your first original draft and trust your own writing and voice. Act like an artist instead of a doormat for heaven's sake.

Second, some scam book doctors you pay are not editors.

If you pay someone, they are NOT AN EDITOR. They can't write you a check. In fact, you are paying them so you can be scammed and your book ruined.

Unless this editor has published fifty or more novels, just STOP!!!

Withdraw the book, count the money spent as learning, and start trusting your own voice and writing. Again, act like an artist.

Again, the only exception to this is if the book-doctor/editor is a major published writer and knows what they are talking about.

But most writers go to "editors" who have published a couple how-to-write scam books.

Seriously?

Think, people, just think.

So what to do with Heinlein's Rule #3?

Follow it.

Completely.

Write the best story or book you can the first time through.

Fix typos and spelling mistakes.

Give the book to a trusted first reader, then fix the nits they find.

Then move on to rule #4.

Yup, that simple.

And really, really that hard in this world of rewriting myths.

As Heinlein said, these rules look simple and are almost impossible to follow.

Why are they impossible to follow? Because simply, you won't let yourself follow them.

You are the only person stopping yourself.

And think about how much more fun you'll have writing if you don't rewrite.

And how much more time you'll have to play with new stories.

CHAPTER SIX

Continuing with the third rule.

Rule #3: You Must Refrain from Rewriting Unless to Editorial Order.

I wanted to go at this rule one more time to make sure I've been clear. Most of the time, in this modern world, rewriting is when you do a sloppy first draft with the intent of "letting it sit" (dumbest thing I have ever heard) and then "fix it" later.

That assumes, of course, that your story is broken.

And that you have suddenly gained a vast amount of new skills since doing the story the first time.

I will often get comments from writers in workshops when I say, "Great job. It works fine." The writer wants to know what is wrong. If I don't say anything is wrong, nothing is wrong.

That kind of thinking, of always thinking something is broken, comes directly out of this myth that everything must be rewritten because it is clearly broken.

If you tell your creative voice to do it right the first time, the story won't be broken.

It might not work the way you feel it should, but it won't be broken and some readers might think it works just fine as is.

Cycling

This modern world of computers has allowed us to use a wonderful new method of writing fiction. That's called cycling.

The first thing you must understand about this new method of working in creative voice to create a clean story the first time through is that you, the author, are the god of your story.

You are unstuck in time in your story.

You could write the last line, the first line, a middle line, and then jump around filling in gaps.

The intent is to make a story that the reader will start into on page one, word one, and end up at the last word.

BUT YOU DON'T HAVE TO WRITE IT THAT WAY.

This is the hardest concept for a new writer to grasp after English classes. English teachers talk about the complexity and all that of fiction, and all of us thought that the authors must have been really brilliant to start from that first word and put all that nifty stuff in at exactly the right moment.

Nope.

You are the god of your own story, you can jump around all you want in your story and do anything you want.

As long as you do it in creative mode.

In the old days, writers would add in pages, or hand-write in sentences in earlier pages that needed to be added because of something that came later in the story.

I would often have a page that was numbered 3a that came right after page 3 in my story.

In our modern world of computers, we can cycle back in creative mode and just add in or take out what we want when we want.

How I do it (and it turns out, many other professionals I have talked to are the same) is that I write about 400 to 600 words (into the dark) and then bog down.

I instantly jump back to the start of those 400 words and run through them, adding in a detail, reading it, touching it, until I am back to the blank page with some speed and I go another 400 to 600 words.

Then I cycle back about 500 words and do it again.

If you graphed it, it would look like I am moving forward and then jumping up out of the timeline and circling back into the timeline of the story and then going forward again.

I'll repeat until I get to the end and the story is done and clean because I have looked at most of it twice. (I talk a lot more about this method in the book *Writing into the Dark.*)

I do this all while my creative voice is in control.

I average about 1,000 words per hour of finished story with this method, which always includes a five-minute break every hour.

Rewriting has been made easy with computers. That is the huge problem.

But cycling isn't rewriting, it's just using the computer tool to do what writers have always done. Jump around in time in our stories.

So remember, just because the reader will read a story from word one to the final word doesn't mean you have to write it that way.

Editors

Let me describe the types of editors there are in this new world just to be very clear.

Traditional Editor

This editor is hired by a magazine or a book company to put together a magazine or a book line. They have very specific things they are looking for and will often ask you to touch up your book, do a pass through the book to help it fit their book line or magazine better.

That's the kind of thing Heinlein was talking about with the last part of Rule #3. **These editors can write you checks for your work.**

Book Doctors/Developmental Editors/Content Editors

All of these types of editors you pay are scams. (With the exceptions of major writers with long careers helping out younger writers for a fee.)

Granted, many of these book doctors have their hearts in the right place. I understand that. They want to help young writers, but the book doctors (or developmental editors or whatever you call them) have no credentials and could no more tell what makes a better book than your neighbor down the street. (Actually, feedback from your neighbor might be better.)

So they are actually hurting young writers instead of helping them.

Do not pay these book doctors. Just trust your own creative voice, your own art.

And focus on learning how to tell better stories over years by how-to books, taking classes, and listening to writers who have forty or fifty novels published.

In other words, learn from those a ways down the road that you want to walk and never grovel and pay someone with no credentials.

Line Editors

Line editors are editors who look for consistency in your story and your words. They look for clarity. Great line editors are extremely rare and most writers can get by without them.

Often great line editors are also buying editors for magazines or anthologies. John Helfers is a great line editor and he often buys for anthologies and edits a volume of *Fiction River* for WMG Publishing every year.

Copyeditors

Every indie writer needs to hire a copyeditor. You can find them in services and locally from newspapers and such. Copyeditors look for nits, mistakes, wrong words spelled correctly.

Great copyeditors are priceless as well, but you must, as an indie writer, hire one. No manuscript should go into print without a good copyeditor looking at it.

I am posting this book on my blog in rough form. It will be run through a copyeditor before it sees electronic and paper print.

Copyediting is not rewriting. Copyediting is simply finding the last wave of mistakes and cleaning as many of then out as they can find.

But no book is perfect. None.

We all do the best we can and release and move on.

Summary of Rule #3

Heinlein was basically trying to help writers learn how to write a story, do the best they could, release and move on.

Forward.

Always face forward.

Think of your writing journey as a walking trip. When you write a story, you are walking forward, helping yourself by learning and practicing and creating more stories that might sell and get you readers.

But the moment you stop and turn around to rewrite something, you have stopped your forward momentum and actually walked backwards to hurt your fiction.

Forward.

Always face and move forward.

The modern world has developed this fantastically powerful myth that all writing must be rewritten to be good. And no writer coming into fiction writing is immune from the pressure of the myth.

Writing is an art.

Good stories come from the creative side of our minds. To tell good stories, you must train that creative side to let go and play.

Write the story, finish the story, release the story. Rules 1-3.

It really is as simple as Heinlein said.

But in this modern world, it is really that hard.

CHAPTER SEVEN

On to the fourth rule.

Rule #4: You Must Put It on the Market.

"It" in the rule refers to your finished and not rewritten story or novel.

On the surface, this rule is very, very basic. And yet it was this rule that I had the most problem with over the years.

This and Rule #5.

Old Traditional Publishing World

What Heinlein meant when he wrote this business rule in 1947 was that you had to send your story to some market that would buy it, publish it, and pay you money.

When I started with these rules in 1982, the meaning was exactly the same. So I started off writing, finishing, and mailing a short story every week to a magazine or anthology that might buy it. I did the writing on an electric typewriter and I didn't rewrite. (I did fix typos.)

I did 44 stories that first year, 43 the second year, (while working three jobs) and was selling regularly by the end of the start of the second year. In fact, by the end of the second year, I had 16 short-story sales.

This was all fine and swell and nifty as long as I was only writing short stories. But then I started writing novels.

I still wrote short stories following Heinlein's Rules, but I would often just show them to Kris and then never get around to mailing them.

Over the years, knowing I had this problem, I started a number of things that were designed to help me follow this rule.

One solution was called "The Race."

The Race was simple. You got one point for every short story you had in the mail to a market (remember, this is pre-indie world), three points for every chapter and outline you had out, and eight points for every full novel you had under submission.

I managed just over 70 different short stories in the mail at the same time during the years the race was going on in my writer magazine called *The Report*.

I was not leading the race.

Kevin J. Anderson and Kristine Kathryn Rusch were always ahead of me in points.

It is amazing, looking back at those old issues of *The Report* from the late 1980s that the names that were on the top of The Race ended up with long careers and the names with only had a few stories out in the race aren't around anymore.

Heinlein said, "You must put it on the market."

But chances are the writers at the bottom of The Race during those years had issues with the first three rules. Kevin, Kris, and I had no issue with those first three. And The Race was a fun way to help us all keep stuff out.

Actually, it helped me.

But to this day, I still find stories that I never mailed.

Wonder why I never sold the stories, huh?

But for the most part, I managed to keep on Rule #4.

The New World of Publishing

Wow, do authors today have more choices for their stories and novels than Heinlein did in 1947.

Or what I did in 1982.

A ton more.

But the meaning of Rule #4 remains solid.

When you finish a story or novel, you must put it on the market.

But what does "market" mean in this modern world?

Well, for short fiction, the traditional rules still work fine. In fact, this is a new golden age for short fiction with as many magazines publishing fiction now as in the 1940s.

So mailing short stories to traditional magazines like I did in the 1980s and 1990s still works great. And I recommend it with short fiction.

As far as mailing novels into the traditional publishing world, I DO NOT recommend it at the moment. Contracts are very bad, advances are so low as to be laughable, and it flat takes too long for anything to get to readers who have grown used to getting it Now!

What to know an interesting bit about Heinlein in his day. Novels were mostly sold to pulp magazines. And ended up in books later, if they were lucky.

When I started writing and mailing novels in the mid-1980s, you sent your work directly to book editors and often sold the editors projects over lunch at conventions.

Those days, both Heinlein's and my early days, are long gone.

For now, stay away from traditional book publishers and their lackey agents. You will be glad you did.

Sending a book to an agent IS NOT PUTTING IT ON THE MARKET.

Sorry. Agents can't write you a check for your work.

Agents are not a market.

Indie Publishing

The new world of indie publishing has exploded since 2009. Now a writer, with some learning, can get a book copyedited and to readers within a month or so from finishing it.

Writers now deal directly with readers.

Getting a book or story out for sale to readers is putting it on the market.

In fact, that is the clear, bottom line of the word "market." Readers are the end product of all storytelling.

Readers are the market.

So Rule #4 now has many, many choices for writers. And that's a good thing. Stressful at times, sure, but a good thing.

For example, in July of 2015, I decided to write a short story per day. It was great fun and I actually did 32 short stories in 31 days.

I followed Heinlein's first three rules to the letter.

But what was I going to do for Rule #4 with those 32 short stories?

First off, I put them all together, plus the blog each night about the process of writing the stories, did a cover for each story, a blurb for each story, and put them all in a book called *Stories from July* that came out just two months after I finished the last story.

So in two months all the short stories were all on the market.

I will be, in 2016, putting some of those stories into my magazine called *Smith's Monthly*. (I usually have four or five stories per issue every month.)

A second market for many of the stories I wrote in July.

I will also be putting many of the stories in short-story collections over the next few years.

A third market for many of them.

And each story will be for sale in 2016 as a standalone story for readers to buy.

A fourth market for all of them.

For a person who has had a lot of trouble over the decades with Rule #4, I'm pretty proud of what I am doing now when it comes to this rule. I think I have finally managed, after over three decades, to wrestle this simple-sounding rule to the ground.

Finally.

Must Talk About Fear

Now, this is a problem area I have observed when it comes to this rule. And I know it is real.

But I have no deep understanding of the problem. My reason for not mailing a story was just laziness or lack of organization or a bad memory that I had even written the story.

But for some reason, many writers are flat afraid to mail their work to editors or indie publish their work.

I guess writers feel that the editor or reader might hate their work and do some sort of mortal damage to the writer.

I guess.

Damned if I know. Just seems really silly to me.

So, let me tell you the reality, folks.

Readers (not jerky critics) don't read or buy something they don't like.

Editors don't read or buy something that doesn't fit what they are looking for.

Over my decades of editing, I can't begin to remember the stories I have bought, which means I loved them and worked with the author and paid the author money.

Why would any author think an editor who only glances at a story, knows it won't work, and passes on it, will remember the author?

Or the story?

Ego. Wow.

I think this fear might come from "my manuscript is my baby" problem some writers have. And of course, every editor's desk is empty, just waiting for the writer's baby to appear in front of the editor so the editor can take their time reading it and remembering every blessed word.

Ego.

But editors don't work that way.

And neither do readers. Even if your wonderful cover catches them, your perfect, active blurb draws them in, if the opening of your book or story doesn't work, the reader will move on and not buy it or read it.

And they won't remember the writer.

Readers are the ultimate editors.

So this fear of mailing is just damn silly on the face and under the surface.

Get over it.

Get over yourself.

Follow the fourth rule.

Summary of Rule #4

"You must put it (your story or novel) on the market."

Very simple, yet scary hard for many to do.

My only suggestion is to figure out systems that work for you to get the story from your computer and on the way to a magazine editor or a reader who can buy it.

And if your system breaks down, change it, fix it, get the stories out there.

Get past the fear, get past your ego, and just do it.

Rule #1 stops a vast majority of people who dream of writing.

Rule #2 stops a vast majority of the people who make it past Rule #1.

Rule #3 destroys stories and sends the writers back into Rule #2 problems.

Rule #4 stops careers of a vast majority of the writers who did make it past the first three rules.

And in the next chapter, Rule #5 wipes out even more.

As Heinlein said, these are simple rules. Deadly if not followed, but simple to understand.

CHAPTER EIGHT

On to the fifth rule.

Rule #5: You Must Keep It on the Market Until Sold.

"It" in the rule refers to your story or novel.

In 1947, when Heinlein wrote this rule, for the most part the only markets were pulp magazines. Paperbacks were just gaining strength and hardback publishers were very, very selective.

So all short stories and most novels were sold to pulp magazines, and the few digest magazines that were starting up, and maybe to the slick magazines such as *Saturday Evening Post*, if you were good and well-known as a writer.

But as with today, there were enough markets in 1947 to make this fifth rule a great business rule.

There are a million stories over the decades of how many times some book or story was rejected before being bought.

I had one story rejected over thirty times before finally selling it to a top market I had never thought of before.

I was following Heinlein's Rules.

Indie Publishing

The new world of indie publishing causes this rule to change slightly to follow Heinlein's intent.

If you put a story up for sale indie, the rule basically means leave it there.

I have heard of so many writers who, for some reason unknown to my way of thinking, gave up on a story or novel because it didn't sell to some preconceived level and pulled the story down.

And never put the story or novel back up.

In the old traditional days, we used to have a saying: "No story sold while sitting in your top drawer."

So, these writers pull down an indie-published story, give up on a story, usually out of fear, and put the story in a drawer. No reader will ever buy it.

Headshaking in this modern world of unlimited shelf space.

So this rule (in this new world) means get the story available to readers and leave it there.

Giving Up

The new world of indie publishing also causes another major problem with this rule that I see and hear about all the time.

It goes like this for short stories:

Writer: I've tried the short story at three markets. I'm going to indie publish it now.

Me: (Thinking) *Dumb.*

I never say that to any writer with my out-loud voice. But I think it.

For a short story, the advantages of selling to major magazines or top anthologies is far, far greater in both money and exposure and free advertising.

Sure, at some point you don't want to go below a 5-cent-per-word market, but wow are there a lot of that level markets out there.

It goes like this for novels:

Writer: I've tried the novel at three agents for two years and rewritten it twice for agents. I'm going to indie publish it now.

Me: (Thinking) *Dumb that you sent the novel there in the first place. You wasted all those years never putting it on the market.*

I never say that to any writer with my out-loud voice. But I think it. Oh, wow, do I think it.

Agents are not a market.

So the new world of indie publishing is causing, with Rule #5, writers to stay up on the business, to find top short-fiction markets, to watch what is happening with the major book publishers, and to learn how to indie publish their own work.

That is all good, if you do it.

Boiling Rule #5 Down

Simple. Keep the story or novel on the market until it sells. For short stories, keep it going to the top short-fiction magazines. For novels, get it indie published and then leave it alone for a few years.

And if you have to touch it after a few years, do a better cover, learn how to write better blurbs, and make sure your formatting is working on all devices.

But past that, leave it alone.

Don't rewrite the story or novel because some reviewer said something. (Really the dumbest thing I have heard in this new world.)

Don't give up on the short story just because it has a few rejections.

Don't pull a story down from indie published because it only sold a few copies in a year.

Rule #5: You must keep it on the market.

For writers who have made it this far in the writing process, not following this rule will often swallow their work in self-doubt and wasted time.

Follow the rule. It's a simple rule.

Don't waste the time.

EPILOGUE

Robert A. Heinlein called these five rules "Business Habits."

I couldn't agree more.

Even though the first three talk about writing, they are firmly in how a writer manages his or her own business.

As Heinlein said, talking about the five business habits:

"... they are amazingly hard to follow—which is why there are so few professional writers and so many aspirants, and which is why I am not afraid to give away the racket!"

After following these rules since 1982 and making a living with my fiction writing since 1987, I can attest to how hard these five simple rules are to follow.

I would fall off, my writing would grind to a halt, I would realize I had slipped, and I would get back onto the rules.

Don't be mad at yourself when you slip off these rules if you really want to follow them. Just keep going at it.

A Few Additions That Need to be Made

First, you can follow the above rules like a perfect clock and they will do you no good if you don't continue to learn how to be a better storyteller.

Learning is critical because the business rules are guidelines to practice.

Learn, then practice, then learn, then practice.

Learning how to be a better storyteller is critical to making these rules work for you.

And that learning never stops. Ever.

Second, there is no place in the five business rules that Heinlein talks about speed of typing or production or all the other favorite topics writers have these days.

You can follow these rules just fine if you only have ten minutes a day to write or if you have ten hours.

However, Heinlein's Rules, if followed, will allow you to have far more fun with your writing, something I hear that many writers have lost lately.

Third, you must keep up with the business side of the industry. Heinlein called these his "Business Habits." You need to also make it a habit to understand the new world of publishing and follow the changes.

The advice I gave above is for 2016, the year this book was published. I have no idea if the indie world will look the same in 2018, or if traditional book publishing will collapse or start giving writers their real value and decent contracts.

But whatever happens, follow the publishing business, stay up with it as best you can.

I hope these five business rules from the great Robert A. Heinlein will help you with your own writing going forward.

I know I owe my entire career to them.

And I still follow them.

Have fun with your writing.

KRISTINE KATHRYN RUSCH

CLOSING THE DEAL ON YOUR TERMS

Agents, Contracts and Other Considerations

A WMG WRITER'S GUIDE

ACKNOWLEDGMENTS

I owe a huge debt of gratitude to my weekly blog readers. Many of them donated money to keep me writing. A large number quietly sent me contracts so I could see many of the things I've discussed in this book. Even more sent me links to various articles online, some of which I've linked to here. Many corrected me on my misunderstanding of the law, and I've tried to incorporate that in here. All mistakes, however, are 100% mine.

I can't name most of the people who've helped me, because they did so on condition of anonymity, but I know who you are, and I thank you.

I can thank Helen Sedwick, whose excellent book helped me organize my thoughts, David Vandagriff (the Passive Guy), Roxie Munro, and Nate Hoffelder.

I especially owe Teri Kanefield for her contributions to the Non-Compete section. She's been lovely and gracious to work with. She's an amazing writer, and I couldn't have done that section without her.

FOREWORD

In 2012 and 2013, I published a series of blogs on contract deal breakers for traditionally published writers. Those blogs became a book called *Dealbreakers.* I've been promising to update it for years now, but I'll be honest: The very topic discourages me.

Still, I have come to the point where I can't ignore the contractual changes in the industry any longer. With the help of my readers, I spent over four months exploring the state of contracts in the publishing industry. I examined everything I could find, from terms of service to existing contracts. I discovered some pretty slimy contract terms, masquerading as "good" contracts. I learned that agent agreements have proliferated, to the detriment of the writer. I learned that publishers are now interpreting seemingly out-of-date clauses in a brand-new, and somewhat frightening, way. I learned that some online services for writers have rights grabs buried in the Terms of Service.

I could have continued writing blog after blog about the things I discovered for the next four months, maybe even for the next four years. I finally quit, not because I had run out of things to say, but because I had run out of the will to continue.

Even so, the book you hold in your hands is five times longer than the original *Dealbreakers* book. This book covers much more than the original book did, and with a different perspective.

Because, in the intervening years, the industry changed dramatically. As the industry changed, so did my opinion about everything from hiring an agent to whether or not a traditional *book* publishing deal is a good idea. If you compare the old *Dealbreakers* to this volume, you will think—at times—that they were written by two different writers.

They were. One writer is older and wiser.

The point of this entire book is to help writers and others make informed decisions about the contracts they sign and the deals they make. I may disagree with your final choice, but I will defend it to the death—as long as your choice is an *informed* choice.

Your career is different from mine. Your needs are different. And your desires are different. You might sign something I would never touch or you might find me too lenient. That's all well and good, as long as you make the best choice you can at the time you make it.

And as long as you continue learning and growing.

That has been the most fascinating part about this process for me. I'm still learning, each and every day. I'm discovering new things. Some of them are things I wished I hadn't seen. Others make some bad decisions in my past even clearer. And still others show me just how different 2016 is from the publishing world I first entered, decades ago.

This book has several loosely defined sections. You can dip in and out of the book if you would like, but it is meant to be read as a whole.

I do have both types of readers in mind. I'll do my best to point out when you need to read a previous chapter to understand the current one. And I'll also repeat a few things in some chapters, so that the people who dip in and out can follow.

I doubt I'll write another version of this book. To be frank, the experience of going through these contracts, and seeing how they've been weaponized against writers, left me very discouraged. Many of you have written to me to help me through some of the darker weeks, and I greatly appreciate that.

I appreciate all of the interaction. This book would not exist without the input from the blog readers, industry professionals, and a few of my lawyer friends behind the scenes. Also, many of you helped by sending donations to keep me writing when the going got tough. *Thank you.*

And now, onto the heart of the project.

I do hope that the information inside this book helps you make the right decisions for yourself and your career.

—Kristine Kathryn Rusch
Lincoln City, Oregon
October 7, 2016

INTRODUCTION

At some point, all writers will make a publishing deal. Whether that deal is with a large traditional publishing company or with a short story house, with a gaming company or a foreign publisher, the writer will have to sign a contract. And the writer needs to understand that contract.

Writers are often desperate to get published. Or, in this modern age filled with easy self-publishing, writers want the "legitimacy" of an agent and a traditional book deal. Once writers have experience in traditional publishing and realize that it's not about legitimacy, but it's about business, those writers might choose to leave. Many of them, however, will do what I'm doing: They'll self-publish some things and publish others traditionally.

There's even a term for us now. We're called hybrid writers.

The bugaboo is the contract. The bugaboo is *always* the contract. Traditional publishing houses used to have relatively fair contracts. They don't any longer. If the writer handles a negotiation with a traditional publisher as if she's working with friends, she's making a very serious mistake.

In fact, any writer who lets her agent negotiate for her without having an intellectual properties attorney first vet the contract is also making a mistake. Traditional publishing contracts have gotten so complicated that agents (who have no legal training) can no longer handle the fine legal details with any degree of competency.

Traditional publishing houses have teams of attorneys developing their contracts. Writers need a team on their side to negotiate the contract.

The main reason is this: Traditional publishers have gone from wanting only the rights they need to demanding as many rights as they can get, not just for the book under consideration, but for all books the writer writes. If the writer wants to remain a hybrid writer—or even if she wants to leave and go to a different traditional publisher—then she must negotiate a good contract for herself.

I know that the idea of negotiating scares writers. I wrote an entire book on negotiation for the timid, called *How to Negotiate Anything.* There is a short course on negotiation toward the end of this book. But if you're truly having trouble, pick up the original book.

I have learned through the course of this series that writers are terrified to hire an attorney to handle their work. I have included a chapter on attorneys at the end of this book. I hope it provides the first step in dispelling the myths about attorneys that so many writers hold.

Before I get much deeper into this chapter, let me make one point very clear: *I am not a lawyer.* Nothing in this book should be construed as legal advice. I do my best to research everything, but I can be (and sometimes am) wrong.

Now, let me define terms.

1. When I say "indie writer" I mean writers who either have their own small publishing imprint or are self-published. I'm not calling all writers who do it themselves self-published writers, because so many of them hire out a lot of the work, from copyediting to layout. At some point, these writers have moved from complete DIY to a small business with contractors or employees. If the writer is serious, eventually, they will become a tiny independent press, just because of the workload.

2. When I discuss writers who want a "long-term career," I don't mean people who write an occasional book and finance their lifestyle through another career. While that's a valid career path for writers, it is *not* the one being discussed here. By "long-term career," I mean

someone who wants to make a *good* living as a writer—with earnings per year of $50,000 or more.

3. When I mention "traditional publishing," I mean the publishing industry that most people are familiar with. Some writers call this the Big 5, but I'm including some smaller houses as well. These are not ground-up businesses, but top-down businesses, with massive overhead, huge staff, and an infrastructure that has been in place for at least a dozen years or (in some cases) nearly a century.

4. You should also know that I no longer sell my *novels* into traditional publishing in the United States. The contracts are too awful, which we will get into here. I do sell my novels overseas, where the contracts are better, although crappy contract creep is happening there as well (especially in firms that are part of those conglomerates). I do sell the occasional anthology into traditional publishing. I publish a lot of short fiction in traditional venues. I still have many novels in print through traditional publishers. This makes me a hybrid writer, with feet planted in both camps.

5. I have not had an agent representing my work for years now. The reasons will become clear throughout this series. With those definitions and caveats in mind, here we go with the body of the introductory material.

I mentioned in the foreword that the topic of contracts discourages me. That's one reason I've put the revision of the original *Dealbreakers* book off for so very long.

I had hoped that contracts would improve. They haven't. They've gotten worse. What has happened is that predictions longtime writers, like my husband Dean Wesley Smith, made have come true: Writers are starting to split into camps. Dean predicted two camps—those who published their books traditionally, and those who published indie.

Unfortunately, we've divided into three camps: those who publish traditionally, those who publish indie, and those who publish through their agents.

That last clause "through their agents" is so wrong, I have trouble typing it. The agents *who still represent the writer as an agent* are breaking the law when they publish a writer's books. The agents are then becoming *publishers*, which makes them violate all kinds of agency law.

Not *literary* agency law, which, anyone will tell you, does not exist in most states. *Agency* law, which governs anyone who calls themselves an agent—from real estate *agents* to insurance *agents* to literary *agents*.

Agency law varies from state to state. I can't tell you what Colorado asks of its agents any more than I can tell you exactly what Oregon asks of its. Because, again, I am not a lawyer, although law fascinates me.

Most literary agents have no idea *agency* law even exists—at least, I hope they have no idea, because if they do, then they are flagrantly violating the law, instead of ignorantly violating the law. Me, I prefer the ignorant to the flagrant.

But law-breakin' is law-breakin' as they used to say on Western TV shows—and ignorance of the law is no excuse.

Above, I mentioned Westerns for a reason. Publishing has become the Wild Wild West. It was always a lawless place, governed by strange rules and ignorance. But much of it was genteel, and prided itself on doing what was right.

Since huge conglomerates have taken over the big traditional publishers, no one even pretends at gentility any more. Smaller publishers which were often a dice-roll (some were great for writers; some were *horrible* for writers) are now as bad, or worse, than the Big Five. Much of this is economic—the economics of traditional publishing, done the old-fashioned way, isn't working as well as it once did, so traditional publishers (large and small alike) are squeezing their writers like never before.

Most writers who publish traditionally can no longer make a living at writing. If those writers only write one novel per year, they *definitely* can no longer make a living at writing.

Most midlist writers are lucky to get an advance of $5,000. Those advances are paid in three installments—signing, acceptance, and publication. Even being charitable and assuming that the advance is paid in the traditional two installments ($2,500 each) or let's be even more charitable, all at once, a writer can't live on that kind of money.

The writer has to be able to write something else.

But most traditional publishing contracts—negotiated by *agents*—have some version of this clause:

The Work [the novel] shall be the Author's next book-length work. The Author represents that there is no outstanding commitment for publication for the first time of another book-length work written or co-written by the Author to a third party and the Author will not offer rights to another book-length work written or co-written by the Author, or accept an offer for such a work, until acceptance of the Work by the Publishers and until the Author has complied with the option in Clause 3(a).

The option clause in most contracts is another problem, which options the author's next work, and allows the publisher to take their own sweet time in deciding if they'll buy the next work.

But note how pernicious the clause above is. I took it from an existing contract that a writer sent me over a year ago. The only thing I changed was adding *[the novel]* for the sake of clarity. The rest is from the contract verbatim.

The contract is for a *novel*, yet this clause restricts *book-length* works. That includes nonfiction, short story collections, novellas, anything at *book-length*, which is not defined at all in the contract. So that means *book-length* could be anything the publishing company deems it to be.

It could also be argued that when a writer *self-publishes* a book-length work, the rights to that work are being offered for distribution. I wouldn't put it past some big book company to argue that the self-publication is in violation of this clause.

Usually, though, there is another clause, buried in the warranty, that says the author warrants he will not publish any other book-length work that will compete with this book. And who determines that competition? The publisher, of course. Certainly not the author.

So...for a measly $5,000 (minus agent fees, which actually will make this $4,250), the author signed away his right to make a living. In the early 1990s, I sold eight novels before my first one was published. I also sold an anthology that I edited, and I was editing a series of hardcover anthologies that we chose to call magazines.

If my first novel contract had had that clause, I could not have done *any* of those things. So, instead of earning tens of thousands of dollars in those early years, I would have been left with a check for $2,125—and some crappy day job.

But what about the dream? The home run? What about earning *millions* on your writing?

What about royalties?

First, most traditional books do not earn out their advances, so the writer never gets royalties. This isn't because the books do poorly. It's because of all of the contract terms, new definitions, and other ways that publishers are managing to keep most of the profit from any published book.

And that home run? That million-dollar advance?

They are rare. They haven't gone away completely, but they're certainly down.

Part of the reason is because traditional publishers—the ones who can spend millions on a project—have devoured each other. When I came into the business, there were at least two dozen publishers who could offer large advances.

Now there are five.

Five.

The dream of having a dozen publishers want your book so badly that they'll bid against each other to get it is just that—a dream. A pipedream.

Don't believe me? Then go to Publishers Marketplace.[1] For years now, Publishers Marketplace has tracked publishing deals on its website. Agents, in particular, love to report their really big coups to Publishers Marketplace. Publishers Marketplace divides the deals it reports into five categories, all by the amount of the advance.

PM defines "major deal" category—the *largest* advance category—as $500,000 and up. In the not-so-distant past, the major deal category was often for one book. If the agent secured a three-book deal that was $500,000 per book, the agent didn't call that a major deal, because that wasn't impressive. Someone might misinterpret and believe the agent got "only" $500,000 for all three books.

Instead, the agents would report a 3-book deal for $500,000 per book as a 1.5-million-dollar deal.

I searched major deals when I initially wrote this chapter as a blog post in March of 2016, and found quite a few major deals. But when I looked at them, they were all for mid-six figures for a lot of books—

usually a three-book deal, although I did see quite a few for five books, and one "major deal" for 11 books.

Believe me, if that 11-book deal had gone to seven figures, the agent on the deal would have said "In a deal worth one million dollars…" Didn't happen.

Searching for fiction only, I found three deals listed as million-dollar deals. They include John Scalzi's 10-year, 13-book, $3.4-million-dollar deal (which comes to roughly $225,000 per book when you subtract agent fees). Only one of the three deals was for a single book, which sold for $1.25 million. The remaining deal was for over a million per book, and that was a $7 million 5-book deal (which comes to $1.4 million per book before agent) for a self-published writer whose books sold $1.2 million all on their own.

Three million-dollar fiction deals in 2015. Only three. And none in the first quarter of 2016. There were nine in 2014, and at least one per month in 2013. In 2012, there were at least two per month.

Why is this important? Because that home run is less possible for *everyone* in traditional publishing, and they're looking for other ways to make money. One of the ways they make money is squeezing writers. Another way is to own the copyright—or at least, control the copyright. (Get yourself a copy of Nolo Press's *The Copyright Handbook* by Stephen Fishman. It's essential these days.)

Here's the really scary part of the changes in the publishing world: Old contract terms, some written in the 20th century before ebooks existed, are being redefined and employed as a justification for publisher behavior. These traditional publishers—particularly those that have been subsumed into a major conglomerate—are not asking permission to change the definition of the terms. They're just doing it.

Things that were pretty innocuous in 1985 are now weapons that are being used against authors.

You'd think that agents, who are supposed to work for the writers who hire them, would prevent this wholesale change of meaning of old contracts. But a handful of agents are complicit in this, preferring to maintain their working relationship with a big publisher than rocking the boat for a small client.

Even more agents are just plain ignorant of what the changes in the clauses mean.

Those who run the agencies, though, do understand that their income is going down, so literary agencies have become pretty Draconian in their own contracts. Those agencies make agreements with their authors, usually requiring the author to give them 15% of the earnings of a particular book if the agent sold the book. That's bad enough, especially if the agent has been fired—as two of mine have (the two who still are entitled to 15% of certain projects).

But the agency agreements are moving into a whole new, and even uglier, place in relation to their writers. Agents are demanding a piece of their writers' copyrights as well. Some agents are blatant about it, stating in the agency agreement that they make writers sign before the writer becomes a client, that the agent will own 15% of the copyright of any book the agent sells for the writer—or in the case of one agency, 15% of the copyright of any book the agent *markets* for the writer.

Other agency agreements are less blatant. You have to read them in conjunction with the contracts the agent has negotiated for the writer, to see that the agent has actually slipped his hand into the writer's pocket and legally stolen copyright. Most writers trust their agents blindly, and never believe it would happen to them—until it happens to them.

These days, most agents have discovered that the best way to control the copyright on a piece of literary property is to publish the ebook. Some agents just publish ebooks through a side arm of their company. A lot of writers object to the quality of those ebooks, but that's the smallest part of the problem.

Under agency law, an agent acts as a go-between for two parties[2], representing one of those parties in a negotiation or business deal. The agent *cannot,* by law, be one of those parties. So unless a second agent with a different agency negotiates the ebook contract, the agent who provides ebook services is violating *agency law.*

Some agents put up a wall between their publishing arm and their agenting arm. Some of these walls are more effective than others. For example, at least one agency has an exclusive arrangement with a big-name ebook company. Many clients are unaware of this exclusive arrangement and think their agent is "negotiating" a deal for them, when really, the agent just funnels the ebook into the big-name ebook company, and takes the boilerplate contract that the agency and the ebook company previously negotiated.

Again, there is no third party here, because the ebook company and the agent have a pre-existing partnership.

So if you think you're indie published, but your agent does all the work, you are *not* indie-published. I don't know what exactly you are, but you don't have control over your rights or your publishing decisions the way a true indie published author does.

In my opinion, being "indie" published through an agent is the *worst* of all possible worlds. Choose. For each of your novels, either go 100% traditional and deal with the headaches and the fallout or go 100% self- or indie-published. Agents in the mix cause too many issues, which I will also deal with in later chapters.

What about indie writers? I mentioned above that they have to deal with contracts as well. Startlingly for many indie writers, they find that they have to *generate* contracts. You want to work with a good local copyeditor? You'll need some kind of agreement to govern your relationship. You want to co-author a book with your best writer pal? You'll need a collaboration agreement. You'll need a contract to delineate who handles the money.

And what about all those 99-cent boxed sets with 9 or 10 authors? I've seen some pretty crappy boxed set contracts that essentially say this:

Suzy, Janice, Alice, Marcy, Mike, Scott, Dan, Jessie, and Madison will put their books in a boxed set that will sell on Amazon for 99 cents. They agree to put 50% of their earnings into advertising and split the remaining 50% among themselves. Suzy will handle the money, and Janice will handle the publishing. Signed and dated, the group.

Oh. My. God. I have not heard about the fights and levels of problems that have arisen because of these "simple" contracts, but I can bet that some friendships vanished, along with a lot of money.

And those are just the indie problems I can think of off the top of my head. I know there are more.

I know, I know. I've just cracked open that huge can of worms. Wait. Let's call it for what it really is, shall we? It's a Dumpster full of worms. Hell, it's probably a garbage pit full of worms.

I dug through the garbage pit full of worms to find an even deeper pit beneath before I finally gave up and called this book done. The pitfalls for writers and the unwary are vast. You'll discover some throughout your career that I've never heard of.

What this book will teach you, more than anything, is to approach each contract as if it were being executed by the Devil himself. Look for anything that might harm you, and do your best to negotiate it away.

What you want for your writing, for your life, really, is control over all of your projects. Which means you should write a tough contract when you bring other people into your own business, and you should mitigate tough contracts when you work with someone else's business.

Ready for a trip to the dark side? Buckle up, and let's go.

THE BASICS

You're in business now—whether it's traditional publishing, indie publishing or hybrid publishing. To be successful, you need to control your own destiny as much as possible. Contracts define your relationships. Contracts define who controls what in the relationship. —From Chapter 1

1

CONTRACT BASICS

Wrapping my arms around a topic this vast is intimidating enough. Often, I will focus on events from 2016 as my hook.

But I realized that I needed to do something right up front: I need to discuss the importance of contracts.

I know to some of you that sounds silly. Traditionally published writers expect to get a contract from their publisher. Hybrid writers expect the same thing, when they have a publisher other than themselves.

Indie writers often have no idea what contracts are or why they're necessary.

In fact, all three groups rarely think about contracts at all.

Over the years, I have become fascinated with writers' attitudes toward contracts. Writers are so very cavalier about them. More than fifteen years ago, a former editor of mine (for a major traditional publishing house that has since vanished) told me that most writers she worked with looked at their 25-page traditional publishing contract like this:

The writer closely examined the lines covering the advance, and the advance's payout schedule. The writer eyeballed the royalty rates, and the writer glanced at the deadlines.

That was it. Out of 25 pages, the writer looked at very little else.

I did not believe my editor. I really believed most writers were not that stupid.

I'm here to tell you now: She was right. Most writers *are* that stupid. Most writers pay no attention to their publishing contracts at all until some term bites them in the ass. Then the writer tries to figure out how to get out of it, not realizing that *they* got themselves into it by signing the contract without examining it.

Hybrid writers are learning the truth of that one. Many hybrid writers want to reprint their backlist. In the early days of epublishing, a lot of hybrid writers simply put their backlist titles up as ebooks, only to receive a cease-and-desist notice from the book's traditional publisher. Writers stopped uploading without permission pretty quickly as the word got out that traditional publishers didn't like that.

It helped that traditional publishers started epubbing their own backlists.

Indie writers have yet another problem with contracts. Indie writers believe they don't need any.

Writers in general—traditional, hybrid, and indie—do not respect their contracts. Writers don't understand contracts, and rather than learning what a contract is and why it exists, writers let "their people" handle the contracts.

For generations now, "their people" are usually their agent and the employees of their agent, which, as you will see in future chapters, is a truly terrible idea. If you want "people" to handle your contracts for you, hire people for whom contracts are a specialty. Namely, a literary lawyer.

But let's talk about contracts themselves, shall we? Most writers expect *someone else* to generate a contract. Most writers *want* their traditional publisher or their agent or their service provider or their mortgage broker or *whomever* they're in business with to provide them with a contract. Most writers have no clue that they can generate *their own* contracts.

Yes, you, traditional writers! You can go to your publisher with your own contract in hand. I personally know several writers who do this.

That puts the contract negotiation phase on equal footing. The writer has their 10-page contract; the publisher has their 25-page contract.

The document the two parties end up with is *neither* of those contracts. It's something unique to that particular negotiation, and probably won't be replicated in the writer's next negotiation with a different publisher.

There, traditional writers, did I just blow your minds? Because it certainly blew mine when I started editing over 25 years ago and some writers provided me with their standard contracts for short fiction. I didn't know that was possible, because, at the time, I did not understand contracts or contract law.

Indie writers, I know many of you are wondering why you need a contract at all. Technically, in many states in the U.S., you don't. But in some states, you do.

There are other, more practical reasons to have a contract, and I will get to those after I define what a contract is.

A contract is a legally binding agreement between two or more parties.

As with anything in the law, however, that simple statement above isn't the whole story. In order for a contract to be valid, it must have *all* of the following elements:

1. Offer
2. Acceptance
3. Valid (legal and valuable) consideration
4. The parties must intend to enter an agreement with each other
5. The parties must have the legal capacity to act in this matter
6. The parties must give *genuine* consent to the terms
7. The agreement must be legal

I'm going to start with the simplest things to explain, and then I'll get to the harder ones.

With that in mind, let's start with #7.

The agreement must be legal

You and I can enter an agreement to commit a crime. However, that agreement, even if it fulfills points 1-6 above, is not valid. There are a million ways to enter into an "illegally formed" contract, and most of them do not apply to publishing, so I am going to skip them. If you want to see a list of possible items that make an agreement illegal, go to this page on the lawhandbook.org, which explains these elements clearly.[1]

#7 generally does not apply to publishing contracts, but the rest of the list does. So let's move to #5.

The parties must have the legal capacity to act in this matter

Legal capacity has a lot of definitions, and we're not going to get into most of them. Generally speaking, the person who enters into a contractual agreement must be an adult, in full command of their mental faculties, and able to understand what they're signing.

If one of the parties is a corporation, then the person who enters the agreement for the corporation has to have the power within the corporation to make binding legal agreements.

This one little fact is why agents *cannot* sign a contract for their writers, unless the writers give the agents power to do so under the law, with another agreement called Power of Attorney. Even then, the ability to sign such documents would have to be spelled out in the Power of Attorney agreement.

All parties to a contract need to have the *legal* ability to represent whatever is in that contract. For example, I cannot sign a *valid* contract selling your novel to a major publisher. I do not control the rights to your novel. I also cannot scan and upload your book to, say, Amazon. When you upload a book to Kindle, you warrant—by agreeing to the terms of service (a contract)—that the book is yours or that you control the copyright to that book. Since I do not control your copyright, I would not have the legal capacity to enter into an agreement for that book.

Speaking of terms of service (which is a contract, by the way), let's go to #6:

The parties must give *genuine* consent to the terms

Have you ever read through a terms of service (TOS) agreement? No? And yet you've clicked *accept*? You have to go through pages and pages of text, plus an offer to have the TOS sent to you via email (or regular mail), before you can click *accept*. Back in the old days (like ten years ago), it was easier to hit *accept* on a TOS. The very ease back then made it possible for attorneys to argue that there was no "genuine consent." (This kind of thing fell under consumer protection laws, usually.)

That's why TOS have become impossible to ignore. You have to willfully *not read* them, and go through a bunch of notices *before* you click *accept*. Then it's your own damn fault if you agreed to something you didn't read.

Genuine consent in most written contracts comes in the form of a signature with a date attached. Sometimes that signature needs to be witnessed and sometimes it needs to be notarized to show its validity.

But on some contracts—particularly verbal contracts—all it takes is a handshake to give genuine consent. Each country's laws differ on this point. In the United States, each state's laws differ. Some states do not honor verbal agreements. Others do. If one of the parties in your contract is from one of those states, then you could be agreeing to something you think you've mentioned casually over the phone.

This one fact alone is why I *do not* conduct telephone negotiations with *anyone* on any project for any reason.

People who want to negotiate with me must do so by letter or, these days, by email. I print those emails and keep them as work product for any agreement that we come up with, or don't come up with, as the case may be.

The best case scenario with your emails is to be clear with the person you're negotiating with that you are negotiating. You say in the first email that you are negotiating the terms of your agreement. If they respond to that email, then you have the basics of a contract.

Now we're getting to the parts of a contract where I'm feeling constrained by the simplicity of this book's format. For every sentence I write, I have paragraphs of "but if this happens, then that could happen" that I could add to this document. I'm not going to.

If you don't understand what I'm writing here, there are many, many, many websites that can help you understand the essentials of contracts, probably better than I ever could. Google contract basics.

But…moving on…and advancing into serious wiggle territory, I present #4.

The parties must intend to enter an agreement with each other

Intent in this instance is really difficult to explain. When you upload a book to an ebook site, you are *intentionally* entering into an agreement with that site. The TOS defines the legal relationship you have. Most writers don't think about that intention, but it exists.

It also exists for you readers. When you pay money for an ebook, you're licensing the ebook to use on your ereader. You are *renting* that book. You have entered an agreement with Amazon or Kobo to rent that book, and those entities may revoke your right to rent that book for reasons listed on their websites. You signaled your intent to rent that book by your actions, not necessarily by clicking agree to a TOS or by signing a document.

This is a very complicated part of the law, and of course, it varies state to state, and sometimes from community to community. If you want to know more, then do some digging on your own.

For our purposes, however, you will be dealing with a written document. You would not be negotiating a document to work with someone if you did not intend to work with them. Therefore, this seems like a small point.

Trust me, it isn't. And it has become more confusing for indies than it has for traditionally published writers, because of things like Terms of Service.

Now that I've muddied the waters with the complex legal wiggle-waggles, let's go to the most basic part of contracts.

Every single contract needs #1: **An Offer.** That offer must be #2: **Accepted.** Tied to that offer is #3: **Consideration.**

I know most of you don't know what *consideration* is, so let's explain it first.

Consideration

What makes a contract special is that it is binding on *both* parties. In return for making the agreement, each party needs to get something. That something has to have value to both parties.

Nolo.com's article on contract basics[2] gives a very succinct definition of consideration:

Each party has to promise or provide something of value to the other.

In many, many cases, consideration has a monetary value. But not in all cases. Essentially, consideration boils down to the very reason each party enters the contract.

Writer A wants to have a novel published.

Publisher X wants to publish that novel.

Writer A and Publisher X decide to exchange services. Writer A writes the book; Publisher X publishes the book. Even with no cash changing hands, both parties have received consideration—in the form of work, time, expenditure, and so on. Both parties have gotten something they value out of the agreement.

We end with the meat of a contract.

A contract does *not* exist without #1 and #2.

Offer and Acceptance

I listed them separately. Many descriptions of contracts list them together. Because a contract does *not* exist without both.

I can make you an offer for your book. If you do not accept my offer, we do not have a contract.

It's that simple.

However, once the offer is accepted, we have a valid contract. Some people mistakenly believe the contract is not valid unless money changes hands. Not true.

The contract becomes valid and binding once the agreement is made.

Let me give you a real world example that, fortunately for the other party involved, I did not take action over.

A representative of a brand new science fiction convention contacted me via email, and offered to pay all my expenses in exchange for my appearance at that particular science fiction convention.

I agreed also via email, and printed out the letter, along with my reply.

These email letters, along with email acceptances, are a common way to do business with a science fiction convention. Those email letters are a contract.

Offer made. Offer accepted. Consideration would happen at the convention itself—for both parties.

A short time later, I received a form email telling me that the organizers had overbooked the convention and they were no longer going to pay any of my expenses, even though they still wanted me to appear at the convention.

I had several choices. They had breached a contract. Our email exchange would serve as the binding contract.

I could have shown up at the convention and insisted on enforcement. Had they notified me with enough time to cancel my plans and get *full* reimbursement for any of my expenses, I probably would not have had a case. However, if they had notified me the night before or the moment I arrived at the convention (which has happened to some writers), then I could have taken them to court.

I had many other options as well, and believe me, I thought about them. This was extremely unprofessional behavior on the part of the organizers, and it called into question habits of a lifetime for those of us who've appeared at conventions.

I was not the only science fiction professional who received the form email. Several other science fiction professionals did as well. We discussed taking action. Instead, the only action we took was to inform the other professionals who had not received the form about the breach of contract. If those professionals had shown up at the convention, they might not have had their expenses paid.

Nothing happened, because the convention imploded shortly thereafter and will not be held. So there will be no appearances and no all-expenses-paid guests. Which is probably good for the organizers, since they had several existing contracts that they were no longer planning to honor.

Most of us think of contracts as those 25-page documents I mentioned above. But we deal with contracts each and every day. Some are implied contracts, and others are actual paper documents. That email exchange with the convention was a contract.

I do not have a written document with the woman who cleans my house. She shows up once a week at a designated time, and I pay her every single week. We made that agreement verbally. We have a contract for cleaning, and it is binding.

Contracts are extremely important. They *define* the relationship between the parties. Written contracts are the best, because each party can examine the terms, think them over, and decide whether or not those terms are acceptable.

You and I might discuss a proposed business plan over the phone. I might think we decided to have you do all the publishing work, from designing the covers of a book to writing cover copy, and you might think we decided that you would write the book and I would publish it. A simple misunderstanding that could happen in conversation would be solved if we had a written agreement.

With a written document, you can examine the terms and see if they're feasible. But you must examine those terms *before* you accept the offer. Once you've accepted, the contract becomes binding.

It's easier to take legal action over a broken contract if that contract is in writing. Taking legal action does not mean you have to go to court. You can have an attorney contact the other party, and let them know they are in breach of the contract. That's very easy to do when the terms are spelled out.

I can't tell you how many times I've taken part of a publishing contract and used that section to show the publisher that they were in breach of the contract.

Once someone is in breach, by the way, they usually have the right to cure. Meaning, if they do something wrong, they have the right to fix that problem within a reasonable amount of time.

I keep catching one of my traditional publishers in a breach, and the bastards keep curing. I want them to breach the contract completely so that I can get my book back. They haven't done it yet. (Sigh.)

Three last points about contracts.

First, both parties have a stake in the contract. You don't have to sign something as is. And, in fact, you shouldn't. You should negotiate. Most writers never do that. I know, I know. You don't know how to negotiate. Go to the chapter on negotiation.

Second, here's an important thing to remember about contracts, which I came across on BusinessDictionary.com[3]:

However, while all parties may expect a fair benefit from the contract (otherwise courts may set it aside as inequitable) it does not follow that each party will benefit to an equal extent.

Traditional publishing has made this one little fact the gold standard of their contracts. Yep, writer and publisher benefit from a traditional publishing contract. Who benefits more these days? The publisher. And I aim to stop that with this book.

I can't stop publishers from asking for more than they deserve. I can, however, dream that I can stop you from *giving* them more than they deserve.

That's where the chapters on contract clauses come in.

Finally (third), indie writers, you need to define your relationships—all of your relationships, from your relationship with your cover designer to your copyeditor—with contracts. You'll probably have to generate those contracts yourself. Some you might want to hire an attorney to help you with.

But for others, you can probably just write up an agreement in plain English, listing an offer, the acceptance, and the consideration. You can always change the agreement (with the approval of both parties) down the road. But cover your asses.

Because, really, covering your ass is what a contract is all about.

2

CONTROL AND COMPROMISE

As I settled into writing this book in weekly intervals on my website, I ordered books to help me. Some of the books cover topics I'm less familiar with, but some look like they might be useful to beginners. I want to be able to recommend books that cover things I don't necessarily cover. (There's a list of the books I recommend at the end of this book.)

I didn't expect to find, in the basic books, things I never even thought about.

I guess it makes sense. I've been dealing with contracts my entire adult life. I've received contracts and I've created contracts. I seem like a different person when I receive a contract than when I issue contracts—or so some of my students would say.

When I receive contracts as a writer and editor, I negotiate the hell out of them. When I issue contracts as an editor and publisher, I negotiate only so much and then I shrug, with a take it or leave it.

In truth, I'm the same person with the same goal both times.

Control.

I want to control whatever project I'm working on. I don't negotiate for more money, but I do negotiate for more control. When I issue a contract, I do my best to foresee what rights I need to license to control the project itself, and then I go forward.

Right now, traditional publishers are just beginning to realize that they can (and often do) control *everything* about a work of art. This should frighten you traditionally published writers, because publishers are going to exploit your works as never before. We'll deal with that a bit next in the chapter on copyright and permissions.

Control. It is at the heart of any negotiation. All business owners want to control as much about their businesses as possible.

How does this relate to my reading? It wasn't until I picked up Helen Sedwick's *Self-Publisher's Legal Handbook* that I realized I had left out the concept of control entirely. As far as I'm concerned, control governs everything, and is as natural as breathing. I had forgotten—if I ever really knew—that most people don't understand this most basic of concepts.

We all know that you can't control everything in life. That rule also applies to contracts. Some large entities do not allow negotiation on their contracts. This is particularly common in Terms of Service agreements (although I do know people who have managed to negotiate some of those as well).

Where do you gain control in a TOS or a nonnegotiable agreement? In your own decision-making.

Here's what you ask yourself:

1. Do I need this *particular* service?
2. Is there a way to do what I want *without* this service?
3. If there is no alternative, can I live with the terms that the service provider has posted on their website?
4. If I can't live with those terms, then I have no choice. I do not hit *agree* on the Terms of Service. I do not sign my name to the contract. I *walk away from the deal*.

Remember, from the previous chapter what the three most essential elements of a contract are: They are *offer*, *acceptance*, and *consideration*.

The Terms of Service or contract acts as the *offer*. It is not valid until you *accept* it. However, sometimes acceptance is not done with a signature or a click of the mouse. Sometimes acceptance happens when you cash a check from the company or when you *use* the service.

In the olden days of websites and online service providers, you could use a service without hitting *agree* on the TOS. There was no guarantee you had even *seen* the TOS. That's why now, most service providers make the TOS obnoxiously hard to avoid when you try to go into their website.

You have to realize that when things like that happen, someone litigated the free-standing TOS and a court found it wanting as an agreement.

The way websites and TOS operate is different from brick-and-mortar stores or services. You don't have to sign a TOS before you enter your local grocery store. But I'm sure there are some implied agreements with that store. For example, they put prices on their food. You know without being told that you cannot remove the food from the premises without paying for it. An agreement—offer (food on display with a price), acceptance (paying for the food), consideration (they get money; you get food).

When I discussed this with my husband, the writer Dean Wesley Smith, he added a few other things to the grocery store analogy. He added that we, as consumers, have an expectation that the food is fresh and won't poison us. The store has an expectation that our money is good (we won't bounce a check, pay with forged dollars, or use someone else's credit card). All of these are implied agreements that we accept as normal, and live with from day to day.

The web is different from brick-and-mortar. Indie publishing is different from traditional publishing. But contracts and agreements remain the same. They are about control.

Which brings us to some of the topics I'll deal with in this chapter. Most of them I got from my blog readers, either in private emails or comments.

Here's my theory: If someone takes the time to comment on something or write me an email on a certain topic, I'm pretty sure that a lot of other people have the same question or comment.

So here goes:

Fairness

Often, you'll see a lot of discussion about fair terms or fairness among non-lawyers about certain deals or certain business behaviors.

Oh, I hate to say this, folks. But when it comes to the law, and when it comes to business, fair does not exist. The law concerns itself with what's legal under statute. And business concerns itself with business.

Some businesspeople are very fair in their dealings with others. Other businesspeople are not.

Whenever you deal with contracts, you don't negotiate the contract for the nice reasonable person sitting across from you. You negotiate the contract with the idea that the nice reasonable person will be fired and replaced with a demon from hell who will enforce every part of that contract to his own benefit.

The best contracts are compromises between the parties to the contract. That means that these contracts are good enough for all the parties, and not great for any of the parties.

The best contracts *are* fair to both sides—at the time the contract is negotiated. However, contracts that were negotiated in 1980 are still being interpreted today, and the world has definitely changed. What might have seemed "fair" then isn't necessarily "fair" now.

Keep that in mind.

Marsha asked a corollary question in a comment on the April 6, 2016 blog post. She wrote:

> With a standard TOS, say with CreateSpace, I assumed that there is little or no negotiating room, and because everyone does sign their TOS, the TOS must be fair to both parties. Am I wrong?

She asked a two-part question: Is there little or no negotiating room? And because everyone signs the TOS, is the TOS fair to both parties?

She's right about the little or no negotiating room. I don't know anyone who has successfully changed the CreateSpace TOS.

But she's wrong about her second assumption. In fact, it's a very *dangerous* assumption both in the CreateSpace TOS and in life in general.

…because everyone does sign their TOS, the TOS must be fair to both parties….

I've heard this assumption a lot and not just in the discussions on my website. The idea that *everyone* signed a document or has a mortgage or has worked with this particular company means that *someone* (who?) already negotiated the contract or the mortgage or the terms and came up with something fair.

Or that the company itself made sure its agreement was fair to everyone involved.

Go back to the opening of this chapter. Contracts are about *control*. They also define the relationship. If you have a hard-and-fast contract that no one can negotiate, well, by definition, that's unfair. You have all the control and the people using your service or buying your product have *no* control.

If you have total control over what's in a contract, and the other party has none, you have no reason to be fair to that party. Some businesses are fair, and some aren't.

But as a consumer—in general—you should assume that no company looks out for your well-being unless that company's existence is governed by certain laws (consumer regulations, etc). Some companies comply with those laws and regulations, and some do not.

Just because a law exists governing behavior doesn't mean a person or a company follows that law. It might mean that there is nothing about the company to complain about. It might also mean that they are violating the law left and right and no one has brought any legal action against them.

You don't know.

As a writer, you run a small business. I don't care if you're a traditionally published writer, a hybrid writer, or an indie writer. You run a business and so the rules of business apply.

One of those rules is this: Protect your own interests. Do *not* expect someone else to do it for you—be that person an agent, a lawyer, a company, a business partner, or a co-writer. Believe promises once they're in writing. Otherwise, remember that a *verbal* promise is worth the paper it's written on. (And for those metaphorically challenged, that means the promise is worth nothing unless it is in the form of a contract.)

If you have trouble with this concept, go back to your childhood. I'm sure at one point or another, someone said to you, "Just because all the kids are doing it doesn't mean *you* should do it." That's one of those lessons learned on the playground that apply to adulthood as well.

One of my great disappointments when I became an adult was the realization that you don't get an extra double-helping of wisdom when you turn 30 (or 40 or 50). You just gain some experience. Some people learn from that experience; most do not.

Be one of the people who learn from their experiences. Or better yet, be someone who believes the best in people, but plans for the worst out of them. When it comes to business, the law, and contracts, it's always better to expect the worst and be happily surprised when the best occurs instead.

Clout

Every time I talk about contracts, either in person or on my website, someone says that they can't negotiate a contract because they lack clout. And every single time I hear that, I sigh and think (but do not say) that the speaker is one of those people who will get screwed throughout their entire life.

You don't need clout to negotiate a contract. You just need…

Balls

And by "balls," I do *not* mean you have to be male. I mean you need to be willing to step up to the plate. When I look up the slang term "balls," most websites use "courage" or "bravery" as synonyms. And yeah, those are good words, but "balls"—at least in American English slang—means more than that.

It means a willingness to put yourself out there in a way that the average person would not.

So…you don't have *clout* to negotiate a contract. You're not James Patterson or Nora Roberts. You aren't already a multimillionaire. You aren't a successful businessperson. So, most people think you should slink into the background and wait for the success pixie to sprinkle you with magic dust. Once that occurs, *then* and *only then* can you negotiate a contract.

Seriously? Please excuse me while I sigh and shake my head.

How do you think people become successful? They become successful by *controlling* their own interests and standing up for themselves. They become successful by learning their business. They become successful by taking risks.

One of the major risks you take in *any* business is that you will hear the word "no." A lot.

What's the worst thing that could happen in a negotiation when you ask for something you want (but may fear you don't deserve yet)? Well, the person on the other side could say "no."

Oh, waaaaah….

But that person could say yes. Or they could say, *I can't do what you ask, but I can do something else that might benefit us both.*

You don't know until you ask.

And here's the thing, people. Anyone who knows contracts, who knows business, *expects* you to ask. So *ask.*

What's important to you might not be important to them at all, and so a yes on your most important thing might be easy to them.

It's not all up to them, by the way. Because it's a negotiation, which is a dialogue.

You might say, *I want X.*

And they might respond, *I can't do X. Sorry, no.*

Then you might say, *I see you want Q. But I can't do Q if I don't receive X.*

If Q is important to them, they might cave on X. And so on.

You don't know if you don't try.

And here's the thing—even if your try fails, you've practiced negotiating. That's a win.

Negotiations

I've been talking about negotiation here as if you know how to do it.

I know most of you are terrified of negotiating. That's why there is a negotiation chapter in this book. I also wrote a book on negotiation called *How to Negotiate Anything*.

And, as I wrote one of the contracts posts, I realized I had left something really important out of the negotiation book because that something was so basic to me, I didn't think to include it. In the comments, Antarespress reminded me that in any negotiation, principals negotiate with principals. Well, duh! And I left it out.

What that means, in plain English, is that the people making the deal —the people who can sign off on the deal—negotiate with each other.

This is a really, really important concept. It ties in with something else that a number of you wrote to me about.

I mentioned that in some states, oral agreements are binding. When this chapter went live as a blog post, two people wrote comments stating that oral agreements are also binding in Denmark and in the United Kingdom. I have no idea where else oral agreements might be binding. I just assume they are whenever I make an agreement.

Oral agreements, by the way, are *verbal* agreements.

The legality of oral agreements varies from state to state. Some states, for example, will accept oral contracts for small things (under $10,000 for example or maybe an agreement to mow the lawn), but not for large things.

Some states have different laws as to what's covered under oral agreements and what is not. It's up to you to know what's legal in your state *and in the state (or country) where the other person is*.

Better yet, never ever ever ever make any agreements over the phone. I do all of my negotiating on paper or online, and refuse to take phone calls *ever* from anyone I'm negotiating with.

Why? Because the other party could claim that the thirty-minute conversation we had on April 12, 2015 was about a contract negotiation when it really was a review of a copy edit. *What?* some of you say. *They would lie?*

Yes, they would lie. Not everyone will, but some people do as a matter of course.

This principals-negotiating-with-principals thing comes into play in *any* phone conversation where you and the other party are able to make an agreement.

Indie writers, who came into the publishing business cold, might have an easier time with this concept. But any writer who started in traditional publishing has a lot of difficulty with it.

Because in traditional publishing, representatives negotiate with representatives, and the principals do not talk to each other.

What do I mean? I mean that agents negotiate with editors. Agents theoretically represent the writer and editors represent the publishing company.

Even then, the negotiation is uneven. In theory, the agent has no power to make or sign an agreement. In reality, the agent shouldn't even be negotiating a legal document. Savvy writers use attorneys to negotiate a contract. We'll get to all of this later in the book.

Here's the upshot: The writer's representative should *not* be able to sign the documentation to make the deal. The writer's representative is not (or was not) a principal. (Many agents are in the process of subverting this these days, which gives me the willies.)

Editors also cannot sign an agreement, and have only limited power to act within certain parameters, as the company's representative. The editor has an offer and some wiggle room, but must get approval for almost everything.

Writers who drop their agents or handle things with their lawyers in the background often forget that the editor can be a representative. Suddenly, the writer is talking terms on the phone with an editor, and it might be a *binding* negotiation, not a casual discussion.

If you end up accidentally making promises while on the phone with someone, do this the moment you hang up: Write an email to that person, recapping the conversation and the agreements you both made. That way, you'll have a real-time written record of what was said.

Be very, very careful when dealing with someone else. Again, don't do it on the phone. Always in writing.

Use a representative when you're not certain you'll be making a final deal or you need someone to be tougher than you can be. Let the representative put distance between you and that nice person you like a lot on the other side of the table.

Understanding the Limitations

As I mentioned above, each party to a contract wants certain things out of that relationship. Some of those things will be deal breakers. Without those things in place, the party will *not* make the deal, because there's no point in doing so.

Each party.

When I act as a publisher or an editor, I try to be as fair as I can. I'll pay what the company can afford to license the rights we will need now and in the foreseeable future. Every clause in my contract has a purpose. Some of that purpose is to get the license, and some of that purpose is to protect me and my business.

When I act as a writer, I try to be as fair as I can. I will license as little as possible, but that license will enable the project to go forward. I will negotiate away any rights grabs. I will also ask for some kind of term limit, because I might want to use those rights in the future. I would like to be paid a good price for the license. Whether that price is a flat fee or a fee with a royalty structure will depend entirely on the project.

I know, because I've been in this business a long time, what a publisher needs in a license and what that publisher is just trying to grab because they can. I do not let a publisher grab everything. If that's a deal breaker for the publisher, then it's also a deal breaker for me. I don't want to work with someone who wants to own my intellectual property outright. I really don't want to work with someone who wants to own my intellectual property and who tries to gain that property through subterfuge, as many new traditional publishing contracts do.

Learning what is and isn't acceptable takes time. It's not something you can pick up in an afternoon.

That's why I recommend you hire an attorney to *explain* the contract to you. Those of you who have agents and ask the agent to explain the contract to you are being foolish. You're asking an English major to pilot a 747 with no training whatsoever. Your English major agent knows maybe a bit more than you do about contracts, but not much more.

However, just because you've hired a lawyer to explain the contract to you and the lawyer does that, doesn't mean you know how to negotiate that contract.

For example, I've had writers (who hired lawyers) negotiate *worse* contracts because of a lawyer's advice. Not that the lawyer gave bad advice, but because the writer didn't know what the advice meant.

The Whole Document

A contract is not a series of disconnected lines. It's a complete item, one thing, in and of itself.

Let me use a metaphor.

A contract is not composed of separate pieces of thread lying next to each other on a board. You cannot remove one thread and have the others remain intact.

Instead, a contract is a delicately woven shirt. You can take a thread from that shirt, but if you tug on the thread, the entire shirt might come apart, or the sleeve might fall off.

A line on page 3 of a contract might have an important corollary on page 2 of the contract. Remove the line on page 3, and that line on page 2 might mean something else entirely.

When a lawyer explains a contract to you and says that Clauses A, C, and F are not in your best interest and should be excised, ask the lawyer what you should do if the other party lets you delete Clauses A and F, but not clause C.

The lawyer might want you to add wording or bring the contract back to them or tell you to keep Clause A in the contract in that instance.

Because it's all interwoven.

I had one writer try to remove the clause that warrants that the writer did not plagiarize the story. Did I think the writer had plagiarized the story? No. I knew what the lawyer objected to. The lawyer wanted the entire warranty clause removed from the contract, *or* to have a clause added that would make my company liable in the same way as the writer was. We might have discussed that.

But the writer heard that the plagiarism clause had to be removed and took it as a deal breaker—which it was for me. Because any time a writer refused to warrant that they did not plagiarize a document, well, then I have to assume they did. As a publisher, I couldn't publish a story with no legal protections for my company in place.

Changes in language, yes. Deleting the entire clause, no. Had the writer consulted with the lawyer about the *negotiation*, rather than about what the contract meant, then we might have been able to come to terms.

But in that instance, we couldn't. Because the writer did not understand compromise.

Compromise

In recent years, "compromise" has become a dirty word, particularly in America. Our politicians refuse to compromise with each other, entire groups demand everything be their way *or else*, and everyone screams at everyone else.

But compromise is the essence of human relationships. No one gets everything they want—or at least, no one should.

That's particularly true in negotiation. The best negotiations are the ones in which both sides end up vaguely unsatisfied—yet with the knowledge that they got the best deal they could under the circumstances.

I began this chapter by talking about Terms of Service which often don't allow for compromise, at least from the average user. But the large user—the big corporation at the other end of the table, or the client who spends a large sum of money on the product or service—might be able to negotiate a much better deal than the small user.

Someday, you as a writer or a business might become a large user with clout. Prepare for that day. Learn what's possible.

In traditional publishing contracts, what's possible is more than most writers ever get. Because most writers never ask. Their agents don't ask either.

When contracts are weighted to one side, often that weight comes because the other side didn't negotiate or didn't negotiate effectively.

This book comes from the perspective that you can ask for what you want. You might lose more than you win. Or you might compromise.

But you should stand up for yourself. You should understand the position of the person on the other side of the table, and you should make the best possible deal for your situation.

Or you should walk away.

Over and over in this book, I will tell you to stand up for yourself. I will tell you to be strong. I will tell you to have courage. I will tell you to take risks.

You're in business now—whether it's traditional publishing, indie publishing or hybrid publishing. To be successful, you need to control your own destiny as much as possible.

Contracts define your relationships. Contracts define who controls what in the relationship.

Start thinking about control and compromise, about risk and reward. About standing strong.

Because you have to do all of those things as a businessperson.

And that, my friends, is non-negotiable.

3

UNDERSTANDING COPYRIGHT

I recently got an email that sent a chill through me. It was a newsletter from a traditional publishing organization. This organization is geared toward publishers and editors, not toward writers.

The newsletter was essentially an ad for a seminar that will teach publishers to understand intellectual property and expand their rights business.

Why did this send a chill through me? Because the one thing that has protected writers who signed bad contracts is the fact that their traditional publishers have no idea how to exploit the rights they licensed.

I know, I know, I just used a bunch of words you're familiar with in a context you don't understand. I'll get to that.

But in short, most publishers ask for more than they have ever used in the past. Publishers have been very short-sighted in how they published books.

Up until a few years ago, those books were simply that to a publisher —a book. Something tangible. Not only was the book tangible, it "rotted" after a few months or a year. In other words, as far as the publisher was concerned, the book had little value after a year or so of publication.

Ten years ago, it was relatively easy to get the rights reverted on a book like that. Essentially both parties agreed that the terms of the contract had been met, that the parties no longer had need of the relationship, and so they severed their business relationship.

It wasn't easy-peasy, but it wasn't hard either. It usually took a letter or two.

By 2005, however, most agents refused to write the letter which severed the contract. The reason was simple from the agent's perspective. Many, many, many agents used a combination of their agency agreement and a clause in the writer's book contract to define their relationship *with the writer*, and determine who controlled the marketing and finances of that book.

It wasn't in the agent's best interest to cancel the contract. In fact, the longer the contract existed, the better it was *for the agent*. (We deal with this in-depth in the section of the book titled *Agents*.)

Writers with agents would have to write those letters themselves—and then, publishers would often contact the agent to find out why the agent was "letting" the writer do this.

What a tangled mess.

I wrote my own letters. I never wrote to the editor (which was what most writers do). I wrote to the legal department. And the legal department and I would wrangle. I wrote so often on one series of books that the woman in charge of the legal department finally gave up.

Even though I wasn't entitled to rights reversions on four of the books in that series, I kept asking whenever I asked for the first two books. I'd make a list of all six books in that series, ask for reversion, and get a grumpy letter from the woman in charge of the legal department.

Finally, after two years of this, she did the legal equivalent of throwing my books at me. She reverted all of them, and sent me a cover letter that basically told me to get out of her life.

I was happy to do so.

In the last year or so, I've been hearing from writers who say it's almost impossible to get their rights reverted. The publishers want to hold onto those rights as long as possible.

The main reason for this has nothing to do with reprinting the book or keeping the book in the marketplace. It has to do with the changes in accounting that have occurred in the big traditional publishing companies.

The Big 5 (4? 3? Whatever. Jeez.) are now part of international conglomerates. Those conglomerates understand that intellectual property has as much or more value than the buildings and land that the conglomerates use to house their businesses.

Those conglomerates put *all* of the intellectual property on their account books as an asset. So your novel—even if it's more or less out of print (or has a $19.99 ebook like my traditionally published novel *Fantasy Life*)—has a value assigned to it that reflects not only its earnings *right now*, but its potential earnings in the future.

The command came down from on high that publishers should retain the assets as best as possible. (I'm pretty sure some of these publishing companies were purchased for their intellectual property assets, not because of their bottom lines. I have no interest in proving that, though.)

So, publishers have kept the assets, doing the minimum to retain the rights to them. But they really haven't maximized their profits.

Think of it this way: Your book is a house in the middle of an older subdivision. The house is paid off, and the taxes are minimal. The publisher has kept the house—hasn't put it up for sale—but hasn't done much more. Until recently, that is.

All of these seminars for publishers on rights and licenses focus on maximizing *profit*. In our analogy, these seminars teach publishers how to rent the house as is, how to improve the house and the property to get more rent, how to interest some major outside company in leasing the house for…say…photo shoots, etc.—all things that haven't happened for years.

The amount of say you have in what these publishers do with your old books depends entirely on the contract you signed way back when.

If the traditional publisher burnishes off the book and exploits the rights, then the book gets revived, and your chances of reverting the rights go down to nothing at all.

But, you're thinking, won't you get money from all of those new uses of that book?

Again, it depends on the contract you signed.

In theory.

In practice, publishers have started to claim rights they never had. They're interpreting the contract terms for something negotiated in 1997 by 2016 standards, and finding ways *not to* pay for those uses.

Big corporations are all about profit for the corporation. The best way to maximize profit is to lower expenses.

That's why, after these big companies merge, you see layoffs a year or so later. That gives the new company time to define itself, find employees with overlapping duties, and streamline production.

Once the layoffs are over, once the agreements with the subcontractors (like printers and distributors) end or get renegotiated, the corporations look around for other ways to cut expenses.

The easiest way is to cut the payments to the suppliers—the writers.

We'll deal with the various ways that publishers cut payments to writers in a future chapter.

Just be aware that publishers often cut payments, and they use the contract as their guide.

Those of us with longstanding contracts with traditional publishers are fighting a different fight from new writers. New writers are being presented with contracts that differ substantially from the ones we old-timers initially got.

We all have something in common, though. We all can use copyright law to save our asses.

As I've written a million times before, writers do *not* sell books. We license copyright. Usually I say, if you don't understand that, get a copy of Nolo Press's current *Copyright Handbook*. Many of you do that, but not all of you have read it.

So I'm going to give you a quick primer on copyright. Very, very, very quick, along with a few links that will answer more of your questions. Or maybe scare you with the wealth of material you have to learn.

By the way, if you Google "copyright for writers," much of what you get is older. It's not necessarily wrong, but it's slanted to a world that no longer exists. For example, as I wrote this chapter I found one article from 1997.

If you want one good newer post that starts to explain copyright, go to "11 Things Every Writer Should Know About Copyrights," from Helen Sedwick's blog[1].

I stumbled upon a relatively good article on copyright basics on a law firm's website. The article is from 2005, but has some clear information. The article is titled, "Know Your Copyrights: A Legal Guide For Writers."[2]

Nolo.com has a copyright FAQ that is about as basic as it gets.[3] And of course, the U.S. Copyright Office has a FAQ for copyright.[4]

And if you want to read the US Copyright Act, you can find it on Cornell Law's website.[5]

All of this, of course, deals with *United States'* copyright law, not copyright law for any other country. The U.S. copyright laws are based in our Constitution, and have been expanded and changed through acts of Congress over the past 200+ years. The trade agreements we sign, the copyright conventions held in conjunction with other countries, all have an impact on copyright.

After I had published this chapter as a blog, a reader shared the best place to find information on Canada's copyright laws, which is Michael Geist's website.[6]

Before you all ask me questions about copyright below, do some research on your own. Use those sites or the equivalent sites for your countries. Do the research.

So…let's give you some basics here, from my American perspective.

What is copyright?

Here's how the U.S. government answers that question:

Copyright is a form of protection grounded in the U.S. Constitution and granted by law for original works of authorship fixed in a tangible medium of expression. Copyright covers both published and unpublished works.

Yeah, that's clear as mud, right?

What it actually means is that works created by someone—music, painting, photography, and writing—are protected under U.S. copyright law. Those works must be in a *tangible* form.

In other words, those works aren't *ideas*. We can all have the same idea. All the law protects is how you express that idea. For example, I have found half a dozen articles on copyright basics. I'm writing one myself. We're all using the same ideas and concepts, but the *way* we put those concepts together—on paper or on my website or in this chapter—is what's protected.

My words and the structure of this chapter are protected. The concepts I'm discussing here are not.

That's very important. Just because you had an idea about a high school girl who encounters a vampire doesn't mean you can copyright that idea. Think about the different ways that idea can be used.

Stephanie Meyer used that idea as the basis for *Twilight*, which some call a romance. (I have issues with a 104-year-old falling for a teenager, but maybe that's just me.)

Joss Whedon came up with a completely different story using the high school girl encounters vampire idea: *Buffy The Vampire Slayer*.

Same idea, two different directions. Both *Twilight* and *Buffy* were copyrighted the moment they acquired a *form*—a novel in the case of *Twilight* and a movie screenplay in the case of *Buffy*, which is why the copyright office lists the fact that both published and *unpublished* works are copyrighted.

What does it mean to have a copyright?

Your copyright is property. You *own* it.

The law protects your copyright in five major areas:

1. Reproduction
2. Adaptation
3. Distribution
4. Performance
5. Display

Only five? Some of you are asking. Many of you have seen Dean's article on "The Magic Bakery"[7] on his website in which he discusses how writers can and do slice up copyright into *thousands* of pieces. That's not a metaphor, by the way.

Those five areas, above, are huge categories. How the writer defines and licenses the copyright determines how the writer will earn money from that copyright.

Let's define the five ever so briefly. Briefly because the more specific I get the more confusing this will all be. There are a million exceptions to everything in the law, and copyright is no different.

But for the sake of education...

Reproduction

The owner of the copyright has the exclusive right to make copies of that copyrighted work. Photocopies are exact copies of a novel manuscript. Books are *substantially similar* copies of a novel manuscript. It gets more complex from there, but you get the point.

Adaptation

The owner of the copyright has the exclusive right to make or to *authorize* derivative works based on the copyrighted work. What's a derivative work? A game, a TV show, a short story, and so on and so forth. There are definitions of derivative works in the law. I'm not getting into that here.

Distribution

The owner of the copyright has the exclusive right to distribute or authorize distribution of copies of the copyrighted work "to the public by sale or other transfer of ownership, or by rental, lease, or lending." Note that this is a different right than the right to make copies.

Performance

The owner of the copyright has the exclusive right to perform or authorize a performance of the copyrighted work publicly. What "publicly" means depends, again, on the law. But those performances can be live or in recorded form.

Display

The owner of the copyright has the exclusive right to display or authorize to display the copyrighted work publicly. What "display" means includes TV productions, movies, and more.

The Owner of the Copyright

Have you noticed that throughout these descriptions, I've been using the phrase "the owner of the copyright" instead of "the writer" or "the creator"? Because if you sell *all rights* to a publishing company, *they* become the owner of the copyright. Not you.

Copyright is property. You can sell it outright. You can give it to someone. You can rent it, lease it, or lend it. You can rent, lend, lease, or sell a part of it.

The owner of the copyright, then, is a legal entity that might not be the *creator* of the copyright. Increasingly, in dealings with movie studios, agents, and publishing companies, the *owner* of the copyright is *not* the creator.

In fact, we just had interest on one of my books from a Hollywood production company. They wanted to "see" the book—from me or my representative. However, before letting them "see" it, I had to sign a document giving them some copyright in the book—*even if they chose not to option the book*. Not kidding.

This, a book they could have bought on any one of a dozen sites or stores. They came to us directly so that they could sneakily get a slice of copyright, just in case I wasn't paying attention to the legalities and niceties of copyright law.

I refused to let them "see" the book, and did not bother to tell them they could buy it themselves, just in case they would take that as an acceptance of their stupid little legal ploy.

This, by the way, was not a fly-by-night production company, but one of the largest in the world, fronted by two very famous hyphenates you would recognize. I always wonder, when I see things like this, how many writers were flattered that representatives of these two famous people were interested in their teeny tiny book.

Slices of Copyright

Dean talks about slices of copyright in his magic bakery. Essentially he postulates that the magic bakery produces pies that can create thousands of pieces. He's right.

You just have to know how to slice the pie.

I listed five major areas of copyright. Realize that they often work in concert. When you sell a book to a publisher, you're licensing part of the right to reproduce the book and part of the right to distribute the book. Not *all* of those rights, I hope, but parts of them.

Let's talk reproduction first. (Imagine if all relationships started like that. Wait! Wrong book.)

You can slice the reproduction pie very thinly. You might give a publisher the right to publish your book in limited edition hardcover with six illustrations, the edition limited to only 100 copies.

That leaves you the right to license the book to another publisher to publish the book in a standard hardcover edition in the territory of the United States only.

Which still leaves you the right to license the book to a third publisher to publish a trade paper edition of the book in the territory of the United States only.

And you can still license the book to a fourth publisher to publish a mass market edition of the book in the territory of the United States only.

And you might want a fifth publisher to publish the book in an ebook version, but only on Amazon in the United States. A sixth publisher might publish the ebook versions in all the other ebook services, but only *outside* of the United States.

Note that reproduction rights only give the publishers the right to make copies of that manuscript, that book. They do not give the publishers the right to *distribute* those books. Publishing companies ask for both for very logical reasons. They want to sell the book, after all, and to sell it, they need to distribute it.

Notice too, that the ebook deals I mention above list where the books will be distributed. Nothing in that grant of rights above specifies what happens if the writer decides to publish her own ebook and make it available only on her website. Since companies five and six are limited only to Amazon and other ebook services, those companies will not have the right to complain about that other ebook, the author-created one, available on the website.

Note too that we haven't discussed any versions outside of the United States. All the rights to books sold in England or France or Japan are reserved to the author.

In fact, every contract should have some version of the phrase "All rights not mentioned herein are reserved to the author" in it, which really covers your ass.

Enough Already!

Is your head spinning yet? It should be. Because copyright is something *all writers* need to understand.

Yes, copyright is complex. Yes, it takes a long time to learn.

Yes, you have to.

Even you, indie writers.

I know, I know. You indie writers will never sign a traditional publishing contract.

Never say never. What about foreign rights contracts? What if someone wants to do a limited edition of your book? What if someone wants to produce a video of you reading your book?

And what about those pesky Terms of Service? Some companies make copyright grabs in their TOS. When you click *agree*, you lose copyright.

Remember that Hollywood rights grab I mentioned. Just by agreeing to let them "see" the book, without a guarantee of a read of the book or even consideration for a film/TV project, I would have had to sign a document giving them a portion of the copyright. That little gem is buried in a nondisclosure agreement, guaranteeing that I would not talk about any business I did with this particular firm.

Since I didn't sign the agreement, and since I told them to bug off, I can tell you about it. But I'm not naming names, since their pockets are deeper than mine.

So, indies, you will have to know copyright. You will have to know it just as well as a traditional writer does. You just need to know it for different reasons.

And you traditional writers, how many of you signed contracts with a grant of rights in it that you did not understand, something your agent told you was "just fine"?

I won't ask for a show of hands, because that would probably be almost every single one of you, although I'll wager some of you only made that mistake once.

The current version of *The Copyright Handbook* from Nolo press is 472 pages long, and it only covers copyright for *written* works. It specifically says it does not cover copyright for music, art, photography or audio visual works. Because copyright is a huge, huge topic, and even those 472 pages aren't really enough to cover everything.

You're running a small business, people. Even you, traditional writers. You traditional writers are a supplier for a publishing company, at worst. You partner with the traditional publishing company to produce and distribute your book, at best.

You need to understand what you're selling and/or licensing. Believe me, the people who negotiate with you know what copyright is and how to best use it. Publishers are learning each day how to do a better job with rights management.

By better, I mean "better for them." Not for you.

Your job is to make sure you do the best job *for you*.

Think of copyright as a house. Each slice of the copyright is another building—not even on the same piece of land. That subdivision I mentioned? It might all be derived from the same manuscript. Each house, each garage, each shed. Think about that.

I have written hundreds of stories and articles, not counting all the novels I've written or the screenplays or the radio plays. Each one could be a subdivision.

It's overwhelming, and yet, I manage.

Remember what I said in the previous chapter. Your job is to retain as much control in your business as possible.

The best way to have control is to *understand* what you're creating. You're not creating books. You're creating intellectual *property*.

Now, use this as a kick in the pants. Go forth and learn what that means.

CLAUSES TO WATCH OUT FOR

Clauses exist in contracts for a reason. Someone put those clauses in that contract on purpose. Double-down on this theory when you ask for a clause to be removed and the other party refuses to remove it. If I ask for a change in a contract, and the other side refuses to make that change or even work with it, then I know that the other side plans, at some point, to exploit that clause in the contract. —From Chapter 11.

4

THE OPTION CLAUSE

In April, 2016, the Passive Guy, who runs the Passive Voice website, posted some thoughts on the way that publishers treat writers versus the way that companies (and the law) treat employees and stockholders[1]. He wrote:

> *Of course, an investor who bought into a mutual fund can sell his/her shares and have nothing further to do with that fund and its managers. A hedge fund that purchased a publisher can sell the publisher and be done with it. Since no US state permits life-time employment contracts, a publishing executive or editor can either quit immediately or wait a couple of years, then bail out on a failing publisher.*
>
> *Only the authors who signed contracts that last for the full term of the copyright are tied to whatever corporate entity once called itself a publisher, but now is a hedge fund asset, for the rest of their lives plus 70 years.*

In the body of the piece, he added this:

> *Under current contract practices, the author is the only person who has to think in the long term while everyone else in the publishing business is focused on the short term.*

Clearly, that stuck with me. I've been thinking about the way that writers think versus the way that publishers think for some time. I've also been analyzing my own out-of-date thinking for quite a while.

I learned to read when I was three. I can't remember a time when I couldn't read. Books were everywhere in my world—my parents' house, my grandmother's house, my aunt's house, the drugstore, the library, school—and somehow, I got the notion that books were forever. I know part of that notion came from school.

Some of it came from my training as a writer. Everything we learned as writers in high school, college, and beyond was how to make our books "art" so that they would be read hundreds of years from now. As if it were that easy to be read forever.

Libraries dump books, bookstores go out of business, and in the old days of print-only books, the print run determined your maximum number of readers—even if your book eventually ended up in a used bookstore. And then there are the behind-the-scenes way that books disappear, such as through badly managed estates (which I cover in later chapters).

I noted in some comments elsewhere about one of my estate posts that people who indie published seemed to think they were immune from a badly managed estate. And I sighed. Because indies might just be the most vulnerable.

But that's another topic...except in the short-sightedness.

Indulge me for a moment.

Some of us write to be read. Some of us write to be entertainers. Some of us write because we have no choice. And a few of us write to be read *forever* like some of the works that we've read throughout our lives.

Yes, I realize that it's arrogant for a writer to believe her work will last through the ages. But, as I've always said, writers are an interesting mixture of ego and insecurity. The ego allows us to think others will find our writing worth reading; the insecurity makes us constantly ask if we're good enough.

We writers are used to long-term thinking. That's part of the "art" argument.

But we writers do very little to protect our work *properly* for the long-term.

Here's the thing, folks: I don't care where your work originally gets published. If someone reads that work and loves it, that someone might want to purchase an auxiliary right to that work. Much as those of us who are indie and hybrid want to, we can't do everything. So we will sell rights in translation or to audio or to television or to some YouTube start-up.

We will sign contracts. And, I hate to say it, we will sign bad contracts.

That's part of the learning experience.

But most writers only look at the amount they'll get paid and what their due dates are. They let others (cough: incompetent agents) handle the messy details. And the others never do it right.

Neither does the writer. For all the dreams of having work last forever, writers are their own worst enemies in making those dreams come true. And the mistakes happen in the little decisions.

Let's take **the option clause.** Option clauses exist in many, many publishing contracts—everywhere from audio contracts to gaming contracts and beyond. But I'm going to focus on a traditional book contract, since that's where most writers will see the option clause.

The option clause in a book contract will say something like this:

The Publisher shall have the exclusive option to acquire upon mutually agreeable terms the publishing rights to the next novel by the Author. The period of this option shall be for sixty days following the acceptance of the last Work in this contract. During the period of this option, the Author agrees not to submit the work or its outline to other publishers. If the Publisher wishes to publish said novel, the parties shall negotiate in good faith the terms of the publishing agreement. If the parties are unable to reach agreement before the expiration of the option herein granted, then the Author shall be free to offer the next work to others, but only on terms more favorable than those offered by the Publisher. The Publisher shall have the right to match the offer of any other publisher.

Realize that all option clauses are different, and this is only an approximation of a clause, *not* a suggested version. Please be clear on that.

Now…to continue:

Once upon a time, in a land before ebooks, an option clause made sense for both writer and publisher. Sometimes, option clauses *still* make sense for both writer and publisher.

But only sometimes.

Let's look at the past for a moment. Before conglomerates took over the publishing world, before ebooks, back when publishing was a smaller business, filled with Mom-and-Pop publishers, there was a lot of competition for good, established writers. When I started in the business, Publisher A might buy the first three books in Really Great Series by Brilliant Writer, investing a lot to get Really Great Series by Brilliant Writer off the ground. Then Publisher B would swoop in and offer Brilliant Writer five times the money for books four through six of Really Great Series, and Brilliant Writer (because he's brilliant) would move to Publisher B.

As publishers became big corporations, and the accounting and business-think changed from long-term to short-term (sometimes as short as the next quarter), the idea of buying books four through six of an established series went away. Now, Publisher B would only consider *all* of the books of the series, if they became available.

But, Publisher B would consider Brilliant Writer's work if Brilliant Writer started a new series for Publisher B. And so Brilliant Writer did. An Even Better Series got excellent reviews. Brilliant Writer even did a few standalone books for Publisher C.

Then time continued marching forward, and companies consolidated even more. Publisher A got swallowed up by Publisher F, and within a year, everyone who worked at Publisher A got laid off. All the plans for Really Great Series went out the window. Early books went out of print, and Brilliant Writer had only Publisher B and Publisher C left.

Brilliant Writer had a brilliant career, but amassed a track record of sales. Some books sold well; others sold poorly. Publisher H absorbed Publishers B and cut writers like Brilliant Writer, because his sales weren't up to expectation.

Publisher C passed on Brilliant Writer's next work—and no other publisher would take Brilliant Writer. Brilliant Writer was done, under that name. No one would buy him.

As you can see, all of these changes had a huge impact on the careers of writers.

The one thing that did not change, however, was the contract writers were offered, and the contracts that writers (and their [cough: incompetent] agents) negotiated. Those writers and agents still seemed to think there was a lot of competition for the writers' work out there.

A well-negotiated option clause always protected the writer and the series on some level. It gave the writer the hope of a home. The writer could offer the publisher a book on the same or better terms, and the publisher would have to consider that book within a short period of time. If the publisher did not consider the book in that period of time, the writer could take the book to the competition.

Then the competition mostly disappeared. Writers were screwed, even though they kept negotiating option clauses as if there still was competition.

Fast forward to 2009 or 2010, and suddenly, writers had opportunities again. Publishers didn't have competition in the form of another big publisher as they did in the middle part of the 20th century. Publishers had competition in the form of the author himself.

Now, Brilliant Author doesn't need the publisher to continue the series. Frankly, there's no real reason to ever sign an option clause—except for the publisher.

Let me speak as the woman who runs a publishing company now:

It makes sense that a publisher, who has invested (at minimum) $250,000 into a book, to want to not only recoup the investment in the book, but to have first dibs on another book from the author who made that publisher money.

No publisher is going to consider buying more books from an author if the author *doesn't* make the publisher money. And no author can tell, not even from royalty statements, how much money the publisher made off that author—especially now, with ebook revenues up.

(Why am I saying ebook revenues are up, even though all the statistics say they're down? Because I'm not talking about ebook sales for traditional publishers. I'm talking about how much money they make off of each sale, which is significantly more than they make off a standard print deal. Ebook revenues have kept many a publisher afloat these past five years.)

The publisher wants to wrap the writer up in a tiny little bow, and hold onto that writer—and the writer's work—as long as possible. Especially now, because a book might not earn back its advance (or anything else) in the first two months out of the gate, but because of ebooks. Because ebooks remain in print, the book might take off a year from now.

Imagine if the publisher has a tight option clause on a particular work from the writer. Then the publisher can decide to take the next book, months or years, after the initial publication.

This used to happen, back in the bad old days, when options were poorly written. Then writers got smart about option clauses (more or less), and publishers started adding non-compete clauses, which I will get to in another chapter.

Now, a publisher must decide whether or not to buy the next book—according to the option—at some point *before* the book is published, when (in theory) sales from retail outlets are just starting to come in. Um...except...the biggest sales are often ebook now, and ebook preorders aren't nearly as big as any preorder from a brick-and-mortar store.

So a publisher will make the author wait until there are actual sales figures.

However, times have changed in a whole bunch of ways.

Now there is only one reason for the author to wait for a publisher to see sales figures before considering the next book. That reason? The author actually wants to work with the publisher, and no one else.

I know, I know. I'm blowing your minds. No option clause? Ever?

Why?

The option clause only benefits the publisher. The publisher has invested a lot of time and money into a project that it has no real ownership of. (Unless the writer didn't follow the other dealbreaker aspects of the contract that are discussed in this book.) So, the publisher needs the writer more than the writer needs the publisher.

The writer has options now. The writer can sometimes (often) self-publish a book or a series better than a traditional publisher can.

In fact, option clauses get in the way of writers. Option clauses no longer help writers at all—and should be removed from most contracts.

I suppose after making a statement like that I should probably remind you that I am no lawyer, and nothing here poses as legal advice. What I'm doing in this series is informational, so that you can make your own decisions, based on your own needs.

Why am I saying the option clause should be removed? I didn't say that in the original version of *Dealbreakers* which I published four years ago.

Removing the option clause goes back to that long-term thinking. Writers need to control the future of their projects. An option clause prevents that.

Say you're happy with your publisher at first, but by the time you've gone through the entire publishing experience, you don't like working with that publisher any more. An option clause locks you into a negotiation—and a timetable—that you don't want.

Let me give an example.

Hardworking Indie Writer has had some luck with her series This Romance Sucks, but she prefers to read mass market paperback romances. She wants to see her novels in mass market paperback. So when Huge Traditional Publisher approaches her (because of her sales numbers) for the next book in the series, Hardworking Indie Author offers them a brand new series instead.

Huge Traditional Publisher takes the brand new series and publishes three books quickly for traditional publishing—one every six months.

But…all of the promises that Huge Traditional Publisher gave to Hardworking Indie Writer were broken. There was a mass market edition, but it didn't get into Wal-Mart like the original now-laid-off editor promised. There was no advertising budget. Hardworking Indie Writer got her money, but nothing else.

In fact, her fans are getting restless because they can't get the new books in the series as fast as Hardworking Indie Writer can write the books.

Hardworking Indie Writer wanted mass market editions, but has discovered that she really hates working with traditional publishers. She's going to publish the next books in her series herself.

However, Hardworking Indie Writer is bound by her option clause, which looks like the one above. It says that the publisher has sixty days *after the acceptance of the last work in the contract* to make an offer for the next book. And the publisher must have exclusivity for those sixty days.

The clause appears to have a timetable, but it really doesn't. Formal acceptance of a book manuscript by a traditional publisher usually comes in the form of payment. Sometimes, the editor might say in a letter that the book is accepted and the check will be forthcoming, but often the writer doesn't know when the check was requisitioned.

Formal acceptance, like that check, will take anywhere from three to nine months after the turn-in of the last manuscript. From that moment, the publisher has sixty days to consider the next book.

So that's another two months, even if the writer is going to say no. But the option clause says both sides will "negotiate in good faith." Good faith is a concept[2] that has a lot of implications under the law. Essentially, good faith in this instance means that both sides will deal with each other honestly, without malice, and with no intention of fooling the other or defrauding the other.

(Sometimes I wonder how traditional publishers can even use the phrase in their contracts, but that's a point for another time.)

Hardworking Indie Writer does not want to continue with her publisher, but she has signed an agreement that ties her to a negotiation on something she doesn't want to sell. In most cases, that's not going to be an issue—most books don't do well enough for a publisher to fight on this point.

But here's where success can hurt Hardworking Indie Writer. If her book in the new series becomes the publishing house's bestselling title of that spring, then the publisher might try to enforce the option clause. And there are a whole bunch of ways to do it.

For example, the clause above says that the writer can only accept deals that are "more favorable" than the one the publisher offers. Who decides what "more favorable" is? If the publisher is going to offer a $250,000 advance is that more favorable than the zero-dollar advance Hardworking Indie Writer will get from her own self-publishing company? Is her company a real publisher according to the terms of the option clause?

Is this something to be concerned about?

Once you start arguing these points, you're starting to argue the way that lawyers will. Often the only way to settle these points is in court or mediation.

Best to avoid this stuff altogether.

And the best way to avoid it?

Delete the option clause.

Does that mean the presence of an option clause is a dealbreaker?

No, at least, not for me. Because an option clause can be just fine. And it should be relatively simple.

It should be something like this:

The Publisher shall have the exclusive option to consider *upon mutually agreeable terms the publishing rights to the next* series *novel by the Author. The period of this option shall be for thirty days following the submission of the last Work in this contract.*

Note that I changed the language from the start. Not the exclusive option to *acquire* the work, which means the publisher can buy it. But the exclusive right to *consider* the work. That means the publisher will be the sole company thinking about purchasing the work. There is no talk of a deal, and there is no talk of how that deal will be structured.

The only thing the clause has is *exclusivity* for the publisher for thirty days after the writer turns in the last book in this contract. Once that thirty-day period is up, the writer can do what she wants with the project.

Heck, even if the publisher makes an offer, the writer can do what she wants. Because there is no obligation in that option clause for the writer to publish her next book with this particular publisher—or with anyone.

Now, lots of writers are either going indie or becoming hybrid or realizing that their jump to traditional wasn't as fun as they thought it would be. They want out, only to find themselves boxed in by a variety of things they signed away in that traditional publishing contract.

Sometimes those things are in the details. Words like "acquire" versus "consider," for example. Or limiting the definition of the next work to the next work in the series or "the next work of science fiction featuring aliens" or something equally specific. (Saying the next novel, or the next book, really ties the writer's hands.)

The time limit is important too. Because it needs to be strictly enforced. I always had tight option clauses on my books. If (and only if) I wanted to work with that publisher again, I would remind the editor that she had thirty days to consider the outline I was submitting *when* I submitted it. Then I would send a reminder fifteen days into the exclusive period.

If I did not want to work with the publisher, I would not say a word about the timetable, and let corporate inertia work in my favor. No editor can get a deal done in thirty days *unless* that new project is worth a lot of money to the company.

As with anything in a contract, the key to an option clause is control. The publisher (or audio book company or gaming company) will want to control the future works of a writer. The option clause is one way to do so.

Delete the option clause and one problem is solved. The writer can still make a deal with the publisher: the writer is just not bound by anything in the previous contract.

If the publisher insists on an option clause, negotiate the clause into something that is toothless—meaning the next work is defined so narrowly that it can only mean one particular project—and make sure that the clause has a strict timetable.

Make sure the clause is *not* about acquiring the next work, but about *considering* the next work on an exclusive basis for a short period of time.

Remember to think long-term. Even though the option clause pretends to be long-term for the publisher, it's really not. It's just a cover-your-ass move for the publisher. Here's the thinking: *If the book we just licensed does really really well, we don't want anyone else capitalizing on the success we built into this project. So we don't want anyone else to license the next book in the project.*

If the publisher doesn't get the next book, no big deal. Sure, some executive editor might have a bad day at the office as everyone piles on about losing the best book of the season, but that's it.

Then the publisher will go on to publish other books.

Long-term for the writer has a completely different meaning. If the option clause says "next book" instead of something narrowly defined, then the writer has to *wait* to do *anything* with the next book until the publisher makes a decision. If the option clause has a crapass timetable like the one in the original clause I put up, then the writer might have to wait a year or more to do *anything* with her next book.

In other words, the publisher can move on to other projects. The writer cannot.

You do not want a contract with a publisher (or any other entity) to limit your future. A bad option clause will limit your future, all because you were not thinking long-term.

Frankly, writers no longer have the time to wait for a publisher to get back to them. Hardworking Indie Writer, above, might want to publish six books in the year after she leaves her traditional publisher, but she can't because of her option clause. She might have to wait. And if she's successful, that wait might involve time with lawyers and maybe the courts.

Yes, I'm deliberately giving you a worst case scenario because in this (and many other instances in book publishing), the worst-case scenario comes from *success*. The more successful the writer is, the harder it is for her to control her own destiny.

Counterintuitive, right?

You think all of that has come about since the ebook revolution? Think again. Publishers want to control as much of a writer's output and her copyrights as possible, especially if that writer has a following. Many traditional contracts, written decades ago and vetted by *agents* (not lawyers), *only* benefit the publisher.

From what I'm seeing, auxiliary rights contracts—like some audio contracts or gaming contracts or contracts for other derivative works— are *worse* for writers than the original traditional publishing contracts ever were.

Remember that copyright protects your work while you live. After you die, copyright protects your work for another seventy years.

You need to be aware of that with every document you sign. Because the future of a work of art (and yes, you literal people, writing is art) is quite long. And you can easily sign your control of that art away, if you're not careful.

So be careful, and as you negotiate your contracts—and you are going to negotiate, right?—make sure you think about the future.

Not the next five years, but the actual future—ten years, twenty years, thirty years.

Because the only person who will protect your work during its long life is you. And one thing you need to protect is the right to have your work published in the first place.

5

THE NON-COMPETE CLAUSE 1

I probably should have called this chapter *Short- and Long-term Thinking*, or maybe just *Thinking*. Because no one should ever sign a non-compete clause.

Ever.

And yet, for the past several years, traditional publishers are trying to control *everything* about a writer, from the rights she sells to the amount of money she makes. They also want what they're calling "a non-compete" clause.

In reality, it's a "do-not-do-business-without-our-permission" clause.

I first wrote about this on my blog in 2011. Then I revised the post for 2013. And now, well, things are much worse than they were five years ago for any writer who wants to become traditionally published.

I'm going to be as blunt as I can here.

If you sign any version of a non-compete clause, you will never *be a full-time professional writer. Writing will* not *be your career. Something else will, and you will write on the side* **for the rest of your life**.

Got that?

Can I be any clearer?

In the past five years, publishers have gotten Draconian about the non-compete clause—and they've also gotten sneaky about it. Many writers have gotten wise to the non-compete clause, and refuse to sign it.

But most writers don't realize that contracts are one long document that works as a whole, not a series of linked paragraphs. Just because you whacked one mole doesn't mean you've gotten rid of the moles altogether.

These days, deleting the non-compete clause is not enough. You must also get rid of all the language about competition in the *warranty* section of the contract. That's the part your agent (if you have one [and if you have one, *why* do you have one?]) tells you is boilerplate so you don't have to read it.

Yes, you have to read your warranty clause. Yes, you have to read your entire damn contract, not just the parts that someone warned you about.

Around 2012, publishers started *requiring* non-compete clauses in almost all of their contracts, and are making those clauses a deal breaker *from the publisher's side*. In other words, the publisher will cancel the deal if you do not sign a non-compete. The choice you are given is this: either you let the publisher control your entire career just because you sold that publisher one book for $5,000 or you walk.

If that's the choice you're given, *walk.* Hell, *run.*

You have other options now. You can go to a different traditional publisher if you want. You can publish that work yourself.

You're even better off putting that book in a drawer and not mailing to anyone than you are signing that clause.

Got it?

Because the moment you sign that clause, you give over your entire career to a corporation that cares nothing for you. Even if the clause does not hold up in court (see the following chapter), you'd have to spend years not writing and litigating to prove me right.

You'll often find the non-compete clause in the same section of your contract as the option clause. The non-compete clause will look something like this:

> *The Author agrees that during the terms of this Agreement he will not, without the written permission of the Publisher, publish or authorize to be published any work under this name or any other, including blog posts, short stories, nonfiction articles, novels, or the like.*

In other words, the contract will *prevent the writer from making a living* at his craft. I saw that clause in my first contract with Bantam Books twenty years ago and hit the ceiling. (The word *blog* was not in it, of course.) I thought I was going to lose this rather large contract because no way in hell would I sign a document with that clause in it.

I demanded the clause's removal and got the removal with no fuss at all. Recently, however, writers have signed contracts with that clause because they were told the clause was a dealbreaker. I know of at least two mystery writers who need their publisher's permission to put up a blog post. I know of several more who have had to get a document granting them blanket permission from their fiction publisher to write nonfiction.

Do you really want that to happen to you? Because it could if you sign this clause. Consider that the contract, like your mortgage, might get sold to another company you're entirely unfamiliar with at the moment. This happened a few years back to Avalon authors who had no idea when they signed their contracts that eventually Amazon would have the rights to publish those works.

Your current publisher might not enforce that clause; the publisher/business your current publisher sells out to might enforce the clause, and make you pay damages for anything you've previously published after you signed the contract (and ignored the clause).

Worst case, right? Yes, it is. But before you sign a contract—*any* contract—you must imagine the worst-case scenario. The contract you negotiate should protect you from bad things, but you have to realize how bad those things can actually be.

Let's go back to the clause: It is ridiculous. It's there to prevent you from controlling your craft. According to that clause, your publisher is in charge of everything you write, *whether the publisher pays you for it or not.* Got that?

I have seen other versions of this clause, negotiated by (idiot) agents for their established clients. Those versions usually read something like this:

> *The Author agrees that, during the term of this Agreement, he will not, without the written permission of the Publisher, publish or authorize to be published any work substantially similar to the Work or which is likely to injure its sale or the merchandising of other rights herein.*

This is only marginally better. Seriously. You're still asking your publisher's permission to write something. Granted, it's only under one name, and if your publisher withholds permission, you can start up a new pen name, but honestly...who signs this stuff? And what advisor thinks something like this is okay for a writer to sign?

Because the problem isn't with the publisher's permission. The problem here is two phrases: "substantially similar" and "likely to injure." Who decides if my funny fantasy novel about fairy-tale characters is substantially similar to my science fiction novels about the Moon? They are supposedly in the same genre—sf/f. Or what about my mystery series set in Chicago in the late 1960s? Is that substantially similar to the mysteries set on the Moon? They are both mysteries after all.

And who determines if those Moon mysteries "injure" the sales of the 1968 mysteries? Does the fact that I'm also publishing romance, a genre that many sf editors don't respect, "injure" the sales of my sf books?

See the problem?

It gets worse when you think about who gets to decide. Most writers will let their publishers decide. Those writers who challenge the publisher's decision will find their books, their careers, their livelihoods tied up in civil court, waiting for a judge to decide.

I have seen several versions of these clauses negotiated to death, with all kinds of phrases added in, but none of them are toothless, and all of them tie the writer's output to his publisher's permission.

For me, this clause is a dealbreaker. No one controls my career but me. No one tells me what to write but me.

The best way to handle a non-compete clause is to refuse to sign one.

So…you take the non-compete clause out and you're in the clear, right?

Hell, no. Lately these publishers have been adding something in the boilerplate section of the contract. A boilerplate section is the stuff that should remain the same from contract to contract—you negotiate it once, and it doesn't change. It's stock or formulaic language that covers expected things like insurance coverage and Acts of God. Some boiler-plate can be changed and some can't.

In the boilerplate section is something called a warranty, and in it, you'll find language like:

The Author Warrants that the Work is original, and uses no material from any other source…

Things like that.

Only cagey publishers have started to add this:

The Author Warrants that she will not publish any other work until this contract is fully executed.

In other words, the Author can't publish anything until all the terms of the contract are met. Meaning that she cannot publish anything until the second or fifth or tenth book of the contract is published, and maybe, depending on the wording, not even then. She might not be able to publish until the book goes out of print.

If the book goes out of print.

Because, people, books generally aren't going out of print any more. Contracts with traditional publishers are becoming contracts for the life of the copyright.

Think, think, think about what you sign. *Think* about the worst-case scenario. You people are supposedly good at imagining things.

Imagine this one.

Seriously, folks, watch out for this stuff. Take clauses like this out of the contract. If your publisher refuses to remove language like this from your contract *and you still sign it*, you will have no one to blame but yourself for your tanking writing career. Because you put your signature on a legal document giving someone else control of your output.

Let's look at the non-compete clause from yet another perspective—one of balance.

Technically, contracts should at least pretend to have balance between the parties. Theoretically, you and your publisher are equal partners in the venture of publishing a book, and your contract should reflect that.

Contract law, from dozens of countries including ours, assumes that both parties are able to enter into the contract equally, with the same kind of knowledge and judgment.

If you can show, in court, that you've been swindled, bamboozled, or forced to sign a contract whose terms actively harm you, then the contract might—and I use the word "might" here on purpose—be canceled.

One of the things a judge will look at to see if one party is unfairly taken advantage of in the contract negotiation phase is balance. If the entire contract benefits only one party, then the contract is unbalanced, and argues—by its very existence—that the other party was taken advantage of.

The judge is not required to act here, and often will not. This is one of the many reasons I tell you to avoid court.

But let's explore balance for a moment:

If you are a professional writer *who makes her living on her writing*, and you have signed a contract that does not allow you to practice your trade, then there must be some similar consideration for the other party to make the contract balance.

In other words, if your publisher wants *you* to sign a non-compete clause, then your publisher should sign one as well.

If you ask for a non-compete as ridiculous as the one the publisher is asking of you, then it would read like this:

The Publisher agrees that during the terms of this Agreement he will not, without the written permission of the Author, publish or authorize to be published any work that might compete with the Work, including blog posts, short stories, nonfiction articles, novels, or the like.

Imagine a publisher signing that. Oh, you can't? Neither can I.

But let's dial it down a notch. Let's say you sell a vampire romance to Publisher A. If the contract has balance, then you can't publish a romance or a vampire book that might compete with yours—*and neither can your publisher.* Even if you limit the non-compete to two years, imagine telling your traditional publisher that they can't publish vampire books or romance books for two years after the publication of your novel.

Now do you see how wrong this clause is? You should not sign it because it's bad for you. If that argument doesn't sway you, then ask yourself if any reasonable business would sign a contract with a clause like that. Or if *any* business would sign a clause like that for *any* reason.

Your writing career is a business. Act like it.

Do not sign something that will stop you from practicing your trade. Ever.

6

THE NON-COMPETE CLAUSE 2

I initially wrote the previous chapter in May of 2016. The chapter caused quite a stir, and a lot of people responded both privately and publicly. Many offered their opinion about the non-compete clause.

Here's what's fascinating about the non-compete. It has become ubiquitous, not only in publishing contracts, but in employment contracts nationwide. In some cases, it was used by corporations to prevent low-paid fast-food workers from getting a better-paying job at a similar company[1].

Because of these egregious examples, the case law pertaining to non-compete clauses in employment and other contracts is changing almost daily.

The chapter below was published as a blog post in mid-June 2016. I write this chapter in October of 2016. Right now, not much has changed. But you might be reading this in 2017 or 2018. I suggest you follow the instructions at the end of the chapter, using this as a guideline, not the be-all and end-all of information on the non-compete.

I know, I know. I've probably confused you. Just read on.

In the previous chapter, I said that I wasn't sure if the non-compete clause in a publishing contract would hold up in court, but that was a bit of fudge. I knew that some states had already litigated the non-compete clause and found it wanting.

I am very aware of the fact that I am not a lawyer. I don't have the years and years of training and life experience that makes some things clear to lawyers and not to the rest of us. I don't write certain blog posts because I'm not a lawyer. I know that I would quickly get in over my head.

I get a lot of letters from lawyers, and they do advise me on the things I get right, and the things I get wrong. I value that.

I've had the pleasure of emailing back and forth with Teri Kanefield for over a year now. She writes books for young readers as well as adults. She also practices law in California. Here's what her website says about her law practice[2]:

> Teri's law practice is limited to representing indigents on appeal from adverse rulings. She believes that when the rights of society's most vulnerable members are denied, everybody's rights are imperiled. She also believes that the purpose of literature is to expand our sympathies.

She emailed me after reading the initial non-compete blog and mentioned that non-compete clauses are mostly illegal under California law, with rare exceptions.

She also suspected that they were illegal and thus unenforceable under New York law.

She had reasons for that. I asked her to send me a few citations, so that I could essentially try to re-create her argument, although I admit, as a non-lawyer, I felt uncomfortable doing that.

Then she suggested doing a guest blog for me on this topic, and I jumped on it. She's written it in the form of a letter. It's fantastic.

I want *all* of you—indie, hybrid, traditional, with non-competes and without—to read this letter, which follows.

I will give you each some non-legal advice on what to do after you've read her letter at the end of this blog post.

So, without further ado, here's Teri:

～

Hi, Kris,

First, all the usual disclaimers: I am a lawyer, but this is **out of my area of expertise,** and I am not authorized to practice in New York.

So, while nothing here is legal advice, maybe we can start a discussion that will help writers deal with these non-compete clauses.

After our email chat, I visited the law library and did a little research on New York non-compete agreements. Here is what I found.

Why I suspect that non-compete clauses in publishing contracts are disfavored under New York law.

As far as I can see, New York has no statutes governing non-compete clauses. The law is entirely case law (meaning that judges make the law according to established principles and follow the precedent set down from other judges).

Case law seem to be entirely in the area of employment law, with employers requiring employees to sign non-compete agreements, which means (as far as I can see) nobody has ever challenged the legality of a non-compete clause in a publishing contract.

That means we have to argue by analogy, even though it's important to remember that the writer is not employed by the publishing house. The writer is paid royalties, not a salary, so the analogy doesn't really work--but employment cases seem to provide the only guidance out there as to what a court is likely to do with publishing contract non-competes.

Leading cases in New York on non-competes are *Reed, Roberts Assoc. v. Strauman, 40 N.Y.2d 303, 307-08 (N.Y. 1976)* and *BDO Seidman v. Hirshberg,* 712 NE 2d 1220 (N.Y. Ct. App. 1999)

Both cases hold that **non-competes will only be subject to specific enforcement to the extent that they are:**

1. necessary to protect the employer's legitimate business interests,

2. reasonable in time and area,

3. not harmful to the general public and

4. not unreasonably burdensome to the employee.

Obviously, it is important to define "legitimate business interest."

Here is what I found on "legitimate business interest" in New York:

Employer legitimate interests include protecting a customer base, trade secrets and an employer's investment in training or educating employees. Business or financial information, such as market reports or market strategies, do not trigger the trade-secrets legitimate interest. Customer lists are generally not considered to be confidential information unless such lists are discoverable only by extraordinary efforts and not through public sources. As a general rule, a restraint against ordinary competition remains against public policy.

Merely preventing ordinary competition is not a legitimate business interest.

Today, a mobile workforce in a digital economy creates opportunities for employees to compete unfairly against their former employers, so courts will prevent employees from using inside information to compete unfairly against a former employer.

In other words, as in other areas of business law, fair competition is allowed. Unfair competition is not.

In addition, non-competes cannot be used to prevent a person from earning a living:

Courts in New York are less likely to enforce non-compete clauses if the restriction would leave the employee without compensation from the former employer and without the right to earn compensation in his or her field. When evaluating the enforceability of a non-compete clause, New York courts may take into consideration whether or not the employer will make any payments to the employee for the period of "garden leave," when the employee is no longer employed by the former employer but is restricted from working for a competitor. See, e.g., *Cornell v. T.V. Dev. Corp.*, 17 N.Y.2d 69, 75, 268 N.Y.S.2d 29, 34 (1996); *DeCapua v. Dine-A- Mate, Inc.*, 292 A.D.2d 489, 744 N.Y.S. 2d 417 (2d Dep't 2002).

A recent (2013) New York case held that a non-compete may be enforceable if the departing employee agrees not to compete in exchange for financial compensation. *Lenel Sys. Intl. v. Smith*, 106 A.D.

3d 1536 (2013). In this case, an employee accepted stock options in exchange for a promise not to work for a competitor for two years.

Now let's have a look at one of the non-competes you posted on your blog:

The Author agrees that during the terms of this Agreement he will not, without the written permission of the Publisher, publish or authorize to be published any work under this name or any other, including blog posts, short stories, nonfiction articles, novels, or the like.

Analysis:

The above non-compete does not protect any "legitimate business interests." All it does is reduce the number of books in the marketplace that are competing with books published by that particular publishing house. It therefore violates the first element.

The clause is not reasonable in time and place because it possibly extends to the end of the author's life, so it violates the second element.

It is harmful to the general public to have an industry stifle writers and limit what they are allowed to publish, so it violates the third.

It is unreasonably burdensome to the writer to be told she cannot publish, and hence cannot earn a living in his or her field, so it violates the fourth.

Every element fails, when only one would be enough for it to be unenforceable.

Given that courts take care to make sure that a person is not prevented from earning a living, it seems clear to me that New York courts would strongly disfavor that particular clause if following the example in employment noncompete agreements.

Options:

It's worth noting that option clauses also restrict what and when an author can publish. Take, for example, this option from a contract I was offered once:

The Author agrees to give the Publisher the exclusive first opportunity to consider the Author's next full-length work with the understanding that such submission may take place no earlier than the initial publication of the Work.

I have had publishers take as long as three years to publish a book, which means an author signing that option can be prevented from publishing anything else for an extended period of time.

Freedom to Contract:

People have a basic freedom to enter contracts without government restriction, with exceptions where necessary for the public good. Exceptions include minimum wage, competition, and price fixing.

This raises the question: Do publishers have a right to say, "We want to contract only with writers who don't self-publish and who are not trying to earn a living through writing and are thus content to publish one book every few years."

Hypothetical: The best yard service in town says, "You can hire us to maintain your yard, but only if you sign here promising never to hire another yard service as long as you live, unless we give permission." The person signs the contract, grateful to have the best yard service in town, and truly believing that she'll never want to hire another service. The yard service does a great job, and for a while, she's very happy. But then something changes...the quality of the service goes down. A better service moves to town. Is the contract enforceable? Can she really be stuck for the rest of her life, regardless of what the yard service does?

Argument in favor: She is a grownup and knowingly signed a contract, from which she received a benefit. She's stuck.

Argument against? That I leave to others.

So there you have my thinking about non-competes, intended as a jumping off point for discussion.

P.S. Yes, you have permission to publish this letter on your blog.

Thank you, Teri. This is spectacular information, and very helpful to all of us.

I have advice for writers at different levels. Please see if any of this applies to you.

For Those of You Who Have Non-Competes in Existing Contracts

Here's a list of things to do *right now*:

1) Find a copy of your contract. Look at the section marked something like "Applicable Law and Modifications."

In that section, it should say something like this:

This Agreement shall be construed and interpreted according to the laws of the State of New York.

Each contract will have a line like this in it, determining venue. Because, in the United States, each state has different laws regarding non-competes. I don't know what the laws are in all 50 states. The state where your contract is litigated might have *stricter* laws about non-competes than New York does. That's for you to find out using point #2, below.

For those of you with contracts from foreign publishers/entities, those contracts will also include a line like this. Sometimes the contract refers to the country of origin (Say, Great Britain). But every once in a while, the contract will refer to the State of New York. (I have Chinese contracts like that.)

2) Find a lawyer to help you with your contract. Yes, even though the contract is negotiated, and even though you've signed it. You're probably being diligent and operating under the non-compete as if goons will show up at your door if you publish so much as a short story without your publisher's permission.

This is hurting you, and your career.

A lawyer will tell you how to deal with your particular non-compete. There are a variety of ways the lawyer can help you. Perhaps a lawyer will suggest modifying the existing contract with addendums. Or perhaps the lawyer can simply inform the publisher that the non-compete provision is illegal, so their client (you) won't follow it. Or they might suggest some other kind of action.

Get advice.

Do *not* let someone else control what you can and cannot write.

The section on attorneys will explain how to hire one, if you feel you need to.

3) Show the attorney this chapter. If the attorney does not understand it, then find a new attorney. This post should be a starting point for a good attorney.

If the contract is governed by the laws of New York, then Teri's work above will help immensely.

If the contract is governed by the laws of another state, Teri's work above will provide a blueprint for the lawyer to find relevant case law and/or statutes. It also provides a way to think about this issue, in regard to writers.

4) Agents can't and won't help you. Agents don't have access to the relevant case law for one thing. For another, they understand it about as well as you do. And for a third thing, most of them don't mind the non-competes. Those clauses keep their clients from producing more work than the agent can handle, and they (usually) give the agent a guaranteed next sale. So do *not* have your agent deal with this.

The neat thing about attorneys is that if you don't like the one you hired, you can fire them and hire a different attorney. That little feature of the relationship is just one reason they're better than agents. An agent usually stays on a project *even after you've fired them.* (Sigh)

For Those of You Negotiating Contract *Right Now*

1) Hire a lawyer, *not* an agent. (See the same point, above.)

2) Show the lawyer this chapter. Then make sure your new contract does *not* have a noncompete clause anywhere.

3) Do *not* sign a new contract with a noncompete clause in it without getting *legal* advice first, and maybe not even then. Be prepared to walk away if the publisher refuses to budge.

For Those of You Involved in Writers' Organizations

Please share this chapter with the contracts arm of your writers' organization. If your organization has a scammer alert committee, send this to them as well.

Organizations have deep pockets and can set up a legal action on the part of members of the organization. I can guarantee you that a lot of writers in your organization have signed non-compete clauses. For all I know, a group of writers may be able to bring a class action.

Again, many thanks to Teri for doing all this work. It's now up to each and every one of you to defend your writing by refusing to sign these clauses, or by getting rid of the clauses in existing contracts.

I am putting the information out there.

I sincerely hope you do something with it.

7

THE GRANT OF RIGHTS CLAUSE

As I dug into the blogs that eventually became this book, I ended up with so much new material that I couldn't finish blogging by a self-imposed deadline. In fact, it took me almost four months of weekly blogging *past* the deadline to give you the book you hold in your hand.

Why is there new material? Because traditional publishing contracts have gotten *ugly* (or should I say *uglier?*). And they're not alone. Contracts for movie deals, gaming rights, comic books, and now works in translation are also getting more and more Draconian.

Corporate entities have finally gotten a clue about the value of copyright and trademark. Now, those entities which own many of the companies you'll deal with—*even as an indie writer*—want to own each piece of the copyright to any property they put their grubby little fingers on.

Before you read this chapter, make sure you have read Chapter 3, "Understanding Copyright." That's a short explanation of copyright, which I am not going to recap here.

You need to understand copyright (even though it sounds dull) because you have to know what you're *licensing*. If you don't understand that sentence, then read the chapter. If you don't understand the chapter, or you want more information, pick up *The Copyright Handbook* from Nolo Press. And for the record, I have no financial interest in Nolo or in the *Handbook*. It's just a great resource.

When I started the revision of the old *Dealbreakers* book, I found a lot of material that no longer applies. 2011-2013 was a transitional period in the ebook revolution. Traditional publishers didn't know anything about ebooks, and writers had a lot more leeway in what they could do.

Now, things are so different that some of the contracts I'm touching feel toxic to me. I want to wash my hands after holding them.

In *Dealbreakers*, I listed six places you, as an author, will want to hold the line in your negotiation with publishers. (I'm saying publishers here, but realize that I also mean people who want to license auxiliary rights like books in translation, audio books, movie rights, and so on.) I'm going to cover three of those areas today.

They are:

1. **The Rights You Plan to License.**
2. **The Amount You Will Get Paid for That License.**
3. **The Number of Books You License in This Contract.**

Let's start with **The Rights You Plan to License.**

In a traditional publishing contract, you'll find that in the **Grant of Rights** section. I'm beginning to think that section should be called the **Grab of Rights** section, because it's so very icky.

Let me show you an example of something **you should never *ever* sign.** This is from a real contract, offered to writers this year, which someone sent me in April of 2016:

Effective immediately upon the execution of this Agreement, the Author hereby grants to the Publisher the following:

1) The sole and exclusive worldwide rights and license to print, publish, distribute, sell and sublicense, and generally exploit the Work, in all languages, whether in print, electronic, digital, audio, video, television, film, theatrical, or any other form or format now known or hereafter discovered or created, in all languages, including any and all editions and formats of the Work, in whole or in part and all revision of the Work and any edition thereof. As used herein, the

term "editions" shall include worldwide rights: the term "formats" shall include
all print, book club, and all electronic formats including download (whether over
the Internet, through an "app" or otherwise), audio, disk, CD, or any other
electronic or digital format known or to be invented, enhanced ebooks, mass
market, large print, and any future formats/technologies for the duration of the
contract term;

The **Grant of Rights** section goes on, with three more points that I'm not going to deal with here, because that clause all by itself is so squiggy that I shuddered as I typed it. Ugh.

(By the way, here's Contracts 101. When you see a phrase like "for the duration of the contract term," the thing you do *immediately* is thumb through the contract to find the length of the term. In the ideal contract, the term is stated in *years*. [Such as: *This contract is for ten years, subject to renewal on the same or better terms should both parties agree.*] In the icky contract, I had to *search* for the damn term of the contract, which is buried in the **Out of Print** clause. The parts of that clause are so favorable to the publisher that this book will *never* go out of print, and the contract will *not* terminate.)

Okay…

Even though this icky contract that I'm quoting from doesn't explicitly say so, this is *essentially* an all-rights deal. (Read that first sentence out loud. You'll see.) The author is giving *everything* to this publisher, and the contract, bless its evil little heart, actually says so, in more than one way. This part of the clause is particularly pernicious:

or any other form or format now known or hereafter discovered or created, in
all languages, including any and all editions and formats of the Work, in whole
or in part and all revision of the Work and any edition thereof.

Any writer who signs this damn thing can't even publish an author's preferred edition with the text dramatically altered. Or compile an omnibus. Or publish half the book in Spanish, a quarter in Italian, and the rest in English. Signing this contract, with this one clause, gives the publisher rights to everything.

The contract goes on in terrible, awful, horrible ways. The noncompete is actually in a section called **Author Rights** (!) and says that the author cannot "publish or permit to be published during the Term of this agreement any book or other writing based substantially on subject matter, material, characters or incidents in the Work without written consent of the Publisher." And then there's another non-compete later, and a third even deeper in the contract.

And this contract *will never end*. (Even though it pretends to.)

Scared yet?

You should be. I am, and I am not an innocent victim who would blithely sign this thing. I can see what's wrong with it, and could have been able to see the flaws even as a teenage writer. (Yep, I was one). I would never sign this. I'm still scared, because the writer who sent me this contract—who was smart enough to run screaming when they saw the terms—says they know many authors who *are* signing it.

So…here's the question:

What should you grant to anyone who wants to go into business with you with regards to one of your pieces of intellectual property?

As little as possible to benefit *both* of you.

Please note how I phrased that question. Most writers ask *"What should I sell to my traditional publisher?"*

That sentence means something completely different than the one in bold.

Since you are *licensing* copyright, you are not *selling* anything. So when you have a deal with a traditional publisher or some other entity, you should only *license* what you need to get the deal done.

So many indie writers dismissed my blog posts as I wrote this series, thinking the posts are only for traditionally published writers or hybrid writers. Whenever I see the dismissal, I think that poor indie writer is hanging out in dangerous country, waiting for someone to take advantage of them. Because someone *will*.

If you're making a deal with a company that produces paper board games, then you need to limit the grant of rights to paper board games, maybe even of a particular type. If you're making a deal with a traditional publisher to produce and distribute paper books, then make sure that contract does not include ebook rights. If you're only making that deal to have a mass market edition of your work, then only license mass market rights.

And so on.

Anything more is unnecessary and harmful to you as the writer.

Remember you are licensing copyright, and copyright can be sliced in such fine layers that you can license mass market paper book rights to one company, trade paper book rights to another company, and hardcover book rights to yet a third, while hanging onto ebook rights, and everything else.

The other aspect to a copyright license is the territory in which you are licensing that copyright. The territory can be limited to North America. Or to Rhode Island, if you so choose.

Make sure you know who you're dealing with when you license a slice of copyright to that company. If the company is based in France, and has no marketing reach beyond France, then there is no need to give that company the right to produce and market books in Canada or Algeria. The company will try to buy World Rights in the French Language, but why give up those rights? You might be able to exploit the rights better than the company can.

And here's the thing: You might not be capable of exploiting those rights *today*, but three years from now, an opportunity comes your way that will enable you to publish a book in French throughout Africa—paying substantially more than the French company above would ever have paid you. If you threw in all French language rights to that company, you would lose the new opportunity.

If you were sensible, and only licensed what you needed to license, then you would be able to make French Language African deal.

Plan for the future. Do *not* license more than you need to.

If a publisher wants more than one thing in its license, the publisher has to pay for the additional rights. You, as the person licensing those rights, need to know how much those rights are worth *to you*.

For example, I would *never* sign that icky contract because they want everything. There is not a dollar figure, even in the tens of millions, that would entice me to license every right to one of my intellectual properties.

So you must consider…

The Amount You Will Get Paid for That License

Each slice of copyright is worth money. So every time a publisher wants to add another right to its license, that publisher should pay for the right.

That icky contract lists *categories* of rights as if they're individual rights: *print, electronic, digital, audio, video, television, film, theatrical...*and more.

But as I mentioned above, print can be broken down in a wide variety of ways. Audio can be audio CDs, audio downloads, audio collections, audio performed by one narrator, audio performed by several narrators (with sound effects), podcast rights, and so on. *Each* of those things can and should be listed in any contract—and accounted for separately.

You know that television is no longer network television, right? It includes streaming shows, cable shows, network shows, shows for the British Market, the Canadian Market, the German market...and on, and on, and on.

Look at all this money that anyone who signed that icky contract had signed away.

I know this whole concept makes your brain hurt. I know it because it makes *my* brain hurt.

But each one of those subrights can *and should* be licensed separately, for a separate fee. Even if those fees run small, say, $1,000 per subright on the audio or the book rights, I've listed six types of audio rights, and four types of book rights. That's a *small* amount of $10,000, and that doesn't include the video or TV or movie or theatrical rights or comic book rights or more.

So if you're licensing all of those rights listed above for $5,000 plus possible royalties, the only person who gets hurt is you. Because many of these companies won't pay full royalties on subrights sales. They'll pay you a 50/50 split of the *net* revenues the publisher receives. The icky contract above only pays a 50/50 split of net revenues on a handful of subrights. On the rest of them, the author gets as little as 10% of the publisher's *net* revenues.

I hope you know what net means. It means the amount *after* the publisher subtracts expenses.

Gross revenues are revenues actually received by the publisher with no expenses removed.

In this contract, the writer gets money received *minus* expenses. And because *net* is not defined in this contract (or in any publishing contract that I've seen of late), expenses might include anything from airplane tickets to Frankfurt to facilitate the foreign rights sales to a daily cappuccino for the editorial assistant's assistant.

In other words, modern contracts issued through conglomerates and other grabby corporations are skewed so that the person who *created* the original product gets little to no money, and the corporate entity gets most or all of the money.

Before you license anything to anyone, make sure you know how much you will take for those subrights and slices of the intellectual property. Then imagine how you would feel if you sold, say, the TV rights (all of them) to XYZ Book Publishing Company as part of your $5,000. Sure you get a 50/50 split of *net* revenues (which are not defined). So your book becomes a TV show—a big one, groundbreaking. Everyone watches it. The show airs on network television. Then the cable rights sell. Then the rights to produce a different version for the Russian market. The streaming rights sell, and on, and on.

You get no money. You contact the original publisher, who reminds you that you get 50% of *net* receipts. They send you their accounting, which they have zeroed out. When they factor in all of their expenses, there is no money left over.

So people *all over the world* are making money off the TV rights to your book, but you have made…wait for it…$5,000. Period.

Oh, maybe you got some additional royalties on the book itself. But the way that the publishers are dealing with the discount clauses these days, you might not even see those. *What's a discount clause?* you ask. A discount clause is something we'll deal with in Chapter 10.

Rather than have the publisher pay for each right they license, make sure they only license the rights they need to complete the deal. That way, you don't have to figure out what all the extra rights are worth.

You have to restrict the license and figure out what that one single license is worth.

That's all.

But that's hard to do. It means you'll have to negotiate your ass off.

It means you'll have to be prepared to walk.

Yes, you will have to do the negotiation yourself or through a lawyer. Because agents won't walk. Agent Andrew Zack of the Zack Company made that point on the topic of contract negotiation in a blog titled "What's Driving Self-Publishing? 'Company Policy'" which he published on the agency website on May 13, 2016.[1]

He wrote:

> But when the [book] offer comes and it ignores that certain rights were on the table or it takes the position that getting World rights including Audio is company policy and those things are not negotiable, I think most authors end up feeling boxed in and bullied into giving up rights they would otherwise have hoped to license for additional advances and income elsewhere. Perhaps we should just be grateful that getting movie rights has not become "company policy" anywhere . . . yet.
>
> And I understand authors can always walk away, but we both know that it's not a realistic move.

When someone tells you that a piece of the deal is non-negotiable, that means they are willing to walk away from the deal. Publishers are doing that more and more (which is the very frustrated point of Zack's blog). But when the negotiator on the other side, the agent, says the author walking away is not a realistic move, then the negotiator has no power at all.

Zack's attitude is typical of most agents. Which is why I'm telling you that you should not hire any agent to make and negotiate deals for you.

Recently, a friend of mine, who wanted out of a traditional publishing relationship that had once been beneficial to him, decided that he would negotiate a new contract with the publisher for the next book in a series. My friend decided to ask for the same contract, except for one detail. He wanted the publisher to pay for each right licensed.

My friend had originally been paid in the low five figures. He asked for mid-six figures.

And believe it or not, the publisher considered the offer quite seriously. In fact, for a while there, it looked like my friend might have negotiated more money, but continued the relationship he wasn't sure he wanted any longer.

(When you make ploys like this, make sure that you can live with the deal if the other party accepts it.)

Which brings us to:

The Number of Books You License in This Contract

In the past, every writer wanted a multi-book contract. It gave us security, and it made sure that the publishing house put an effort into publishing our work. The publishing house had a lot of money and future profits at stake, so the house worked harder on multi-book contracts.

Now, with things changing as rapidly as they are, multi-book contracts no longer provide security. They might harm us by locking us into contract terms that won't be good for us in a year or two.

Always go with a one-book contract. It gives you flexibility to negotiate better terms for you in the future, terms we may not even be able to envision now. (Did you know what an app was in 2008? If you signed a multi-book contract that year, you are probably still fulfilling that contract. And it's out of date.)

So, let me summarize this entire chapter.

When you make a deal with another party to license part of your copyright, make sure that:

1. **You Limit the Deal to *Only* the Rights Needed.** Include nothing extra, such as rights that have nothing to do with the one thing the other party does best. Limit the territory you license the copyright in, limit the time the other party can produce the product, and limit the rights granted. If the other party needs more rights, you can amend the contract to include those extra rights...for extra money, of course.

2. **You Get Paid for *Each* License.** Do not bundle bits of copyright together. Slice those rights very thin. Don't license "book rights." License mass market paperback rights in the United States. License Limited Edition Hardcover Rights in Germany. License Ebook Rights for a Translation in Italian in Italy. Each license is worth money to you. Make sure you get that money.

3. **You License One Book at a Time.** Do not make a multi-book deal. The markets are changing so quickly that a long-term contract with one publisher or corporation will end up hurting you. For example, almost everything I wrote in the *Dealbreakers* book three years ago on the rights to sell to a publisher is out of date now. *Three years later.* Imagine if you have a five-book contract, negotiated in 2013, for one book per year. That contract will reflect those out-of-date terms, and hold you to them for five years. That means you won't have a chance to get a better contract until 2018 or 2019—if you want to have a traditional publisher *at all*.

One book at a time, one narrow slice of copyright at a time. Think about the future, not about the present.

Finally, writers too often sell themselves short. Clearly that agent was doing so above. He figured writers should take what they're offered because walking away "is not a realistic move." Too many writers think that.

Yet walking away is always an option. And it's an even better one now than it was in 2013, when I published the original *Dealbreakers* book or than it was in 1993, when self-publishing was hard and frowned upon. Writers have opportunities now.

Writers who aren't tied to long-term contracts, writers who have retained the bulk of their copyrights, writers who know how to exploit those copyrights, are making a fortune on their writing.

Writers who haven't reached the "making a fortune" part of their careers are reserving the right to make a fortune when the opportunities present themselves.

Here's the clearest way I can say this:

If your writing is good enough to attract another company that wants to buy up your copyright for very little money, that means the company believes your copyright has value now and will have even more value in the future.

Why let them make money off you? Why shouldn't *you* make the most money from your copyrights?

Don't sell yourself short. Stand up for yourself and your work. License only those rights needed to partner with another company (if you want to work with someone else) and if the company balks, *walk away*.

You'll get a better deal in the future. Heck, that better deal might simply be one you've created by doing the work yourself.

But I guarantee that the *worst* thing you can do is sign a Grant of Rights clause like the one above. Stop begging for scraps at the publisher's table. Realize you hold all the cards. Negotiate from a position of strength.

You have created something valuable. Protect that asset. Treat it with respect. If you do that, others will too.

8

THE CONTRACT TERMINATION CLAUSE

This chapter deals with the termination of contracts. The first blog post I did on this subject, five years ago now, is unrecognizable from this chapter. I'm basing this chapter on the one in the *Dealbreakers* book from 2013.

However, that book dealt with traditional publishing contracts only. What I didn't foresee was how many contracts indie writers would end up signing. Some of those contracts are with foreign publishers for translation rights; some are with game companies for gaming rights; some are with app developers for rights to use a story in an app—and so on.

So, the advice I'm giving below doesn't just apply to traditionally published novelists. This advice is for all of you who have writing careers.

I am going to keep the writing below in the context of a traditional publishing contract, however, because so many indies are still signing contracts with traditional publishers, selling everything but ebook rights. (Which is a mistake, imho, but hey! It's your career, indies.)

Just think about some of these things when you sign a gaming contract or developing a web comic based on your fantasy series. These general rules do apply.

Got that?

Here we go, with the slightly revised chapter on the contract termination clause.

It feels odd to talk about how a contract ends when you're entering a brand new relationship with a publisher. Both of you feel like this is a Great Thing, and it's all shiny and celebratory and marvelous. And maybe your relationship will be that way.

But the law is all about planning for the worst-case scenario, not the best case. It's all about protecting *someone,* so that someone, in my opinion, should be the writer, not the publisher.

Since 2009 or so, publishers have gotten quite nasty about contracts. In short, they're refusing to let any contract terminate.

This is causing all kinds of problems for writers.

Here's the thing: A valid contract must have some sort of ending. A contract cannot be "forever" or unlimited. It must have a limitation. For the past fifty years or so, the limitation in the U.S. publishing contracts has been what is called sales velocity. If the sales dip below a particular amount, then the writer can ask for a reversion.

In the past, sales were impossible if a book wasn't in a brick-and-mortar store. So if you couldn't find your book in a bookstore, and your friendly neighborhood bookseller couldn't order it, then the book was officially out of print. You would write a letter demanding your rights back, and your publisher would have six months to put the book back into print or the rights would revert to you. Simple (more or less), even if it was contingent on action by the writer (composing and mailing that letter).

The rise of print-on-demand and ebooks changed the bookstore calculus. Now, a book could remain "in print" and "available" forever. With the click of a button, a publisher could send another copy of that book to the interested party.

However, book agents still recommend a limitation clause of some kind—based on book sales and/or royalties.

I've seen the clause written one of two ways: the book must sell a minimum of 200 copies per year in any format to remain in print. Some agents have raised that threshold to 1,000 copies, or more, but that doesn't help.

Because all the publisher has to do to hang onto the book is a 99-cent sale on the book, advertised via BookBub or through Amazon's Deal of the Day, and the book will cross that 1,000 copy threshold.

Years ago, I recommended that authors define out of print like this:

The book shall be deemed out of print if, after five years in print, the author is not receiving a royalty check of at least $500 per six-month period.

In other words, your book has to have earned out its advance, and be paying you royalties of at least $1,000 every single year.

Publishers are loathe to agree to this because it's not in their best interest. Negotiate on the number of years to recoup the advance—three years, five years, ten years—but never on the money. You have to be earning real money on this book for them to hang onto your rights indefinitely.

Shortly after I published that suggestion, a publisher friend of mine pointed out that such a small threshold is a tiny price for a publisher to pay to hold onto a book indefinitely. If the book doesn't earn $500 in real royalties in a time period, then the publisher could pay a $500 "bonus," to buy the right to remain in print.

Since then, I have had a publisher do this very thing. I'm still trying to get the rights reverted on that contract, and the publisher's practice of paying me money like a continual slow-moving advance is creating some problems in doing so. I'm going to have to hire a lawyer to get me out of a contract I should have been able to get out of, based on sales, five years ago.

Here's the thing: Any threshold that is based on sales or velocity or money can be worked around in the modern market.

So instead, here's what I suggest: limit the term of your license.

Technically, because contracts cannot exist in perpetuity, all copyright licenses are limited. But I'm talking about a limitation in *years*, not in dollars or sales.

A limitation in years would work this way. The publisher would ask for the right to publish your book for five or ten years from the publication date. You would also limit how long it would take the publisher to get the book into print. So, they might have a year from turn-in to publish the book and ten years to keep the book in print.

At that point, all rights would automatically revert to the author *unless* the publisher asks for an extension or a new contract *for the same or better terms.*

I have contracts that now contain such limitations. My newer contracts no longer contain a contract termination clause. Instead, the matter is dealt with in the Grant of Rights section, and usually says something like this:

> *The Author grants and assigns the Publisher the following rights…* [paragraphs of rights granted, very explicit language]. *The period of this grant shall be for ten years, at which point, the contract may be renewed on the same or better terms, provided both parties agree.*

Usually that agreement of both parties requires a written document. Sometimes it's an addendum. Sometimes it's a new contract. Sometimes it's a simple letter.

The term limit in years probably sounds unusual to you full-time professional midlist writers. Most contracts negotiated by agents do not have term limits in years. Why? Because if the license is limited, the author can renegotiate the deal without the agent attached or with a new agent to handle the negotiation.

I do know that many long-time major bestselling authors—those who use attorneys to negotiate for them instead of agents—have time-limitations on their licensing deals, rather than sales limitations.

It just makes sense.

Think about it: If your publisher is doing a crapass job with your book, you can wait through the publication period and then find a new publisher to take the work. Or, in this modern era, publish it yourself when the license expires.

That's why so many bestsellers have the time limit instead of the sales limit. Because bestsellers might never sell at a low level, so if they want to jump ship, they need a way to do so. It keeps their publisher on his toes, and it ensures that their writing gets the best presentation possible.

Such limited-time licenses are common in other countries. Every foreign publishing contract I have signed *since I fired my foreign agents* is a limited-time deal. The contract will expire at a particular date, which then goes into my calendar, so I am aware of it. No sales velocity to worry about, and no earnings amount.

The Hollywood options that I've had are also limited-time. Just last month, I renewed—for the fifth? time—a property that continues to provoke interest, just not a full-fledged commitment from a studio. The producer holding the option is keen to renew and, in this case, so am I.

In the past, however, I've used the time-period limitation to jump from a mediocre option deal to an excellent one. The new producer and I just waited for the old deal to expire, and then we made our agreement. Of course, the old producer wanted to renew on better terms, because she knew that the new producer was waiting in the wings.

Suddenly, I was in the position of choosing between two good offers, instead of taking whatever came along.

Aside from convenience and an ease in future negotiations, why am I suggesting a limited-time contract?

Because of what publishing has become. Even back in the day of the handshake agreements, the relationship between publishers and authors was uneasy. Now it's worse.

And the future is hard to imagine.

Dozens of people who work in traditional publishing companies follow my business blog, and many of them write to me about their experiences within the company. They often ask me to make their comments without attribution.

Often, when I get letters from these folks, it's because they're seeing a trend inside their company that scares them. Or because they have heard rumors that make them worry.

I got a letter on term-limited contracts in 2012 from a production editor who worked at what was then one of the Big Six publishers (and who has worked at others in the past).

Note how prescient this editor is, since we're now dealing with the Big Five, instead of the Big Six.

This editor said some interesting things, which I excerpted in my book with the editor's permission. I'm reprinting those comments here.

I have kept the details about this editor's job, gender, and past history to myself all these years. I initially did it so that the editor didn't get in trouble at work. Now, I have no idea if that editor is still employed with the same company, but just in case...

Here goes:

> *I was thinking about your post on term limits for contracts. I think this is especially important right now [2012], given what's going on in publishing. Amazon just bought Avalon, and is in the process of buying Dorchester—for the purpose of putting up their backlist, probably as Kindle exclusives. I think you're going to continue to see Amazon buying up small presses, and I don't think it's out of the question that they'd buy one of the Big Six. The big companies do get sold by their parent divisions from time to time. In the past, those divisions have been bought by other media companies and have continued on, business as usual, just in a different building.*
>
> *Amazon has way, way more cash reserves than other potential bidders. I think, if [Amazon] wanted it, they could buy a major publisher. And then you would suddenly see an enormous portion of the backlist of the last twenty or thirty (or seventy) years on Amazon, probably as Amazon exclusives.*

The editor goes on to point out—with examples from the editor's current and former employers—how hard it is to get rights reverted "even if the book was truly out of print." I'm still dealing with rights reversions from one recalcitrant company whom I will eventually have to take to court. I'm waiting until I have the rest of my backlist in print, because I'm hoping someone else will fight this issue out before me.

The editor's point on rights reversions is an excellent one. (I will be doing a rights reversion blog next week.) The editor then goes on:

> *What I mean is, rights sold to a publisher now could end up—anywhere. Most contracts have very broad language allowing the publisher to sell a book how they want to and at a price they want to. And with Amazon entering the publisher market (and I don't think it's impossible to think Google or Apple might as well), there's no telling if five or ten years down the line an author's book might wind up being sold, or offered for free, in a way [the author] never anticipated or intended.*
>
> *I think authors still think that if they sell a book to the publisher, the publisher will follow the traditional path publishing. And even if that is the*

acquiring editor's intent, and the publisher's intent, things are changing so fast now, there's no guarantee of anything.

We exchanged a number of emails on this point, and as the editor mentioned, all of this might get settled in court. But my goal here, folks, is to make you stay out of court. How do you stay out of court? Have the best damn contract going into an agreement with another party (in this case, the publisher).

I always tell writers that when negotiating a contract, you must imagine this: that the very nice person sitting across the desk from you negotiating for the other side retires or gets fired, and is replaced by the meanest, nastiest person you can imagine. Think of some movie villain if you have to, but imagine someone who cares nothing about you and will twist every piece of that contract to their company's benefit at the expense of you and yours. Ideally, that person wants to pay you nothing for your book or your property and wants to do it legally.

When you're negotiating your contract, imagine you're negotiating with that vile person. Because as this kind editor is pointing out, your publishing company (even one of the so-called Big Five) might get sold to That Guy. And if That Guy runs the company, do you think he cares about promises some fired employee of the bought-out business made to you? Of course not. You and your book have become a widget, made for generating profit for That Guy's company, and nothing else.

You can argue reversions and velocity and sales and money in court. Or you can have a limited-time contract, that automatically expires in five or ten years after publication. Then you leave That Guy's company legally with a minimum of fuss.

See why I want authors to consider limited-time period contracts as the only kind of contract? It benefits us all.

You have choices now, including publishing the novel yourself. Remember that. You don't have to take a bad traditional publishing contract just to see your book in print. In fact, that's probably the worst thing you can do. It'll tie your work up for decades, and you'll have to go to court to set that work free.

And, um, going to court means you'll have to hire an attorney.

So when you sign a contract, make sure that you consider how that contract will end. If you can't figure out how the contract will end, then you have a serious problem. Don't sign that contract. Add a term limit in years or months—with an option for renewal *on the same or better terms*.

Then mark the end of that contract in your calendar, and act upon the renewal (or cancelation) in a timely fashion.

Believe me, you'll benefit from this.

I know, because I have. Repeatedly.

9

RIGHTS REVERSION

When a writer signs a contract with a publisher to have a book published, that contract includes which rights the publisher is licensing and at what cost/percentage of that cost. All of this is based on the copyright, which can be sliced down to minute fractions, and each fraction licensed.

For example, a writer might license worldwide rights to publish the book as a hardcover novel in the English language. The other rights, from ebook to audio to mass market paperback, would not be included in that particular contract.

While contracts are short, others are ten and twenty pages long. Each contract will delineate what the rights licensed are, what the publisher will pay the writer for the use of those rights, and when the contract expires. All contracts need an end date to be legal, and so you'd think that book contract would have a set time period. It's pretty convenient: both parties know the contract expires on a specific date. The contract can be renegotiated around the time of expiration or renewed on a yearly basis, until one party decides to cancel the contract, or, or, or...

Before we go any further, I want to make something very, very, very clear. Often, writers in the comments section of my business blog ask a question about contracts that assumes that *all* book contracts are the same. Some writers might understand that contracts differ, but those writers then believe that all bestsellers have the same contract, and all midlist writers have a different one.

Here's the truth of it, folks. You—one writer—can have twelve book contracts *with the same company*, and each contract might have different terms from other contracts. For example, let's pretend that you have spent your entire publishing career with one publishing house. You write the same type of book year after year, and you *still* would have twelve different contracts, with twelve different terms, including twelve different reversion clauses.

I know that's hard to wrap your minds around, but it's an important thought, because if you believe that all contracts are the same, you'll end up signing something that's bad for you. After all, Famous Writer (who publishes with the same publisher) signed that contract, right?

No, not right. Famous Writer One is different from Famous Writer Two. One is a great negotiator who hires an IP attorney. Two is a terrible negotiator with an even worse agent. The great negotiator with the IP attorney might have a better contract. But he might not. Because the terrible negotiator might be too famous to piss off, and the publisher automatically offered terrible negotiator better terms than great negotiator.

You don't know, and can't know, and probably never will know.

So you must make decisions based on your *own* career.

Now, back to reversion clauses. They are not created equal. But there are some commonalities in book contracts that I can talk about *in general*.

As I mentioned in the previous chapter, book contracts evolved over to avoid the time-limit. Instead, the ticking clock would start once the book was officially "out of print." Generally speaking, "out of print" was usually defined in a contract (if defined at all) as "unavailable for sale." Once the author realized that the book was unavailable, she would notify the publisher that she wanted all rights reverted. Once the writer notified the publisher, the publisher either had to revert the rights, or would have a set amount of time (generally six months) to reissue the book.

Of course, there were a dozen permutations of that. I've seen some contracts that would not allow a rights reversion for seven years after the date of the contract even if the book went out of print in the very first year. The publisher in that case had no obligation to reissue the book and could sit on the rights for six years. At the end of the seventh year, the publisher would *still* have the option of putting the book back into print if the publisher did so within a six-month window after the writer informed the publisher that she wanted the rights back.

Why would a publisher have this clause? Imagine this: in the six years that the publisher ignored this out-of-print book, the writer went from relative unknown to a bestseller. Even if she became a bestseller under another name, the publisher would want the right to reissue that old book. That's why you often saw things like *Famous Writer writing as Not-So-Famous Writer* on book covers, particularly in the 1980s and 1990s. Those writers had signed bad contracts early, and were paying for it years later.

In the past, when a novel went out of print, it was pretty obvious. No one could find a new copy of the book in a bookstore. The burden was still on the writer to ask for a reversion. Back in the 1980s, publishers often required a letter from a bookstore along with the author's reversion request. To prove that the book was out of print, the bookstore letter had to say that the store tried to order copies of the book and failed to get them.

Note that even though it was the publisher's responsibility to print and distribute the book, the author had to prove that the book was no longer in print. Needlessly adversarial? Not really. The problem was that then, as now, the publisher seemed to be the only one in the equation who understood that the control of the rights was the important thing. Writers, for the most part, just wanted to get published.

In fact, back then, only weird or pushy writers would ask for rights reversions. In the 1970s and earlier, rights reversions were important because other publishing houses would buy backlist, but by 1990, that concept was disappearing. So writers just didn't ask. Or they'd instruct their agent to get the reversions, and the agents either wouldn't do it at all or wouldn't follow up.

And getting reversions, even then, required a lot of follow-up.

By the late 1990s, printing technology changed, and print-on-demand books became easier to do. Publishers started using print-on-demand suppliers to do second, third, and fourth printings of backlist titles. Those printings might have been as small as 100 copies. By the mid-2000s, such practices were common.

As usual, writers and their agents were behind the curve on this thing, and only recently started adding the phrase along the lines of "the availability of a print-on-demand edition of the book does not count toward the in-print definition in this contract."

The only reason I can't get my rights back on my last remaining title with Simon and Schuster is because my very old contract with them does not have that line, and S&S counts the POD availability as "in-print."

If contract terms can be bent or stretched to the publishing house's favor, the publishing house will do so.

The print-on-demand technology changed the in-print calculation. At that point, the bookstore letter became irrelevant. If the bookstore waited long enough, it could get an edition of the book.

So agents and authors tried to define the end of a contract by sales velocity. If a book sold fewer than 500 copies in a six-month period (for example), then that book would be considered out of print, and would, for the sake of the contract, be eligible for reversion.

The problem here? The only way the writer knows what the book's sales are is through the royalty report generated by the publisher. And, as I have discussed in various blog posts, those reports are rarely accurate.[1] Plus, if the book sold fewer than 500 copies in a six-month period, the writer would have to wait until the reporting time after that period ended. Which gives the publisher even more time to hang onto the rights.

For example, the six-month period from January 1 to June 30 royalty reports arrive from many traditional publishers at the end of October. That gives the publisher an extra four months to goose sales, if goosing is needed.

At that point, the end of October, the writer can then request a reversion, and will probably have to wait for six more months for a reply. If there's any chance the book will sell well, the publisher has plenty of time to remedy any out-of-print or sales issues. Too much time, in fact.

Why do I say that? Wouldn't a writer want a book to stay in print?

Not always. Sometimes the reason a writer wants a rights reversion has nothing to do with book sales and everything to do with mismanagement in the publishing company. In 2012, when I posted the blog titled "A Tale of Two Royalty Statements,"[2] saying one royalty statement from one company was accurate and a royalty statement from another company was an unmitigated mess, many writers wrote me privately asking who the good company was so they could sell books to that company.

I didn't tell the writers anything. My problem was this: the company with the accurate royalty report had also provided me with my worst-ever editor experience (in a career filled with bad editing experiences) and I wanted the hell out of that company because of the editor. The company with the god-awful royalty reports had an excellent editor and editorial support staff. Companies the size of most traditional publishers are not all good or all bad. They're a mixed bag, and that bag might be different for different writers.

So, back to our overall reversion topic. At the dawn of this new century, it became very hard to get rights reversions. It became even harder in the past several years as the ebook revolution hit traditional publishing.

If an old publishing contract contained ebook rights, and that ebook was available, did that constitute in-print? Traditional publishers said yes; writers and their advocates said no. The courts will eventually decide a lot of these cases.

Writers and agents again tried to close the barn door after the horses got out by trying to define ebook velocity as out of print. If, for example, the ebook sold fewer than 100 copies in a six-month period, then the book would be considered out of print. But that barn door remained wide open, since most writers and agents did not exclude free ebooks from the sales figures. So if a publisher wanted to hang onto rights, he could offer the book for free for a few days, the "sales" would go up, and the book would not revert.

As the writers and agents have changed the contracts again, the publishers are now discounting ebooks to 99 cents or less and counting those sales toward the on-sale total. (Such discounting is often not counted the same way as full-price books in the print book part of the contract. I deal with that in Chapter 10.)

Slowly, traditional publishers have realized that backlist titles are worth a lot of money. So they're buying—and holding—rights. Years ago, when I got angry at a publisher for their misbehavior, I offered to buy back the rights to one of my books. It caught that publisher flat-footed. No writer had ever done that, and the publisher had no idea how to estimate the book's value to the company.

Now, I'm hearing from more and more writers that their publishers insist on the writers *paying* to get rights reverted. While this is in part good news—the publishers are willing to let go of the books—it's also bad news. Writers are being asked to pony up as much as two-thirds of the book's initial advance (on books that were already published) to get the rights reverted.

The publishers claim that this is how much the books will be worth to them in the next ten years, which leads me to wonder if that's just some accountant's valuation on a spreadsheet, done to estimate the value of an existing asset.

What you need to know is this: Traditional publishers are doing everything they can to make these old publishing contracts (and even the new ones) into contracts that exist in perpetuity while seeming to follow contract law. It's a dicey proposition which will take a lot of legal wrangling to settle.

Which is why I've started recommending to writers that if they want to have a traditional publishing contract for their book, that contract has to have a limited term. The contract can exist for ten years from the date of the contract (or seven from the date of publication, which may not be unreasonably delayed), and can be renewed at the same or more favorable terms. I explain this more in Chapter 8.

So, if you don't have a limited-term contract, how can you get your rights reverted?

Writers sometimes ask me why they even need to bother the publisher to get the rights back. After all, if the sales go below 200 copies or whatever that agreement is in the contract, don't the rights automatically revert to you? And I always shake my head in wonderment that the question even came up. Because… um…your relationship is defined by a contract, and contracts require communication.

Besides, most publishers, as I mentioned above, reserve the right to "cure," meaning they can try to repair the damage to the book's sales and put the book back into print.

So it might look like your rights have reverted, but you don't have full legal title to those rights until you have a release letter from your publisher.

A note here: I'm dealing with book contracts, but many short story contracts also have rights reversion issues. Each contract is different. If you're going to reprint a short story that you've previously published, then you need to make certain that the rights you're about to exercise belong to you.

If you didn't understand that paragraph, you *really* need to go back to Chapter 5: Understanding Copyright. As I mentioned earlier, you're not selling a book when you sign a contract. You're licensing part of the copyright.

Okay. So…you want to reprint one of your backlist titles or put up an ebook of an out-of-print novel or sell the Japanese rights to your first novel.

Time to haul out the contract and read it. See what the terms are, what you signed, and what you still own. If the contract is old enough, you might not have licensed erights at all. They might not have existed. Make sure you didn't sign an addendum to the contract in the last few years granting erights, either.

If you believe you own the rights you're about to exercise free and clear, if you're *positive* that there are no existing licenses on those rights, then proceed.

But if you're in doubt, then you need to do some research. You might even need to hire an intellectual properties attorney to help you figure out what you own and what you don't. (See Chapter 23 "How To Hire A Lawyer.")

Let's assume, though, that the book is out of print by whatever standard is set in the contract. Then you have to go through the hoops that the contract establishes for rights reversion.

Generally, those hoops are pretty simple. You must write a letter asking for the rights to revert to you.

The letter should be formal. It should cite the contract, the date on the contract, the clause that pertains to reversion, and the proof you have that the book meets the definition of out of print. Then you should ask for a letter reverting the rights to you.

Send this letter to *the legal department* at your publisher by snail mail with a delivery confirmation attached. Also send it to the legal department by email.

You probably won't get a response from the legal department. Usually, they'll just put the reversion letter into a pile and deal with it at a biannual meeting on rights reversions.

Avoid both your agent and your editor in this process. They both have a vested interest in keeping that book under contract. In fact, contacting your editor before writing the letter might get that back-in-print process under way before your letter even hits the desk at the legal department.

If you get no response in a month, go through this process again. And then do so a month later. By then, someone will respond. They'll be pretty irritated and they'll probably tell you that they will get to you when they get to you.

Remind them that they have six months from the date of your original letter to put the book back into print, or they lose the right to publish the book. (If, indeed, that clause is in your contract. If it isn't, simply state that they must respond to this legal request in a timely manner.)

What you want to do is get them to release your rights. You want to be that annoying person they grant the release to because they don't want to deal with you anymore.

You must remain polite but firm. And if you can't do this comfortably, after the first letter, hire an attorney to do these letters for you. Believe me, that will pay off in the end.

If the publisher says no, but doesn't put the book back into print, then repeat this process six months later. If the contract calls for them to put the book into print six months after the notification, and they haven't, they're in breach of the contract. Notify them of that—or better yet, have an attorney do it.

Most publishers are hanging onto publishing rights these days because it's easy. The publishers believe the rights will be worth money down the road. Writers generally don't push to get books reverted, so publishers have had free reign over this process for decades.

If you want your rights reverted, then you need to be proactive about getting them back. You have to show the publisher that this is important to you, and you will continue to push until you get your way.

Because publishers have so many writers and so much backlist, they won't push back against a squeaky writer unless they believe that writer's book (reissued) will make a lot of money. In most cases, the publisher won't even do enough research to learn that the book would make money.

If you push consistently and politely, you will succeed more times than you'll fail. But it'll take a concerted effort on your part.

What if the publisher wants you to pay them money for the license? They'll say that they'll revert the rights if you pay them ten or twenty or fifty or one-hundred thousand.

Take a moment to gather yourself before responding. And realize that the response is *good* news. They're willing to revert. Now, all you have to do is settle on a price.

As you calculate what the reversion of the book is worth to you, revisit the contract. Figure out what rights you licensed to the publishing company. If it's only First North American book rights, it might not be worthwhile to you to get that license back.

Chances are, though, it's World English and audio and serial rights and T-shirt rights and a whole slew of other rights. Remember, each slice of copyright is worth money in and of itself. You're not just asking so that you can republish in the States (or Europe or whatever this contract licensed). You're asking for an entire group of rights.

I figure any rights reversion is a good one, even if you don't make money right away.

Just be prepared to negotiate. If they say it'll cost $100,000 to revert the rights, counter with "you reverted for free in the past." If they hold firm, then counter with $10,000. Chances are, they'll come back with another figure, say $50,000. Now you're in a negotiation.

And if you don't know how to do that, read Chapter 25: A Short Course in Negotiation or pick up my short book *How To Negotiate Anything.* If you're not *comfortable* negotiating—which is a whole different thing than not knowing how—hire an attorney to negotiate for you. But still look up the proper way to negotiate, so you don't freak out as the process goes along.

You can do this. Worst case scenario is the one I find myself in: The publisher won't revert the rights. Even that can be fought with enough money, time, and legal fees. Just pick your moment.

Even if you fail at getting your rights back from your publisher, you will have one more chance at recovering those rights. Thanks to a change in the copyright law, authors can request the rights back to their work 35 years after signing those rights away. *However,* the author *must* start the process two to ten *years* before recovering those rights. (25-33 years after signing.)

You can find out more information in a 2012 article titled "Reclaiming Your Copyright after Thirty-five Years"[3] on dearauthor.com. You can also find out more at the MIT Library site[4], or through the U.S. Copyright office.[5] (Thanks to Roxie Munro who reminded me of this, after I posted the most recent blog on this topic in July of 2016.)

Take advantage of this, folks, especially if you signed a terrible contract back in the day, and the terrible company refuses to work with you.

And remember: Don't reprint your book if you're in doubt about whether or not you own the rights. The key to success in rights reversion is this: Read your contract, follow the law, be polite, be consistent, and don't give up.

Good luck.

10

DISCOUNT ABUSE

As I write this, I am covered in contract dust—quite literally, *dust*—and growing sadder by the moment. A number of my blog readers have shared their contracts with the personal information excised, and I've been going through the documents. Some of these contracts which the readers received and *did not sign* (thankfully) are the worst of all.

But wowza, are some of these contracts *awful*. No wonder readers sent them to me. Sigh.

Besides the general ickiness of these contracts, I found something else in those contracts which bolsters my memory of things. I have a memory of the way contracts used to be. They were much kinder to the author than current contracts are. I now know that for a fact. I have some contracts that go back to the 1970s and early 1980s thanks to my readers, and while those contracts are similar beasts, they're not the same as today's contracts.

The old contracts are more of a partnership agreement. Oh, there's still some yucky stuff in them. A lot of yucky stuff, to be honest, but most of it can be excised with the strike of a pen. (Some of that is because the contracts were written on *typewriters*—and who wants to type extra unnecessary words? Now, contracts come from computers, with icky yucky boilerplate added into the template.)

Contracts have gotten worse, *much* worse in the past thirty years—and that's with agents (so-called experts) negotiating them.

Other chapters are dealing with the horrid stuff I found. But this chapter deals with something that has come into being in the past thirty years and has been horribly misused.

In this chapter, I'm going to focus on the *discount clause*.

Before you indie writers go heading off to the hills thinking none of this applies to you, look at the title of this chapter. *Discount Abuse*. Many of you indies are as guilty of discount abuse as traditional publishers are.

You just do it in different ways. If you want to understand how to properly discount your books, look at my blog. I have an entire series on Discoverability that I have posted for free. Part of what I discuss there is pricing[1]. If you have the *Discoverability* book I wrote (from those blogs), you'll find an entire section on discounting and pricing.

And before your eyes glaze even more, let me add three things:

First: Do *not* discount *any* of your titles until you have at least three books. Do not discount your first book at all, if it's hanging out there all by its little old self. (I know, I know, how will you get readers otherwise? That's not the question. How will you *keep* readers? By giving them something else to read after they've finished that wonderful book of yours they got for a low price.)

Second: Do *not* do what traditional publishers do when they discount books. Generally speaking, traditional publishers do it wrong. Or their strategy is aimed at promoting *their company*, not at promoting *an author*. Your strategy is to grow your readership. A totally different thing.

Third: Be glad, as you scan this chapter, that you're an indie writer. Even if you screw up and decide to discount your first book, you'll make more money than your traditionally published friends do on *their* discounted books. (Unless, you put your book up for free. Sigh.)

And—a bonus **Fourth: Read this chapter now in case you decide to get a traditional publisher to publish your paper copies.** *Especially* if **you had (or will have) an agent negotiate the deal.** Because much of what I'm going to discuss here applies to paper books, not ebooks. This is one of those areas where you, the indie who has gone hybrid, is most likely to get screwed.

In fact, this area is where writers have been getting screwed since some publisher thought to change their contracts in the late 1990s—and then all the other publishers followed suit. (How is this not collusion? Oh…Department of Justice…)

Discount clauses always send a ting of discomfort through me, and not just because the things are damaging to writers' careers and writers' incomes. But because they are one of those let's-screw-the-writer clauses that got added into contracts in the past twenty years or so.

I had a hunch this was true, but I didn't have proof of it until I was sorting through the contracts some of you sent me. I got my first book contract in 1989, although I'd been reading book contracts ever since I worked for a textbook publishing company in 1984.

My own contract is buried deep in files that I haven't searched through, but I have in my hot little hand a contract from a still-existing Big 5 (or Big 2 or whatever they are now) imprint. That publisher used to be an independent publisher, and in 1980, it did not have a discount clause in its contract.

It had a *remainder* clause. And it's really simple. It says:

The Publisher shall promptly notify the Author whenever it desires to sell copies of the Work at a discount of seventy-five or more percent (75%) of the list price if after making such sale no more copies of the Work will remain in stock. The Author shall have the right to purchase all of such remaining copies within twenty (20) days after such notice is sent at a price equal to the best price which shall be offered to the Publisher. The Publisher shall not have the right to remainder the Work until twelve (12) months after initial publication.

Wow. How fascinatingly reasonable. The publisher has to *notify* the author when it plans to sell books *significantly* under cover price. The publisher is doing this to get rid of inventory of the book on hand, say extra hardcovers to prepare for the paperback edition. And the publisher cannot discount this book for at least a year after publication.

Wow. Shades of another era, huh?

Because modern remainder clauses are not at all the same as that thirty-six-year-old clause. And on top of the new remainder clauses in modern contracts, there are clauses for cheap editions, discounted editions, "other book publications" and all kinds of other "we-don't-have to pay-you-the-royalties-we-promised" editions.

Most modern contracts I'm seeing don't have a remainder clause at all, because nothing is going out of print any more. Editions continue to exist. A handful of contracts with a remainder clause have something like this:

> **Remainder sales.** *On all copies destroyed, given away, or sold at or below cost, no royalties shall be paid. On overstocks or damaged copies, a royalty of ten percent (10%) of the net amount that the Publisher receives in excess of manufacturing cost if the Publisher, at its option, disposes of all or a part of the stock at the best prices it can secure.*

But who cares, really, right? Because these are overstocked or damaged items. They're not a big deal—except that publishing has changed, and is often done with much more sophisticated presses, and overstock and damaged items rarely exist anymore. But pretend they do. It doesn't matter much, right?

Wrong.

Because as I've said repeatedly, a contract is a *full* document, like a story. And these modern documents have lots of let's-screw-the-writer clauses. Sometimes they're bunched into a single clause marked "the discount clause" and sometimes they're spread out, such as these clauses from a fairly recent contract:

> **1. Discounted sales.** *Some sales of the Work in the forms specified in [another part of the contract—forms like hardcover, trade paperback, mass market] above may be to jobbers, chain stores or others at substantial discount. Where the discount is fifty percent (50%) or more from the Retail Price, a royalty equal to one-half the regular royalty. Where the discount is sixty-five percent (65%) or more from the Retail Price, a royalty equal to ten percent (10%) of the Net Receipts per copy sold.*
>
> **2. Cheap editions.** *On all net copies sold of any cheap edition that the Publisher publishes at a price not greater than two-thirds (2/3) of the original*

retail price, a royalty of ten percent (10%) of the Net Receipts, but if the Publisher licenses publication of such edition by another publisher, a royalty of fifty percent (50%) of the Net Receipts.

   3. Other Book Publication. *For other editions (including but not limited to premiums, mail order, schoolbook and book fair editions, and other special editions) sold in the United States: Ten percent (10%) of the Net Receipts.*

This lovely publisher starts screwing writers right from the start. Chain stores or *others?* Most of the large stores get discounts over 50% *as a matter of course*, so that means that most of the royalties paid from a writer's book are paid at half the usual royalty rate.

Oh, wait! It gets worse. These "discounted" books have no time limit, so if your book is really popular, and it sells to Barnes & Noble (chain store) or Wal-Mart (chain store) at *publication*, the publisher can discount the royalty rate too. Right from the moment of publication. None of this waiting a year, as in the 1980 contract.

And lookie here! The publisher doesn't have to pay full royalties on books sold by mail order. Many publishers now consider books sold off their website as mail order. In fact that entire clause that mentions other editions? It's pernicious all by itself.

It says *"For other editions (**including but not limited to…**)"*

In other words, the publisher can publish the definitive book, and then all kinds of other editions, because the author didn't *limit* the kinds of books the publisher can publish. And believe me, there are a million different editions the publisher can think up, *none* of which the publisher has to pay full royalties on.

Things get even worse for writers. For example, this lovely publisher from whose contract I'm quoting has an even lovelier clause in its ebook royalty rate. That clause says:

Royalties for Ebook Editions sold in the United States, except as described in paragraphs 1-3 below: Fifteen percent (15%) of the Net Receipts.

Guess what, folks? Paragraphs 1-3 are the clauses I excerpted above. The *discount* clauses. So if your publisher has this clause in their ebook editions royalty rates, then your publisher can sell your discounted ebook and pay you *even less*. So that wonderful $1.99 sale they're doing to "promote" you? Well, that $1.99 is significantly less than 50% of the cover price of your $9.99 ebook, isn't it? Guess who doesn't get paid a full 15% of net receipts on the ebook edition.

You.

By the way, the contracts I'm using for this modern stuff were all negotiated by agents, not attorneys. Just pointing this out.

I don't agree with the Authors Guild about much of anything because they don't advocate well enough for their authors. But I agree with them on the discount clause—which they call "The Discount Double-Cross."

In fact, the Guild nicely does the math for us using a book with a cover price of $10 in an article on their website titled "End The Discount Double-Cross"[2] from November, 2015. I have excerpted a paragraph from the article here, but I'm going to add some paragraphs to the excerpt for clarity's sake. I'm also making one part of this paragraph bold just so you see it:

> At a 55% discount to retailers, the publisher would receive $4.50 per copy, minus the author's 15% royalty of $1.50. That leaves the publisher $3.00 before printing and other expenses.
>
> Increase that discount to 56%, and the publisher receives only $4.40 from the sale.
>
> But under some "deep discount" clauses, the author's royalty would suddenly plummet to 15% of that $4.40—just 66 cents—thereby magically increasing the publisher's take to $3.74.
>
> But what's magic for the publisher is misery for the author, who takes a haircut of more than 55%.
>
> **With a clause like this in effect, why would any rational publisher maintain a higher wholesale price when a lower one would deliver 25% more to its bottom line—entirely at the author's expense?**

Why indeed? Realize this comes from an organization that's deeply in the pocket of traditional publishers. The Authors Guild is trying to climb out of that pocket—the fair contracts initiative is a beginning—but the Guild is not doing very well.

Because the "solutions" the Authors Guild poses in that article are not worth quoting. They still assume that the publisher needs deep discounts.

The publisher *doesn't* need the deep discounts the way that those discounts are being applied now. The publisher might need a pass on paying standard royalties for books sold *below* cost. But even then, the writer should get a payment of some kind.

My solution is to go back to 1980.

First, the publisher can't discount anything without seeking the author's permission.

Second, the publisher can only discount a book *after* the book has been out for a year or more.

If the publisher wants to discount titles to promote sales in the first year of publication, let the *publisher* eat the difference in the cost. *Not* the writer.

Here's what Roxana Robinson of The Authors Guild told the attendees at the Rights and Content in the Digital Age Conference put on by Publishing Perspectives[3]:

Many contracts have clauses that will allow the publisher, under these circumstances of deep discount, to pay no royalties. The publisher gets paid by the middleman. And the middleman gets paid. Only the author will get nothing at all for the sale of this book which she just wrote…The publishers know this. But they do it [sell at discount to middleman vendors] because they want some money now.

In fact, right now, in the existing system, the only person involved in the creation, production, and distribution of a book who does *not* get paid when the book is deeply discounted is the *writer*.

And the reason for that injustice is the contract, which the writer signed.

As I was researching this piece, I found several blogs by agents who basically said that a bad deal for a writer is better than no deal at all. That's ridiculous. It was ridiculous back in the days before the rise of indie publishing, and it's even more ridiculous now.

It's truly ridiculous coming from the person who is supposed to (in theory) negotiate better terms for the writer. Clearly, that's not happening. One reason it's not happening is that agents don't understand these contracts any more than the writers do.

Let's look at this problem in terms that indie and hybrid writers understand. When an indie writer puts her ebook on sale for 99 cents, down from her usual $4.99 "cover" price, she knows that she will receive 35% of that lower price instead of 70% of the higher price.

She's losing roughly $3.15 per sale, but she has *chosen* to. I'm assuming here that she chose to lower the price to achieve some goal—to get readers into her series, to increase sales of her other books, to offer a special for a few days to entice new readers—and she knows what she's losing.

Traditionally published authors have no idea what price their book is selling for and what royalty percentage they will get on that book. Without a full-blown audit of their publisher, there's no way the traditionally published writer *can* know.

These discount clauses—which the authors have freely signed—are the way that publishers are increasing their bottom lines. This is also why so many #1 *New York Times* bestselling authors are seeing their royalty rates decline. It's not because the books sell fewer copies (although that's happening as well); it's because the authors are being paid less per copy sold—significantly less.

These terms crept into contracts one by one. As the business changed, as publishers consolidated, as chain stores rose and the margin for big publishers got slimmer, the money that publishers made came out of the writer's pocket.

If you insist on selling your book to a traditional publisher, especially one of the Big Whatevers, then accept that you will lose that book for the term of the copyright, and you will not get rich off that book's sales *even if the book is a bestseller.*

Do your best to negotiate out these pernicious clauses. If you do manage to get those clauses out of your contract, be prepared to audit your publisher regularly. Because they'll probably still act as if the clauses are *in* your contract, and figure you won't catch them at it.

And you probably won't—not without an accountant at your side.

My solution? I go traditional for short work and the occasional editing project, but not for my novels. I'm still hybrid, but just barely.

I'm a *professional* writer. I make my *living* at writing. Clauses like these make it *impossible* for writers to make a living at writing.

If your goal is to be validated while you work another job, then go ahead, sign contracts with big traditional publishers. If your goal is to be a professional writer with a long-term career as a writer *and no other job*, you have to stay away from contracts and clauses like these.

Because, as we saw in other chapters, getting out of contracts is much harder than getting into them.

11

MORAL RIGHTS AND EDITING CLAUSES

Back when I was writing a lot of tie-in novels for the *Star Trek* division at Pocket Books, a brand-new editor asked me to help him rescue a story in an anthology. It seems that the main writer on the project had quit unexpectedly. The writer had outlined the story, and the outline had been approved by Paramount, which was a major hurdle. What the editor needed from me was an actual draft of the story.

In other words, none of the characters were mine. The plot, setting, and theme were not mine. The editor needed my style as a writer and my name on the cover. That was it.

I had never worked with this editor before. My usual *Star Trek* editor advised me to stay clear. But, I figured, it was just a short story. What could it hurt?

Well…it didn't exactly hurt. But it was perplexing. Based on a 2,000-word outline, I wrote the 6,000-word story as requested. Turned the story in on time. Got an acceptance, and the ridiculously high acceptance payment.

Then I got the copyedit.

Which wasn't a copyedit. The editor himself had *rewritten every single sentence* of the story. Every single one. Sometimes adding passive voice. Sometimes making the meaning unclear. Always dumbing down the content and the voice and the point of each sentence, let alone each paragraph.

I looked at that, glanced at my contract, and realized that even though this short story was written as work made for hire, I could make a huge stink about this. I could pull my name or pull the story or cause all kinds of grief.

In the end, I decided to leave it alone. If you look up this short story now, you'll see the most poorly written thing ever published under my name.

But the outline hadn't been that good in the first place, the story was a rescue, and the other author's name was underneath mine, so I figured anyone who saw my name would think that the collaboration went poorly.

It had indeed. I found out later that this editor rewrote every single sentence of everything he bought, from short story to novel, and got a reputation inside the publishing house for being the slowest editor in the entire company. Gosh, I wonder why. And his writers *hated* him. Yep. I refused to ever work with him again, and I told other authors to stay away from him.

Nice man in person, though. Sweet, charming, congenial. And a total doofus.

I mean, if you're going to hire half of the team (me and Dean) writing most of the *Star Trek* novels in that period of time, then you should trust her abilities to appeal to the fans. But there was nothing of me in that piece. Nothing at all.

That is the only time in my recollection that I can recall allowing an editor's or copyeditor's full rewrite of my work to get into print. I've had worse rewrites in my career, including a copyeditor who changed every single piece of punctuation in one of my romance novels, but I never let those rewrites stand.

I cited contract terms, refusing to allow the changes. I pulled books from publishers because of shenanigans like this. I got copyeditors fired. Repeatedly.

I *defend* what I write. My writing in some story or novel or nonfiction article might be awful, but it's *mine*. If I put my name on it, guaranteed—except for that one short story—every word in the piece is a word I wrote or approved. Every single one.

I've written about defending your work before, most recently in March, 2016 in a post titled "The Copyedit From Heck."[1] Usually when I write about these things, I'm writing to younger writers who don't believe in their own abilities. These writers—indie, hybrid, and traditional—need to trust their inner rule-breaker and go with the way that they had written their stories in the first place.

But today, I'm writing about contract terms. And the ones that I check for first are the ones that most writers ignore.

Remember, early on in this book, I told you that most writers check their traditional book contracts for the advance, the payout, and the due dates. They don't look at anything else. Writer after writer, and editor after editor, have told me this.

I always look toward the editing clauses first. Because if they're ugly, the rest of the contract usually is as well.

This applies to *all* kinds of writing for traditional markets, including for nonfiction and short fiction. I've seen terrible editing clauses in contracts, and what's ironic is that those clauses often seem to be the most innocuous.

What you want is complete control of the content of your work. For example, in every single short fiction contract I sign, I change the publisher's right to "edit the Work" to "*copy*edit the Work." I always add a line that ensures I must approve any changes, including those copyedits, to the Work.

If I don't like the copyedit, my version stands. If my version isn't going to stand, then the story doesn't get published. Period.

Usually, most publishers—both book publishers and short form publishers—allow those changes.

But in 2011, I started encountering some publishers who refused to allow me to control the content of work published under my name. These clauses first appeared in British contracts, and then migrated to the U.S., which I found (and find) odd, since it usually works the other way around.

I had just negotiated a book deal with a British publisher, getting rid of a ton of this messy stuff. Then a friend of mine, a writer I respect greatly, asked me to contribute a nonfiction piece to an anthology he was putting together.

No problem. I wrote the piece and he approved it.

Then I got the contract.

First off, the contract started out badly with this:

In consideration of a fee of £50.00 (fifty pounds) and 2 (two) paperback complimentary copies of the Work to be delivered to the Author on publication of the Work by the Publisher, the Author hereby grants to the Publisher the sole and exclusive right and licence throughout the world to produce, print, publish, copy, store in any medium by electronic means and otherwise exploit the Contribution or any part of the Contribution or any derivative of the Contribution in all languages in every form or format whether now known or hereafter invented, including without limitation print, audio, digital and electronic form and in each case to license others including without limitation associate companies of the Publisher to do any or all of the same. The Publisher shall have absolute discretion as to the exercise, sale or other dealing of the rights granted herein.

Yuck. We've discussed this kind of thing before, particularly in Chapter 9 "The Grant of Rights." According to this grant of rights, the publisher would control all of the content in my article in any means forever without limitation. I knew how to change that control, but the publisher and I didn't start our relationship well. I was making notes. There were a lot of other problems, all noted.

Then I hit this:

The Publisher may make such editorial amendments to the Contribution as the Publisher considers necessary.

Um, what?

The contract gave the publisher the right to do exactly what that *Star Trek* editor did. Under this British contract, the publisher had the right to change *everything* in the document if the publisher deemed it necessary to do so. The writer would have no say. In fact, the writer did not get to see copyedits or proofs or anything.

The publisher got total control.

Then, this lovely publisher added this:

The Author hereby asserts to the Publisher and the Publisher's licencees the Author's moral right of paternity in the Contribution. The Author irrevocably and unconditionally waives the Author's moral right as provided in the Copyright, Designs and Patents Act 1988 to the extent the Publisher deems necessary to allow the Publisher to exercise and license the exercise of the rights granted to the Publisher under this Agreement.

I know most of you don't understand this or why it's so horrifying, particularly in the context of the rest of the contract. So to explain, let me tell you my theory of contracts.

Clauses exist in contracts for a reason. Someone put those clauses in that contract on purpose.

Double-down on this theory when you ask for a clause to be removed and the other party refuses to remove it. If I ask for a change in a contract, and the other side refuses to make that change or even work with it, then I *know* that the other side plans, at some point, to exploit that clause in the contract.

Remember that I am not a lawyer, so I can be wrong about this, and nothing I do here constitutes legal advice.

But…with my theory of contracts in mind…let's look at "moral rights" for a moment.

"Moral Rights" differ depending on which country issues the document. The United States does a crap job with moral rights. Europe pays a lot more attention to moral rights than the U.S. does.

But the protections differ. And nowadays, writers generally sign contracts that license World Rights. In theory, the U.S. law should apply to U.S. authors. But…that's not how things always work, especially in the law. And I also know that a lot of you who read this book are not writing here in the U.S.

So…on moral rights, here's the short version. Moral rights in a work do *not* refer to morality. It might be better to call this Integrity Rights or perhaps Reputation Rights. Those aren't entirely accurate either, but they're helpful in understanding what I'm about to say.

Essentially, an important part of moral rights protects the use of the writer's name. Usually moral rights are affirmative—the writer has the right to *put* her name on something.

But as with most things contractual, I prefer to look at the downside. The writer also has the right to *pull* her name from work that no longer represents her.

There's a lot more to moral rights. For example, in Europe, it's impossible for a writer to give up her moral rights by contract. However, many companies ask the writer to *waive* her rights (not license them or transfer them). According to lawyerly blogs I looked at as I wrote this chapter, the European courts probably won't uphold that either, but who knows? It's courts, and you don't want to get to a court. You want to negotiate bad clauses out of a contract entirely.

So...let me give you the skinny on this contract as it is written in regard to *editing only*. The British publishing company has the right—if the publisher deems that right necessary—to completely rewrite my article. They could change *everything*. They could add stuff I find objectionable—political points of view, for example. They could libel someone through careless writing or even deliberately. They could take a piece in which I say I *love* something, and change it to say I *hate* it.

They can do all of that, because I would have signed away that right. Then I would have *waived* my right to remove my name as the author of the piece. So they could write all this stuff, and claim I meant it, because my name is on it.

And...the article stays in print in collections and other anthologies and online and in newspaper articles and in skywriting—all for the lovely exchange of 50 pounds and two authors copies of the original book.

Seriously.

Honestly, these weren't even the worst clauses. There were other ugly clauses—a minor non-compete, and then a clause that said they were under no obligation to publish anything.

Oh, and one that drives me as batty as the editing clauses: They have the right *to my name*. Not just to use my name in publicity. I "empowered" them to use my name in any situation they "considered necessary."

My *name*.

I see this clause a lot. Writers give up the right to their own names to a corporation for a few thousand dollars and the publication of a novel. Or in this case, about $100 and two copies of an anthology. Nope, no, never, nuh-uh, not happening. Not *my* name or my pen names or anything else.

Or my likeness. Or anything about me.

No.

Horrid.

And these clauses—all of them—are turning up in short fiction contracts, article contracts, and other agreements. Not just in novel contracts.

So, you're wondering, what did I do in this circumstance? I looked at this contract and decided that it wasn't worth negotiating. The contract would have to be thrown away, and we would have to start over. It wasn't worth the effort.

I really didn't care about getting published in this project enough to spend weeks negotiating the contract. I doubted the publisher was going to pay me more than fifty pounds, and my time is worth way more than that.

I wrote to my editor friend, and told him that regretfully, I couldn't sign this contract, so I was bowing out of the project. He wrote back, asked what I objected to, and I told him my problems with the contract. He didn't comment. He said simply that he would see what he could do.

Next thing I hear is a clarifying email from the "commissioning editor." She offered to change some of the clauses. And then, on the editing clause, she offered something that went on for nearly a page.

Buried in the middle of that was this lovely addition:

The Author expressly acknowledges and agrees that: (a) in the event she does not undertake the Revisions as requested by the Publisher pursuant hereto, the Publisher may use its absolute discretion: (i) withdraw the Contribution from any and all subsequent edition and/or versions without any ongoing liability or responsibility on the part of the Publisher (or any authorized third party thereof) to the Author in respect of the same (including without limitation by way of remuneration, publication and/or credit); and (ii) freely substitute the

*Contribution and/or **itself (or by a third party on its behalf) undertake the Revisions...***

In other words, she was adding a clause that *still* gave them the right to rewrite my work. Or have someone else rewrite it.

Then she added that they refused to change the moral rights clause at all.

So, with all that lovely language, they said the exact same thing and did not change the contract *at all*. They just made their intentions clear.

I wrote back, very politely, saying that I could not sign the contract with the stuff above, and they needed to remove it (along with any other similar language in the contract which I specified). I also insisted, again, on deleting the clause waiving my moral rights.

She wrote back, refusing to change the editing clause, and then said this:

I'm afraid the moral rights clause is not one that I am able to make any alterations to. It is a standard clause across all of our contracts and our lawyers will not accept changes to it. As you say, this is a clause that relies somewhat on trust; I can only assure you that we will not act unreasonably, as it would not be in our interest to do so....

I kid you not. She wrote "Trust us. We won't hurt you."

After I stopped laughing, and showing this around to my writer and lawyer friends, who also laughed (except for one lawyer friend who got incensed), I wrote her back politely, *again* withdrawing my article from the volume.

By now, I had spent more time on the stupid contract than I had spent writing the piece.

One month later, I got a response from her.

She said they were willing to have me sign a non-exclusive "permissions request" rather than a contract. She enclosed it. Three paragraphs, giving them the non-exclusive right to use the piece. They could not revise it or alter it. They did not ask me to waive moral rights. They had to ask my permission to translate the piece or use it in other formats.

A very simple, very sensible contract.

And again, she browbeat me with a somewhat stupid argument. Her very polite language said that because I'm an idiot, I would be hurting them. Her words:

> We will no longer hold exclusive rights across the whole collection, which makes it much harder to sell as any potential translator, for example, would have to seek to reclear permission to use your work.

Um…in other words, if you do this, Ms. Rusch, you will hurt the sales of this book and you will hurt all your little friends who have articles in it.

I ignored that part of the letter, signed the non-exclusive agreement, and the book came out in various countries, with permissions recleared no problem.

I thought I was the only person who had trouble with the original contract but it turns out that about a third of us had trouble. Earlier communication with this company made it sound like I was the Big Bad Wolf. The problem was, I didn't care.

All I wanted to do was withdraw the article if they didn't give me a better contract. *They* were the ones who kept negotiating. I kept walking away.

I wasn't trying to hurt my little friends or tank the collection—and surprise, surprise, surprise, I didn't.

Some quick takeaways here:

Make sure the editing clauses in your contracts—from short story contracts to article contracts to novel contracts—limit what the publisher can do to your work. You essentially should allow the publisher to change some things to house style (like whether or not you put a capital after a colon). You should have the right to review a copy-edit—and to have the final *say* on that copyedit.

You also need a clause that limits revisions. When there's a clause in the contract that says that the finished book must be "accepted" by the Publisher, then you have to define what that means. If it means revisions, then those revisions should be limited to no more than two or three before the contract terminates.

I've known writers who rewrote their books for *years* before the books finally were tossed back as unacceptable by the publisher. One author I know rewrote her book every year for ten years for a textbook publishing house I worked for. When my boss left, and the next editor took his place, that editor saw this continual revision, and canceled the contract. The writer had to *repay* her entire advance.

She did ten years of work, revised a textbook *ten times*, and lost money on it.

Yep, see how I learned how bad contracts can be?

Learn about moral rights. I'm not including moral rights as a deal-breaker in the contracts here, because I'm an American author, and in theory, American authors don't have moral rights in their books. We have other protections for our name and our content under our copyright laws.

In theory. Which is subject to change whenever the laws change.

I don't think it's worth tanking a contract over the possibility that the laws might change in the future. But you might feel differently.

Learn about the ways that other countries' laws differ from ours. For example, libel laws in Great Britain are much more Draconian than they are here in the United States. And the punishments are more severe.

Suddenly, protecting your content against the things I mentioned above becomes very, very important.

And you indie writers, think about those libel laws when you publish something wide on Amazon or Kobo. If you have a dicey section that might libel someone—even sniffs at it—then you could run into trouble *outside* of the United States.

Guard your name and your likeness as well as your content.

Make sure you are the arbiter of what gets published under your name, not the publisher or some employee of a multinational corporation.

The ironic thing about the story that I just told you is this: I could easily have removed my name from that *Star Trek* edit. I could as easily requested another editor or deleted every single one of those changes.

And that was a work made for hire, with a good contract behind it.

If I had signed that nonfiction contract for an *original* work, I would not have been able to do *any* of the things I could have done with a *Star Trek* short story.

If I were to ask a group of writers to judge sight unseen which contract they thought would be the worst—a work-for-hire contract for a media tie-in novel or a standard contract with a reputable publishing house—every author would have said the work-for-hire contract. And they would have been wrong.

I hope this piece helps you understand a little more about contracts. And about how to protect yourself and your work. I also hope it shows you that sometimes walking away is the best option, particularly when very little money is involved.

Sadly, that British editor was right when she told me that the contract I saw was standard. It is. I've seen many more like it both before and after. These contracts aren't getting better, folks. They're getting worse.

12

OTHER EVIL CLAUSES

I've spent eleven chapters now on contracts, and there are still a million clauses to go. Just this week, I heard about a new one—contract termination fees—thanks to an article on Writer Beware's website[1].

I could spend the rest of my life writing about bad contract terms, and telling you how to avoid them. And that doesn't even start to count Terms of Service clauses that no one reads, such as the very scary initial ToS for July's popular game, Pokémon Go[2]. In theory, Niantic, the makers of the game, claim that they have patched the problem. But not before they collected information on millions of users, information they did not promise to delete from their servers.

It's a minefield out there, and not just because so many of us have been playing Pokémon Go outside without looking where we're going. (A friend says he saw a woman walk into a telephone pole this weekend, which isn't that bad, considering there are reports of people falling off cliffs near the Pacific Ocean in San Diego County. Those men are alive and not seriously injured. If they had fallen off a cliff in my hometown, they would be dead.)

Writers tend to go through their business life like Pokémon Go players, looking for something that isn't there, hoping to score a magic number of points, and not seeing what *is* there.

It's impossible to show you all the bad contract terms. I've delineated several that you need to watch out for. I'm going to go through some important ones quickly in this chapter, and then look at a few more major things before we go to agents and attorneys.

After that, folks, you're on your own.

So, here are a few more things to watch out for, in no particular order.

1. Definitions: Make sure all of the important and dicey terms in your contract come with an attached definition. And make sure that definition is in your favor, extremely clear, and very narrow. The biggest and most important definition in modern contracts is the definition of the word "net."

Most contracts leave out the definition of the word "net" altogether. Those contracts assume, apparently, that we all agree on what the word means.

Here's the thing about contracts, folks. Contracts create their own language and their own definitions. So if the word "net" is undefined, it means whatever someone wants it to mean.

If the publisher does define the word "net," the publisher often does so in a way that benefits them. (Horrors! They don't do that in other things…oh, wait, never mind.)

Publishers have moved to "net" in royalty payments at the same time as the rise in ebooks. But that's not why publishers did it. They did it for the same reason that they have discount clauses in the contract, such as the ones discussed in Chapter 10, to make sure the writer gets almost no money for the books the publisher sells.

If the publishing contracts end up defining the word "net," then the clause usually looks something like this:

As used herein, the term "Net Receipts" means monies received by the Publisher on the sale or license of the Work after all discounts, fees, and returned copies have been deducted, and before addition of freight charges and/or handling charges.

It's all very, very loosy-goosy. Monies received by the Publisher. I suppose you can audit for that, but there's lots of room for dispute in that language. And lots of room for abuse.

Daniel N. Steven, who runs the website publishlawyer.com in a blog post titled "The Net Revenue Royalty Clause,"[3] suggests that you define "net" this way:

> *"…actual cash receipts from all sales of the Work in any media or format less shipping costs, returns, and sales or value-added taxes remitted to Publisher by the purchaser."*

Frankly, I don't like that definition either. I would rather have net defined as "actual cash receipts from all sales of the Work in any media or format" without the "less shipping costs…" The price of the book has already been lowered from "cover" price or "standard retail price." Why should the writer be further penalized for something like taxes which vary from state to state or "shipping costs," a term which many mail order companies use to jack up their prices.

Since the publisher is already shorting you on the price of the book, try to get as high a percentage as possible as well. Not 15%, but 25%, if possible or 50%. In theory, you should be a co-equal partner in this publishing thing, although publishers don't treat you that way.

Ask, though. You'll be surprised what you might receive.

Remember though, in all definitions that you add to a contract, define narrowly. Define to *your* benefit. And be very, very clear, leaving *no* room for publisher interpretation.

2. The Reserve Against Returns Clause: Traditional publishing works like this: The publisher solicits the book to bookstores. The bookstores order books. Many, many bookstores have the right to return those books if they don't sell.

That's a hold-over from the Great Depression—yes, the 1930s Depression. Back then, publishers wanted bookstores to survive. Such things are no longer necessary now, but those practices continue for most brick-and-mortar stores.

(And yes, bookstore owners, I know how hard it is to order inventory, and how costly it can be. I own *two* retail stores, and have owned several others—none of which allowed me to return anything for full price. Not a one.)

Because of computer ordering, returns are much less of a guessing game than they were years ago. When I came into the business, returns could be as much as 50% of the print run. Now, it's more like 20-25% or even less. This little figure will be important below.

The reserve against returns usually looks like this:

> *In making accountings, the Publisher may retain a reasonable reserve against returns on any accounting statement, provided the amount of the reserve is clearly indicated.*

But that clause is unclear—and, hello!, there is no cap on the reserve. The *entire print run* can be counted as reserve against returns. Because the only way you can know if the publisher deems the entire print run a "reasonable" reserve is to, again, go to court over that clause.

Better to define everything.

Cap the number of copies of the reserve at 15-20%. So if the print run is 10,000 copies, then let the publisher keep 1500 to 2000 copies as a reserve against returns.

Since most publishers only ship print copies to bookstores in the first month of a book's life, cap the time that the reserve can be held to six months. The reserve *must be* lifted after six months.

Finally, make sure your reserve against returns *does not count against ebooks*. That clause above? It can be applied to *any kind of book*. I've seen the royalty statements from the company that issued that clause. They keep a reserve against returns *for ebooks*.

So limit the clause severely. In fact, I would love to see you strike it out, and figure out if the publisher even notices. If they do, they'll go bonkers. Then anything else you suggest after you tried to cut the reserve against returns clause would seem reasonable.

But I'm bratty, and I'm tired of elucidating all the ways these freaking publishers will, can, and do screw writers.

Seriously. It's ugly out there. And this clause is just one more screw in the coffin.

Sigh.

3. Basket Accounting: speaking of screwing the writer, let's look at this old favorite, that has existed since the 1970s. Basket accounting refers to the fact that the publisher throws all of the books in one contract into the same "basket" before paying out royalties.

So if you have a three-book contract, and book one sells 5 times its advance, but books two and three never earn out, you probably won't see a dime in royalties.

If each book were accounted separately, then you'd receive royalties for book one, making you significantly more money.

The clause is not called the "basket accounting" clause. Every contract does it differently.

And I have to tell you: In this modern world, it's a lot more probable that you'll get a basket accounting deal if you have a multiple book deal with a publisher. That publisher will guarantee that you don't see a dime in royalties by underpublishing at least one of those books.

The best way to avoid this?

Have a one-book contract. Never ever ever sign a multiple book deal, no matter how much they offer you.

Traditional publishers and agents will tell you it's in your best interest to sign a multiple book deal. After all, you'll get money for years, and you'll know how much. But you won't necessarily *get* actual money for years, especially if there's an "acceptance" clause in your contract. (Meaning your book is not considered publishable until the publisher deems it "accepted.") And there's no guarantee, in this publishing environment, that your publisher will be around five years from now.

Besides, if you have a one-book contract, and your book is *successful*, then you have the opportunity to negotiate a *better* contract for book two. And with the rise of indie publishing, if you can't get a contract for book two, who cares? You can publish it yourself.

Now, you're thinking you're safe, right? You won't have to ever worry about basket accounting.

Not true! Because there's an even sneakier clause that can show up in your later contracts. And it's…

4. The Cross-Collateralization Clause: Oh, yes, this one is ugly. And you'll find it mostly in bestseller contracts.

It goes something like this:

> *All Works covered by this Agreement or any other agreement between Publisher and Author shall be considered one account and shall be accounted for jointly or collectively.*

This little beauty should simply be deleted. This probably should be a dealbreaker. If your previous novels haven't earned out, but your fifth did, and then you got a contract for your sixth for twice the advance of the previous, you might find the cross-collateralization clause in that contract for the sixth book.

It means that the publisher wouldn't have to pay you the full advance for the sixth book. The publisher could subtract all the unearned advance payments from that sixth book advance.

And God forbid that any of your books becomes a bestseller, because those royalties that you expected (diminished as they are, from the undefined net royalty calculations and the discount clauses) won't come. They'll be counted against *all* of the previous books you've done for this company and *any other book* already under contract, even if it's not published.

Holy crap. Yet another major screw-the-author clause.

(Why do you people want to have your novels published with a traditional publisher, again? Really. Why?)

5. Time limit on publication: This one is sneaky. It caught me on my very first novel. What you want here is for the clause to read in your favor. Something like:

If the Work is not published within two years of the date of this contract, the contract terminates, and all rights revert to the author.

Usually this clause isn't quite so writer-friendly. But something like this clause is in most *good* publishing contracts.

The contracts that leave it out—well, the publisher *never* has to publish the book.

I was lucky: the publisher wanted to publish my book advantageously, so he kept pushing the pub date back and giving the novel better and better placement on the list (with more advertising). The book came out more than 2 years after it was bought. By then, I had sold eight other novels to other publishers. If I had signed a noncompete like the ones in Chapters 7 and 8, I couldn't have done that.

But I have had friends who have had a different experience with this lack-of-definitive publication date. One friend lost his editor, and the editor who replaced the previous editor *hated* my friend. The new editor just buried the book. Took it off the schedule and never ever scheduled it.

My friend eventually bought back the book by repaying the advance *five years* after the book initially sold to the publisher.

Make sure there's some kind of date. And again, make sure it benefits *you*, not the publisher.

Are you seeing a pattern here?

Speaking of getting out of a contract...

6. Termination Fee: I have never encountered this clause in any of the contracts I saw, signed or vetted for writers for this chapter. However, this nasty little clause turned up on Writer Beware as I was writing this piece.

Termination fees are simply that: fees charged to terminate the contract. The contract listed on Writer Beware has two different fee schedules—a $500 fee plus expenses incurred by the publisher if the contract is terminated before publication, and a substantial percentage-based fee system if the contract is terminated *after* publication.

The case Writer Beware cited showed that the publisher in question used these fees to bully a writer who was trying to extricate herself from a bad publishing situation.

I've got nothing to add in regard to these fees because they are new to me. Except to express a dull sense of horror at the permutations that publishers, both large and small, are going to in order to make sure writers never ever ever make a living at their work or get their books published.

Sigh.

So… you've got the best contract possible. You've negotiated every single point I've mentioned in this book. You have great royalty rates, no reserve against returns, a toothless discount clause…everything.

And yet, you're still not making money. Well, that might be because you left out this clause:

7. **Audit Clause:** All of this work you're doing on your contract don't mean shit if the contract lacks an audit clause. The audit clause, like the definitions, needs to benefit you, not the publisher. I've seen too many audit clauses that, in effect, make it impossible to audit the publisher because of all the restrictions placed in the clause.

What you want is the right to audit your publisher as often as your royalty statements appear. If you get six-month royalties, then make sure you can audit every six months. And make sure that you have the right to send in *your own* auditor. I've seen audit clauses that restrict the author to using the *publisher's* choice of an auditor. (Seriously.)

The clause needs to be short and to the point. You have the right to audit your publisher's records as they pertain to the books you've published with that publisher.

Why have the audit clause? Because right now, you're going on faith that the publisher will be honest with you. They have no reason to accurately calculate your royalties and payments. Publishers have never been accurate in their royalty calculations. *Never.* Why should they start now?

So, get an audit clause on your book. Be prepared to use that clause, especially if you have royalty clauses in your contract that are different from the norm. Because publishers might "accidentally" default to the old way of doing things, and only shape up if you prod them.

An audit clause prods them.

Also make sure that elsewhere in your contract, there's no clause about binding arbitration or mediation or anything like that. Buried in those clauses are often damage limitations as well as something that will *rescind* or cancel out the audit clause. (The publisher giveth, the publisher taketh away.)

You want the right to audit, and the right to dispute any claims you might find *in a real court of law.*

Got that?

8. Reserved Rights: Make sure your contract has this language in it somewhere:

All rights not expressly granted to the Publisher are reserved to the Author.

That will cover a lot of ground for you, should you ever have to take your publisher to court.

And…that's a wrap, at least on some of these clauses.

I can't cover everything. As the termination fee shows, there's too much everything to even contemplate.

So you should look at all of this, not as legal advice—because I'm not qualified to give legal advice—but as an object lesson.

And I do mean "object." Object to everything you can object to in these contracts. Yes, *negotiate.* You have to.

As I tell my students, you are responsible for your own career. That means you own the successes—and the failures. And the crappy contracts you signed. Not your agent, not your best writing buddy.

You.

So learn everything you need to, in order to protect yourself. No one else will do it for you.

OTHER THINGS TO CONSIDER

The only person who can watch out for you in the real world of business is you. The only way you can protect yourself is to educate yourself. —From Chapter 13.

13

SNEAKY MONEY GRABS

On June 1, 2016, I posted a blog about a sneaky money grab that Nate Hoffelder of *The Digital Reader* alerted me to. Sometimes, when I write blogs, I use current events to make a larger point.

I used the blog to explore something I've seen more and more in modern contracts. It's the sneaky money grab, and most writers and agents miss this until it's much too late.

Rather than modify the blog to make the tense correct for October (which is when I'm updating this book), I'm going to let the blog stand as it first appeared on the website.

Here goes:

I've been emailing back and forth with Nate Hoffelder of The Digital Reader all day about Booktrope, the "team publishing" or "hybrid publishing" company that got $1.2 million seed money a year ago to help writers publish books. Booktrope announced very suddenly at the end of April that it would completely shut down on May 31[1]. According to the original announcement, Booktrope said it would remove all published books for sale by May 31, 2016, and it would return all rights to the writers.

Writers are caught in a bigger mess, though. Nate covered this well in Digital Reader Wednesday (June 1)[2]. Essentially, because of a contract clause, writers whose books were *published* believe they are still supposed to pay their "team"—the editors, cover designers, and anyone else whose fingers have touched the published book. Or rather, the now unpublished book. Unless the book was in special programs, like Amazon Encore, the book is no longer available.

Nate helped me find the sample contracts[3] that Booktrope once used to entice writers. (Thank you, Nate!!!!) Booktrope did try to be above-board—it had all this stuff on its website.

And like most of these companies that purport to help writers avoid doing the publishing work themselves without going to a traditional publisher, Booktrope was 100% buyer beware.

I was going to write a blog on why you never hire people for a percentage of your sales for the life of the project. I wrote a different version of that blog in August of 2011, titled "Common Sense and The Writer,"[4] before indie publishing really took off.

Back then, the problems were your agent or your best friend's neighbor who happened to be good with computers. Both the agent and the best friend's neighbor promised to do the work for you for a percentage. In those gold-rush days, you both were learning what it meant to indie publish a book—just how hard covers were, why copy editors were necessary, and how exactly do you upload a file to turn it into an ebook.

I knew then that those arrangements would dissolve into icky, awful, nightmares. I also knew that if the writing gold rush followed every other gold rush in human history, it would only be a matter of time before Big Money came in with bigger frauds.

Well, fast forward to spring of 2015. Booktrope appears, and hits the news when it gets $1.2 million of the $2.5 million seed money it believes it needs to run a successful business.

Booktrope did an SEC filing, which meant that it had actual accounting behind it, a good business plan, and something that would entice investors besides some pie-in-the-sky ideas. I remembered looking at that, and wondering vaguely where the promised revenue to the big investors was.

I found the promises. Today, as I looked through the contract.

My initial goal was to look through the contract to see if the writers are actually tied to their "teams." There are two groups getting screwed here: writers who signed on with Booktrope, and the copy editors, graphic designers, artists, and others who provided the "book publishing services." In fact, the teams probably got screwed worse[5], because they signed work-for-hire agreements[6], and, generally, never saw a dime for all the work they did.

I scanned the agreements—there are two that are linked—and frankly, it'll take a lot more investigating on my part to figure out what really is the case here. Because these agreements are badly written. They look like pieces were cobbled together from other contracts, some traditional publishing contracts, and some from work-for-hire agreements found on the web.

You'd think with $1.2 million in seed money, Booktrope could afford lawyers. Apparently, they didn't think they needed any—or worse, they hired really bad ones.

I know that the writers think they're in hell right now, and I know they're worried about whether or not they have to pay their "creative teams" for the rest of the book's life. I have no idea. I'm not a lawyer.

I suggest that anyone who has this worry hire an attorney to vet these really bad contracts and see if they hold anyone to anything.

I know, I know. A lot of these writers are broke and don't know where the next dime will come from. But usually the first consultation with a lawyer is free, and lawyers often set up payment plans for impoverished clients. A consult on a contract like this one shouldn't take more than an hour or two tops, and it's going to be well worth the money spent, particularly considering that most of the writers involved with Booktrope are looking at paying a percentage to other people *for years*.

A one-time fee to get yourself out of that or to negotiate a settlement if one is needed is much better than sucking it up and paying money you might not have to pay.

Okay.

I was going to expand on that, and look at some of the contract terms that writers should be wary of, from companies like Booktrope, companies that still exist.

And then I choked on a big gigantic paragraph in the Booktrope sample author agreement. This big gigantic paragraph is the one thing that allowed Booktrope to raise millions of dollars.

And, my friends, according to an article in Geekwire in April, "hundreds of writers,"[7] signed this agreement.

Hundreds.

Think about that as we go through this little nugget of pure nastiness below.

This nugget of pure nastiness was on page four of a six-page contract, under Clause 7 "Accounting and Reports; payments for subsidiary and derivative rights."[8]

Part A in Clause 7 deals with payments of royalties to the author. Okay. There's some stuff in that which is…bizarre. But fine.

It's Part B that made me shout out loud and change the direction of this blog. I'm going to give you Part B in chunks. By the end of this, you'll see all of Part B. But I can't stomach doing it as one big lump, because it's just so very ugly.

Wade through the legalese, people, because you'll see the problem soon enough.

Ready? Brace yourselves.

Here goes:

(b) ***Revenue from subsidiary rights:*** *Author agrees to pay Publisher the following share of any net proceeds in excess of $2,500 received by Author from third parties based on sale or license of subsidiary rights in the Work or from derivative works:*

ten percent (10%) for any sales or licenses arranged after the first publication date of a Booktrope edition by author or author's agents independently of Publisher during the term of this agreement, or

twenty percent (20%) if such sales originate with the purchaser or the purchaser's agent contacting the Publisher directly or if Publisher arranges for the sale on behalf of the author. Author authorizes Publisher to negotiate sales of derivative or secondary rights in the Work (such as film, TV, recording, or other dramatic media) anywhere in the world and to receive payments on Author's behalf on any sales of such rights arranged by Publisher, provided that Publisher will not enter into such an agreement unless the Author approves it.

(Okay. Breathe, Kris. Breathe. The company went out of business.)

Here's where the multimillions that the investors hoped for came in. What Booktrope did, through the guise of being a service that "helped" writers by publishing their works and putting them up online, was grab a percentage of *all* sales of subsidiary rights and other derivative works, *the moment the book got published by Booktrope.*

First, let's clarify one thing. The use of the word "agent" in that block of text does not mean literary agent. It means anyone acting on behalf of the author—the true meaning of agent.

Now, let's look at the implication of that section. For example, let's pretend that the author and/or the author's agent licenses a movie independently of Booktrope. And let's say that the movie deal was being talked about *before* Booktrope published the book, but the deal was put on paper *after* Booktrope published the book. Booktrope would get 10% of the net proceeds *after* the first $2,500.

That means proceeds *to the author.* Authors generally don't practice Hollywood accounting, so authors would have paid their agent, then subtracted $2,500, and paid Booktrope 10% of the rest.

Here's how it would have worked:

Say *Really Good Book* ends up with a $50,000 option with Hollywood Company, negotiated by Tough Broad Hollywood Lawyer who charged the writer $1,000 for her services.

The writer would end up with $49,000. Subtract $2,500 from that (this is the amount the writer can keep without paying a percentage, according to this contract), and the writer has $46,500. And, according to this contract, she now owes Booktrope $4,650 of that money.

Booktrope did *nothing.* It would get nearly $5,000 for *nothing.* And it would get ten times that or more if the movie actually got made. For doing *nothing.*

The second part of the clause is just as bad. Booktrope could negotiate on behalf of the author, undercutting any deal that was in the works or superseding it.

Booktrope—and their investors—were not book people. They said so in a bunch of interviews. (That was part of their hype[9].)

And because the Booktrope folk were not book people, they were subject to the same misconceptions that the general public has about books: things like all books sell lots of copies; it's easy to get a movie deal; subsidiary rights like gaming rights will bring in tons of money.

And so on and so forth.

Lucky for the authors that Booktrope vanished. Because guaranteed in that mass of books that Booktrope kept publishing, there would be a few books that would sell really really well. Those books would garner subsidiary rights attention, and those books would have earned hundreds of thousands of dollars. It's the law of averages.

And then what would happen? Well, in addition to all that stuff above, there's this ugly honking paragraph, that's part of Clause 7 (b). It follows right after the 20% paragraph.

> *Examples would include movies, TV shows or other productions based on the work or payments for use of characters, features, sales of foreign rights or excerpts from the work. Author shall pay Publisher within sixty (60) days of receipt of such payments; if publisher receives payments on author's behalf; publisher shall pay Author any amounts due within sixty (60) days of receipt of such payments. This paragraph applies to any revenues from subsidiary rights, where Author was contacted by the buyer or licensor of such rights during the term of this agreement. Author's obligation to Publisher under this paragraph shall continue as long as this agreement remains in force or for five (5) years from the date on which Author first receives revenues from sale or license covered by this paragraph, which ever is later. Payments to Booktrope based on subsidiary or derivative rights under this section 7(b) shall not be included in "net revenue" under the creative team agreement and shall not be shared by Publisher with author.*

By the way, all the typos and inconsistencies in these passages are in the actual sample document, which is only one way I suspect no lawyer drew this up. Lawyers are taught to be anal in law school. One misplaced comma and an entire document changes meaning.

(However, in the comments on this post and other posts, some reader/lawyers assured me that many lawyers are *not* that anal, and do make these kinds of mistakes often. Sigh.)

Which is why I'm not exactly 100% certain, but I'm like 99.99% certain that the last line of this honking paragraph means what it says:

that if the Publisher negotiates a big movie deal, then the writer gets some percentage of that deal—maybe 80%, we hope, kinda sorta, but the "creative team" gets nothing on those pass-through royalties for book sales.

But I could argue, if I had a law degree, which I do not, that the wording of that last sentence means Booktrope didn't have to pay the author *anything* if Booktrope brokered a subrights deal. All the monies could have gone to Booktrope, and there might have been some fun litigation to get those monies out of Booktrope.

All of which is theoretical. As of this week, Booktrope is no more.

Even if you were part of it, do not mourn it. It tried to shuffle big money away from writers into the pockets of big investors and its owners, and it failed.

Yes, writers are having to deal with some pretty serious problems for them. But had they actually read the agreements they signed…well, they wouldn't have signed on with Booktrope in the first place.

This is why you hire lawyers to vet contracts for you, people. *All* contracts. You can't eyeball this stuff and think you know what it means.

Why am I telling you about a company that no longer exists?

Because Booktrope is symptomatic of a dozen other companies I could name and won't. These rights and money grab clauses are *common*. I'm seeing them everywhere these days.

What's really disturbing to me is that they're not just in traditional publishing contracts. They're in contracts that are essentially service contracts.

Hire a company to print your book on a web press, and you might encounter one of these clauses.

Hire a tech company to digitize and upload your book to various sites, and you might encounter one of these clauses.

Hire a marketing company to publicize your book, and you might encounter one of these clauses.

Seriously, people, these clauses are *everywhere*.

You have to learn this stuff. And you can't blindly sign your rights and your future revenue away. *For any reason.*

Please, please, educate yourselves. And think before you sign *anything*.

Then hire a lawyer to explain the contract to you.

And then believe in yourself. Walk away if there is anything bad in that contract that happens to be non-negotiable.

What non-negotiable means, in real world terms, is that the party you're negotiating with is walking away if *you* don't agree. They're playing hardball.

You need to as well.

Indies, I know you think you're immune to this stuff. You're not. No one is.

The only person who can watch out for you in the real world of business is you. The only way you can protect yourself is to educate yourself.

Part of that education is learning contracts and copyrights. These blogs I'm doing are just a start. Keep reading, keep digging, and keep questioning.

And never, ever, sign a contract out of desperation. Because believe me, the people on the other side of that contract will see you coming. They'll take advantage of your desperation.

You think it doesn't happen? It did to hundreds of writers who signed on with Booktrope. Fortunately for those writers, Booktrope is gone. It (in theory) reverted the rights and canceled contracts and now its writers are free to republish their works, once they figure out their relationships with their "teams."

But I can guarantee that other companies are filling the void right now. And who knows what evil lurks in the hearts of their contracts?

14

PRINCE, ESTATES, AND THE FUTURE

The death of Prince hit me hard. I was in the middle of teaching the Romance Workshop, here on the Oregon Coast, and working my tail off. A satellite radio station that I always listen to had breaking news—something they never do (which is why I listen to them)—that I could barely hear. I heard "prince" and "died" and "young" so I'm wondering Prince Harry? Prince William? I pick up my iPad across the kitchen to look up the news, and that's when I see it.

Prince Rogers Nelson.

Prince.

I burst into tears—and shocked myself.

While I love some of Prince's songs, I would never have called myself a Prince fan. I didn't love his work like I loved Michael Jackson's or David Bowie's. Jackson's death hit me hard, Bowie's hard as well, but not as hard as Prince's.

I was thinking maybe it was the exhaustion from the workshop, but no. I realized it was because Prince had a huge influence on the way I go about handling business. Doing my work. Taking control of my contracts, my royalties, my *art*.

I immediately planned an entire blog post on Prince and business, although I wasn't sure I was going to write it yet, partly due to the aforementioned exhaustion, partly because I knew a lot more informa-tion would come out in the next few weeks about his business, his craft, his work—everything.

So I niggled with doing a post on another topic, sparked by The Passive Guy's response[1] to my post on copyright (which is now Chapter 3 "Understanding Copyright.")

PG said:

Under current contract practices, the author is the only person who has to think in the long term while everyone else in the publishing business is focused on the short term.

Spot-on, and something quite important to the themes of this book.

I was still on the fence about how I was going to approach the blog—Prince, control, business, or thinking long-term and contracts—until I saw on the news that Prince did not have a will[2].

I sighed. I was afraid of that.

Now, before I get into this, realize that six days after Michael Jackson died, the family also assumed he had no will. (Or maybe the family *hoped* he had no will.) The attorney who held it, John Branca, submitted the will six days later, after he returned from a vacation he had started before Jackson died.

The will had to go to probate court, along with any other will that any other attorney might have had. Branca did not believe the will he had was the final will because it was seven years old, and Branca hadn't been Jackson's attorney in the last few years before his death. But no other will appeared[3].

And so far, no will has yet appeared. Prince's sister had to go to probate to have Bremer Trust, Prince's long-time bank, act as special administrator for Prince's entire estate for six months[4].

To say that this is a mess is an understatement. Right now, the finan-cial press values Prince's estate at $300 million, but that is probably low. The financial press figures out the value of celebrity estates through public filings, news articles on deals made, and guestimates about the net worth of things like Prince's "right of publicity"—in other words, the value of his image and his name[5].

Dean and I handled a small estate several years ago, and that took six months of Dean's life (while I kept writing) full-time. Prince's sister's request to appoint Bremer Trust showed some good sense and savvy at a dark time. Thank heavens. Because no family can handle this, particularly a mess like the one Prince (might have) left behind.

Why would someone as smart as Prince about business make this kind of mistake? A million reasons, some of them psychological. None of us believe we're going to die, not really. And Prince had no children to leave things to. He was famously private, and putting together a will that would handle an estate of that size, with all of its future earnings potential, means that lawyers, financial advisors, and estate planners would have been combing through every aspect of his life, trying to figure out what would happen past his death.

Prince would have turned 58 in June, which sounds old to many of you, I know. But he was at the height of his creative powers, and if he had lived a normal lifespan, he was probably counting on another twenty years at least. Putting together a will was something he probably thought he could worry about later.

Trust me, he had a lot to worry about now.

Like so many of us, Prince handled his own business. He hired help, of course. Otherwise continuing to be creative would have been impossible. Sometimes he partnered with a record label, sometimes he did not. But he had his fingers in everything.

He had his hands full. Estate planning was probably something he figured he could do later. Of course, later never came.

I'm sure that a lot of projects died with him. A lot has been written about all the music he kept in a temperature-controlled vault at his Paisley Park estate. Speculation about what's in that vault is rife[6], but Prince was clear about it. He believed the music in that vault was raw, not ready to be released, for whatever reason. He made conflicting statements about what he wanted done with that music—burned upon his death or eventually released, once it was ready.

It's not ever going to be ready now, not the way that Prince envisioned, anyway. It'll be up to whoever ends up managing the estate.

I've been working with estates this past year, and let me tell you that estate managers vary as greatly as people do. Some estate managers don't give a rat's ass about what they're managing. Others see it only as a cash cow. And still others forget that they even have an estate until reminded by someone like me.

Only a few estate managers seem to be aware of the legacy they're entrusted with. I'll deal with some of this in Chapter 19, "Agents and Estates."

But let's return to Passive Guy's quote, shall we?

In the past, traditional publishers saw their role as that of manufacturing and distribution. (In fact, look at some of the discussion in the comments of PG's post to see how clear that used to be.) Now that major conglomerates have taken over publishing, traditional publishers are more interested in the intellectual property rights they're buying than they are in the actual physical books they're producing.

Not that the traditional publishers plan to do much with those rights besides sit on them at the moment. But the fact that they do means they are looking at books as income properties, *investments*, not as products.

Which leads to this analysis by PG in that blog post mentioned above:

Of course, an investor who bought into a mutual fund can sell his/her shares and have nothing further to do with that fund and its managers. A hedge fund that purchased a publisher can sell the publisher and be done with it. Since no US state permits life-time employment contracts, a publishing executive or editor can either quit immediately or wait a couple of years, then bail out on a failing publisher.

Only the authors who signed contracts that last for the full term of the copyright are tied to whatever corporate entity once called itself a publisher, but now is a hedge fund asset, for the rest of their lives plus 70 years.

Think about that, people. When you sign a traditional publishing contract, you're tying up the rights to that book for *decades*. There's no way out of that analysis—unless you can get a term-limited contract.

But it's not just traditional publishing contracts any more. Recently, I was digging through the rules for a major international contest. The contest, which has a huge prize pool, is open to *all* writers, not just beginners. I've submitted work in the past, and have had no problem with the contest at all. I was thinking of using the contest deadline to jump-start a project.

Before I even put the deadline on my calendar, though, I looked through the contest rules, and I'm glad I did.

Because, in the years since I last submitted to the contest, the rules have changed.

By *entering* the contest, you give the contest and its designated publisher the right to distribute the work. If you win one of the prizes, you give the contest exclusive rights to the work in four different languages *worldwide*, "including the rights to reproduce, distribute, publicly communicate and transform the work." If you look at Chapter 5 on copyright, you'll see that you're licensing (for a few thousand dollars) the *entire* copyright to the work for one year, with no guarantee of royalties or any other fee.

Once the work is published in ebook *only*, the rights become non-exclusive. But the contest still has licensed all the rights to the work. So they can make a movie or a game or whatever they want to from the work. What kind of compensation does the writer get?

A portion of the income derived from those rights as laid out in the agreements that the publisher has with its other writers.

Huh? What does that mean? I have no idea, because I've never seen that publisher's contracts, nor am I privy to what other writers have negotiated.

And then there's the kicker. The winners *must* sign all documentation that transfers these rights—

Simply from entering this contest.

Needless to say, I have crossed the contest off my list and will never participate again.

But let's pretend that I have participated. Let's pretend that I sent the manuscript to the contest, immediately giving the contest the right to distribute the work. Then let's assume that I die tomorrow.

How would my estate ever know that the contest has these rights? Because if I'm stupid enough to submit a story to this contest, I'm probably too stupid to print out a copy of the rules from that contest and attach that printout to the documentation that I have about entering the story in the contest.

Tiny decisions that I make every day, lost in my files because I'm spreadsheet challenged (and I started writing before this massive computing power that we all take for granted), have an impact on my work in the future. If someone got my estate tomorrow, they'd be able to figure out what rights I've licensed, where the contracts are, and what rights are available for resale, but it would take work.

I have a cover-your-ass will, something that would give my heirs some guidance, but not a whole heck of a lot. More than Prince (might have) had, though, so (in theory) the state of Oregon won't be involved.

But I know how much work it will be to manage my estate. A friend of mine, with maybe 20 or so novels to his name, wrote an eight-page single-spaced sheet of instructions to the person who will inherit under his will, explaining terms (like intellectual property) and where the heir can look for more information on things like copyright.

In the middle of this document, he writes that he has attached a spreadsheet which is a master file to *all* of his work, including the name of every work published, the ISBN of the print publications, date of publication, what channels the work has been published in, and whether or not the work has been registered with the copyright office. He added a separate file of all his passwords, and then a map on how to find the files (and their backups) for everything he's ever written.

Okay. I am not that organized. Not in a 2016 way. But I have paper files of everything, and most things filed away in folders in filing cabinets for my work, as well as computer backups that are up to date, and the computers themselves (several of them) which are within one week of each other as to being up to date.

Will that help someone who inherits my estate? Not really. They will feel like they've had a small city dumped on them. (We felt, when our friend Bill died, like we had a large house dumped on us.) But within that small city, there are maps, and those maps provide guidance.

Here's the point I want to make, though.

Like Prince, I have spent decades protecting my work and my copyrights. I have thought clearly about what I want to do with the work in the future, and I know what I want to do with each item in my backlist and catalogue.

Most of that information—the information on what *I want*—is in my head, which means it will all disappear when I die.

If I'm okay with that, I can leave things as they are now.

If I'm not okay with it, I need to plan as meticulously for my death as I have throughout my writing career.

It does no good to protect your work during your lifetime only to lose it upon your death.

All of those negotiations, all of that hard-fought work, all of those copyrights returned, reserved, and never licensed, mean nothing toward your legacy if you don't plan for that legacy.

I can guarantee that Prince did not plan to die in April of 2016. I'm sure he thought he had decades ahead of him, time to plan all of that. Maybe he has an as-yet-undiscovered will. Maybe.

But if he doesn't, his musical legacy now resides with the disparate members of his family. If they prove to be more mature than Michael Jackson's family—less interested in money and more interested in preserving Prince's work—then his legacy will survive just fine. Maybe not in the way he intended, but in a way that will give future generations access to his music.

Let's hope.

But we can do nothing about the Prince estate. We can only handle ours.

If we sign contracts that tie our work to a publishing company that might or might not exist for the next hundred years (lifetime plus seventy), if we submit stories to contests that will own them for decades to come, if we sign away the right to make a film from our work just by signing a non-disclosure form, then we are doing a disservice to ourselves right now.

But we're also doing a disservice to our heirs and to our fans. Because we are creating intellectual *property*. And property continues to earn revenue for decades after our deaths.

That's how the laws work. If you're only planning for this year or next year or the next ten years, then you are failing not only yourself, but your future.

If you want a legacy, if you want your work to be read long after you die, then you need to provide for that.

The first step in providing for that is at least a CYA will, like I have. Ten years ago, Neil Gaiman posted a sample will for intellectual property on his website. Use that as a template for making your will *with the help of an attorney.* You can find that will under the blog post "Important. Pass It On" which he posted on journal.NeilGaiman.com on October 30, 2006[7].

The next step is to make sure you *never* sign away or license your copyright to an entity that can control it for the lifetime of the copyright. That means traditional publishers.

That means you have to learn how to stand up for yourself. Learn copyright, learn to negotiate, learn contracts.

Learn it all, then leave the proper documentation and maps for your heirs. The easier it is for them, the greater chance you have of leaving a legacy.

Pay attention to the news on Prince over the next year. It'll be educational.

Maybe it'll even scare you into providing for the future of your work. I know it scared me into updating my will to reflect 2016, not 2011.

And that's a good thing.

Good luck.

And just an FYI: the Prince song stuck in my head today isn't one he sang, but one he sold to the Bangles thirty years ago. "Manic Monday." I don't have manic Mondays. I have manic Wednesdays. The soundtrack of our lives...

AGENTS

The agents are doing this to make money *for themselves and their agencies. If you think that agents are on the side of the writer, then I have a bridge to sell you. —From Chapter 15.*

15

THE AGENT CLAUSE

So, you decided that you need an agent.

Do me a favor: Read this chapter with an open mind.

Maybe you've decided to hang onto an agent because you believe that the agent will sell your foreign rights better than you can (as if this isn't an international market already), or because you've always had an agent, or because you've always *dreamed* of having an agent. Fine. As I tell my students, you are responsible for your career.

Which means protecting yourself in *all* circumstances, even with the people you employ to help you with that career. And yes, in case you've forgotten it, you *hired* that agent. They work *for you*. (In theory. Generally, in practice, their interests align with the publishing company.)

So what this means is that you have or you will sign contracts *with your publishers* that reference your agent. And you will sign an agreement with your agent, creating a document that governs your relationship with them.

Writers rely on their agents to negotiate contracts, which means that agents will negotiate things into those *book* contracts that benefit the *agent.*

Writers who rely on their *agents* to negotiate book contracts generally are afraid to hire a lawyer to vet those contracts, and that opens the writer up to a whole ton of problems.

Because writers who rely on their *agents* to negotiate book contracts generally sign agreements with the *agent* or the agency which the agent is attached to without negotiating that agent agreement *at all*.

Sigh.

I dealt with this in the original *Dealbreakers* book. Of course, things have changed *for the worse* in the intervening five years. So I'm redoing the old section below. Chapter 16 focuses on agent agreements in particular, including the newest wrinkle in agent agreements, for those of you who "retain" your ebook rights while your agent negotiations your "book" rights.

Why am I putting those words in quotes? Because, the agent agreements that readers kindly sent me make those arrangements something other than black and white. They're not even really shades of gray. They're more…puke green.

Anyway.

This chapter, however, deals with the clause that agents insert into your book contract with your publisher.

(This is the book contract that your agent negotiated *for* you. Yes, I'm telling you the agent inserted something into that contract that benefits the *agent*, but doesn't benefit you.)

The Agent Clause

Agents have been abusing this clause for years now. *Agents*, not publishers, even though this clause is in a publishing contract between the writer and her publisher.

Once upon a time, publishers paid the writer directly and the writer paid the agent. Which is, frankly, how it should be. After all, the agent is someone *you* hired, not the publisher.

However, some brainy publisher got the idea that if Agent A has 20 clients with the publishing house, it's easier to write one check to Agent A than it is to write 20 checks to the writers. Agents liked this because that meant they didn't have to browbeat their writers to get the commission.

If the contract is between the publisher and the writer, the publisher cannot just pay the agent. That's illegal. The author can't just say, "Oh, pay my agent," because that's not legally binding.

If the author wanted the publisher to pay the agent directly, it had to say so in the writer-publisher contract. So some lawyer came up with the way to do this. *That* was the origin of the agent clause, which was, in reality, a payment clause.

Back when this started, the clause looked like this:

The Author hereby authorizes the Author's agent, Agent A, to collect and receive all sums of money payable to the Author pursuant to any of the provisions of this Agreement.

And that's it. That's all. Really simple, right?

The net effect was this:

Checks sent to Agent A (at such-and-so address) counted as payment to Writer Z, and thus fulfilled the contract. *That's all.* If the writer signed the contract, then the clause became activated, and all payments went to Agent A.

The problem with this is, if you fire Agent A, you need an addendum to the contract, so that payment would go either directly to you or to Agent B, who is now your representative.

Well, that might screw Agent A out of money that you might owe him. So the agent started adding words like "irrevocable" to the agent clause which, of course, he negotiated with the book publisher.

Then things went crazy. Agents started adding all kinds of things to the agent clause which are in the agent's interest, but no one else's. The agent would add things like "the agent represents the author on this book, and all foreign sales of this book" and so on.

Then the agents all seemed to come up with "agency coupled with an interest." The clause, which you find in most agent-negotiated publishing contracts, now says things like:

The Author hereby appoints Agent A irrevocably as the Agent in all matters pertaining to or arising from this Agreement...Such Agent is hereby fully empowered to act on behalf of the Author in all matters in any way arising out of this Agreement...All sums of money due to the Author under this Agreement shall be paid to and in the name of said Agent...The Author does also irrevocably assign and transfer to Agent A, as an agency coupled with an interest, and Agent A shall retain a sum equal to fifteen percent (15%) of all gross monies due and payable to the account of the Author under this Agreement.

Authors blithely sign this stuff. When I had an agent, I refused to sign anything like this and cut things like "fully empowered" and "agency coupled with an interest" from my contracts. I authorized payment only. A few of my former agents balked; I fired them.

Why? First of all, I'm not assigning anyone anything "irrevocably"—certainly not someone I can fire for cause. *Especially* if my money goes through their account first. I will not "fully empower" anyone to act for me.

(Some agents go so far as demanding general legal power of attorney —which is something you should never give anyone. What that means is that they then have the right *to be you* in all legal matters. No. Do not give general legal power of attorney to anyone without good cause—like you're dying and need someone to handle your accounts [and even then, it might not be a good idea].)

Finally let's discuss "agency coupled with an interest." What that means is this: *You are giving the agent ownership in your novel.* Ownership. They now have a 15% ownership of your book.

In theory. Technically, a two-party contract cannot hold one party to third-party terms. In other words, if you and Publisher K have a contract, it cannot bind you to do things for Agent A, because Agent A did not sign the contract.

Still, what's to stop Agent A from trying this? A lot of agents are doing it, and backing it up with a separate agent-writer contract, which I'll touch on in Chapter 16. Absent the agent-writer contract, these clauses should not hold up in court. (And so far, have not.)

When I first wrote this series on my blog, two examples backed up my non-lawyerly reading of these clauses. First, the Ralph Vicinanza Agency tried to sue its writers under this clause. Ralph, who ran the business for decades, died suddenly[1], leaving his agency to heirs who had no idea how the publishing industry worked. However, Vicinanza's heirs wanted their money, and they threatened to sue authors who wouldn't work with them.

A lot of negotiation happened, and a lot of behind-the-scenes maneuvering, which took nearly a year before everyone settled out of court. Writers lost entire books in time trying to hang onto their own income and reserve the right to hire an agent who actually knew what he was doing, instead of some relative of Ralph's who had no idea what an agent was before Ralph died.

That's but one example. The other, more important example, is an actual court case[2]: *Peter Lampack Agency v. Grimes et.al.*

In 1996, Martha Grimes hired the Peter Lampack Agency (PLA) to represent her works. For those of you who don't know, she's a *New York Times* bestseller and a Grand Master in the mystery field.

In 2007, she fired PLA. At the time, she had a four-book contract with Penguin. That contract had an option on a book called *The Black Cat*. Grimes eventually sold *The Black Cat* to Penguin through another agent, and PLA sued, claiming—under the agency clause—that it had rights to any work deriving from that original contract.

Long story short, the case made it to New York court. The court decided that the agency clause only entitled PLA a 15% interest in the four-books named in the original contract, not in *The Black Cat*.

A victory, yes, but a minor one. Because Grimes fired PLA, and yet has to deal with them to this day on books still in print.

And maybe she still deals with them even if the books are out of print. I don't know what her publishing contracts say, but given the fact that Lampack sued over the sale of a new book after the publishing contract mentioning him terminated, I would assume he had other icky tricks in his contractual agreements with Grimes.

You think it's unusual that an agent would make a revenue grab on a book that he didn't sell?

Not at all. It's *common.*

For example, in 2014, Claire Cook detailed her breakup with her traditional publisher and her agent in a post titled "Why I Left My Mighty Agency and New York Publishers (For Now)" on Jane Friedman's website[3]. Cook wrote the book *Must Love Dogs*, which became a movie with John Cusack and Diane Lane. Cook wanted to self-publish the sequel, and her agent, with a really big famous Big Name Agency, contacted her, demanding 15% of Cook's *self-publishing* revenues.

Unlike many agent agreements nowadays, Cook didn't seem to have any agent agreement in place that would have *given* the agent that 15% automatically. (Or else they wouldn't have written to her.) Many agent agreements now have that clause—and we'll deal with that in Chapter 16. (These agreements are separate from the clauses we're dealing with in this chapter.)

No, the agent apparently had no right to that 15%. This revenue grab was Just Because. *Most* authors cave when their agents tell them to do something. That Cook didn't is a tribute to her.

She was angry and confused. Her attorney tried to comfort her with the "bright side." Her attorney said, "They never would have bothered if they hadn't smelled money."

Her attorney was right about that. The agents are doing this *to make money* for themselves and their agencies. If you think that agents are on the side of the writer, then I have a bridge to sell you.

So…

If you're thinking of hiring an agent *ever* or if you have one now, I suggest you go to the end notes, find the link, and read Cook's entire post.

Here's the real bright side. It's now two years almost exactly since Cook wrote that post, and she has published not one, not two, not three, but *four* sequels to *Must Love Dogs* and hit *The New York Times* list with her self-published book, *Life's A Beach*[4].

You can survive this stuff, with the right attitude.

In fact, you can not only survive, but do much much better.

The above examples, especially Vicinanza, occurred in agencies with either handshakes with the clients to cement the relationship or old-fashioned agent agreements between the client and the agent. Those old-fashioned agreements were very loosely drawn. However, because of a series of lawsuits against agents (many of which *did not* end up in the press), agent agreements have become Draconian.

Nowadays, agents do not rely solely on that clause in the publishing contract. Most major agencies now require their writers to sign an agreement *with the agency* stating that the writer will follow all the terms of an agency clause in publishing contracts.

That's Chapter 16.

But let's come up with a solution to the agency clause in a publishing contract right now.

Delete it.

Even if you have an agent, let your attorney negotiate all of your contracts. Pay the agent out of your own pocket. If the agent wants 15% of the book sale, fine. Pay the agent *after **you** *receive the advance. Your money should never go to someone else first.

Most agents will balk at this. That reaction alone should give you pause. Why isn't the agent trusting *you* to pay them—which is a standard business arrangement? Why does the agent expect you to *trust* them, and get all the monies first, which in most businesses is *not* standard?

Think about it: The agent is getting the money *and* the paperwork explaining what that money is. Paperwork that can easily be changed or fudged.

Yeah, yeah, I know. Your agent would never do that.

Okay. But maybe someone in that giant agency where your agent works will do that. You have no idea. I know of more cases of embezzlement involving agents than I do of any other active business I've studied. I personally know more than a dozen people who have had their agents embezzle from them.

I've caught *two different* **reputable** agents (or their agencies) embezzling from me.

If you really want to hire an agent who balks at cutting the agent clause from the contract, then do this: have your *attorney* revise the clause so that the publisher splits payments. What does that mean? It means the publisher will issue two checks when it comes time to issue payment. The first check (the *larger* check) will go *directly* to the writer. The second check (the *smaller* check—15% or less) will go *directly* to the agent.

That way neither of you can "forget" to pay the other.

But if you take anything out of this chapter, please take this: let your attorney negotiate all of your contracts. Do *not* let an agent touch your money or your contracts.

Of course, if you have an attorney negotiate your contracts, and you're dealing with the publisher yourself, why do you have an agent in the first place? Maybe it's time to get rid of this vestige of mid-20th century publishing and branch out on your own.

Just sayin'.

16

AGENT AGREEMENTS

I wrote some of these chapters on agents at the end of the contracts/dealbreakers blog series. I can't tell you how dirty I felt looking at some of these agreements. And in many ways, the agent agreements were the worst.

One of the things I discovered was that many indie writers tuned out the series because they believed it didn't apply to them. Yet, I read all the time about indie writers who sign with an agent to sell the print versions of an ebook and to sell foreign rights and auxiliary rights.

Bad move. Really, really, really bad move.

First, you're signing traditional publishing contracts if you sell your paper book rights. You're also signing traditional publishing contracts if you sell foreign rights. And I'm not even going into Hollywood options or movie deals or TV deals—

Except to tell you one thing. A writer I know forwarded a *shopping agreement* to me and Dean a few years ago, as *proof* that her agent was doing a good job.

A shopping agreement is an agreement that a writer will make with another person, often a producer, to *shop* the work (whatever it is) to film, TV, movies. Essentially, what that person wants is an exclusive to see if they can make a deal that will result in an option or an actual movie/TV deal. Generally, no rights change hands. There's not even a promise of rights changing hands. Just a short period of exclusivity where this person shops the project around, in exchange for the possibility that they would be attached to the project.

Whenever I negotiate a shopping agreement, I make sure I get paid for said agreement. If someone wants to be the only person representing a project to potential buyers, that someone needs to pay for that privilege. And lots of people do pay. I won't work with those who won't pay even a token amount. That's a *sign*, and one I don't like much at all.

Okay...so back to this professional writer, trying to prove the worth of her agent, and the shopping agreement the agent negotiated with a third party.

Think about that for a moment: This writer hired an agent to represent all rights in the book, including movie and TV rights, and the agent had the writer sign a *shopping* agreement with a third party. Right there, that's suspect. Because the agent should *already have* representatives from the agency (or a partner company) shopping the property.

This shopping agreement had no termination date, allowed the third party to shop the book to anyone who might make a film, a game, *anything* that moved, in technology developed or not yet developed, in territories around the world *and the universe* in perpetuity. For the duration of the agreement, the third party and the agent controlled *all* of those subsidiary rights in the project.

And the kicker? No money exchanged hands. The writer lost control of all subsidiary rights in her book project for no money and no reason, in perpetuity. All because her agent told her to sign the damn agreement. And the writer did.

And then she sent it to us as an example of the agent doing a *good job*.

I know, I know, you're thinking scam agent.

Nope. "Very good," "very reputable," boutique agency. Long-time agent.

(Please note, *every* example I have ever used in these agent chapters comes from reputable boutique and big-name agencies.)

I must tell you. That agent did a good job—for herself and her friend in Hollywood. Terrible job for her client. Awful. Horrid. Disgusting.

One of the (many) agents I fired, back when I believed the myth that you needed an agent, gave a free option to a very famous actor on one of my works. This actor had contacted me directly, and stupidly, I put the agent on the job, thinking she would negotiate a good option deal for me. Nope. She gave him a verbal option, free, for two years. No paper agreement *at all*.

Verbal agreements are binding in California, where he was calling from.

She's still working. She's got many clients, many of whom you've heard of. She works for an agency that represents some of the biggest writers in the business.

But, even after hearing these commonly occurring agent horror stories, you indie writers still want an agent to represent your subsidiary rights. Okay. Fine. Let's go with that.

And along the way, you traditional-only and hybrid writers, you should pay attention as well.

In Chapter 15, we discussed the case mystery writer Martha Grimes won against the Peter Lampack agency[1]. For the record, that case is binding in New York and California. But so far, not anywhere else.

Still, that case put the fear of God and the law in a bunch of agents, so they decided they needed more than a clause in the traditional publishing contract to protect their interests. At that point, most major agencies made certain they had a contract with their writers, governing the relationship. Before that, many agencies worked on a handshake.

At first glance, these agent agreements, as they're called, seem pretty benign. Most are no more than three pages long, and seem to be written in English. In fact, most of them are written in chatty language, usually in the form of a "letter," so the writer thinks they're signing something informal, when really, they're signing a *contract*.

The worst one I've seen comes from a huge, very famous agency, whose chairman (and lead agent) apparently figured he could save money on legal fees, and cobble an agreement together himself.

It looked like it was made of spit and glue, and had many unenforceable clauses. I'm sure it's been revised since by lawyers, because I know two writers who challenged the thing in court.

But the version I have gave the *agency* 15% of the *copyright* in every project the agency represented. It said so flat out in the agreement. (I'm sure the updated version says the same thing, as well. I'm sure it says all the same things, except in better legalese.)

The agency also decided to cover its tushy by adding some version of this:

The writer agrees to follow any agent clause in a publishing contract to the letter.

In other words, that agent clause in your traditional publishing contract, the clause we discussed in Chapter 15, the clause stuffed full of things that benefit the agent? Well, if you had no agreement like this with your agent, that clause is toothless.

If you have an agreement saying you will abide by the clause in that traditional publishing contract, then suddenly the clause has teeth. And so does every version of that clause you signed from the beginning of your relationship with the agent.

Many agency agreements have a point that says the writer must agree to abide by the agent clause in a publishing contract. Such points have become the norm. Now, let's look at more norms.

The agreement I have before me, from a long-time agency, founded by one of the big name agents of the mid-20th century, has an agency agreement that looks like the chatty letter-type agreements I saw in the 1980s.

Until you read it.

And then you find clauses like this (the emphasis in bold is mine):

*You hereby **irrevocably** assign to us and we shall be entitled to retain a sum equal to fifteen (15%) percent of all gross monies and other considerations paid to you or on your behalf with respect to any and all contracts negotiated and concluded under the terms of this agreement...*

Well, you can delete the word "irrevocably" and the clause isn't that bad, right? If they negotiated something, then they're entitled to their percentage, right?

Um, the clause doesn't stand by itself. Combine it with this baby:

*This agreement is effective immediately and continues in effect until terminated by either party…**We will continue to function as your agent** and to receive our commission on all contracts negotiated and concluded during the term of this agreement, or within six (6) months following termination, if negotiations were commenced during the term hereof, and any modifications, replacements, extensions, and supplements of such contracts **regardless of when made or by whom negotiated or when payments were received…***

So imagine this: You *fire* the agency because they screwed up your negotiation. Say, maybe, they tried to give a *free* option to a big name actor, or something stupid like that.

You do the negotiating yourself on the deal (with a lawyer back-stopping you), get a movie option for six figures, that's then made into a film for seven figures, plus the book the movie is founded on stays in print, and becomes a bestseller, and you **renegotiate** the contract and, according to this stupid agreement, you **still** have to pay the fuck-up agent her 15%. The agent you *fired* because she was *bad* at negotiating.

(So are you, if you sign anything like this.)

I'm hoping that those of you who signed agreements like this didn't then turn around and sign with another agency. Because that means you would owe 15% to Fired Agency and *another* 15% to Brand New Agency. *Now* you're out 30% of your earnings on this project for the life of the project, **all because you thought hiring an attorney to negotiate for you for a one-time fee would be too expensive.**

Holy crap, folks. Seriously.

And then there are you indie writers who are *so* smart. You've hired an agent to sell your print rights *only* (and the subsidiary rights). You've "retained" your ebook rights, haven't you?

I put "retained" in quotes for a reason, because let's go to one of those agency agreements that "allow" self-publishing.

Remember, these agreements—or contracts, which is what they really are—must be seen as one complete document. Each clause *builds* on the other clauses in the agreement.

So, this particular agreement with another Very Big Name Agency, starts like this:

This is to confirm our understanding under which you appoint [Very Big Name Agency] in the person of [Very Famous Agent] (hereafter "us" or "The Agency"), your sole and exclusive literary agent throughout the world to counsel and advise you professionally and to negotiate the terms and conditions for the publication, lease, license, sale, and any other disposition of material created by you (the "Work") in all media.

It goes on to describe the Work in the broadest terms possible, taking that Work out of the realm of book manuscript and into every other right you can think of.

Okay…I hear some of you thinking, yeah, that's what you hire an agent for. To "counsel and advise" as well as to "negotiate the terms"…

(Hmmm. Kris pauses here, goes to the Very Big Name Agency's website to see if they have a legal department with actual lawyers on staff. And after a quick scan, it doesn't appear that they do. Which is what I remembered from way back when. Heh. So they're signing an agreement with writers, saying they will act as lawyers, when they're not lawyers.

(Well, well, well. Draw what conclusions you may. I know the one I just drew.)

Anyway, this agreement you're thinking of signing with this agency has a clause that says it includes special permissions detailed in the "addendum" attached to this agreement.

The addendum is another chatty letter. And it says:

It is agreed and understood that some of your book-length work may be best suited to self-publishing, and if we together agree in good faith that a Work should be self-published, the agency shall not commission income earned directly from such self-published work, unless previously agreed to.

Okay, ick. The condescension drips. The agency says you can put your terrible unsalable books up as self-published work, after they decided they can't do anything with them. And the agent won't ask for money earned *directly* from that work, even if it sells well. But what about *indirectly*? And what does that all mean?

I'm already asking questions, and the stupid clause isn't done yet.

The Agency shall act as Agent for all subsidiary rights in the Work (including but not limited to) theatrical, television and film, translation, audio, and other subsidiary rights and income from such sales, shall be commissionable by us.

Okay, this tortured language has more wiggle room in it than I've seen in a while. In essence, they still represent the book in all subsidiary rights—and other rights, because of that lovely parenthetical phrase "including but not limited to." And if the writer sells this book anywhere on their own, all income from that work "shall be commissionable by us."

The agency will get their 15% if the writer sells it or they do, even though they gave the writer "permission" to self-publish.

Because, you see, the writer agreed in the very first paragraph of the original agreement to let this agency exclusively "counsel and advise professionally."

Folks, the point of this thing is to make the writer consult with the agent on every single project the writer finishes, so the agent has a record of that consultation and that work, and should that *self-published* work make the writer money, the agent can reach around sideways and put their grubby paws on at least 15% of that money.

However, this lovely clause gets *worse*.

It adds this:

This provision applies to other Works self-published before our association began as well as to self-published works created after our association began.

Do I really need to point out why that sentence is bad?

Writers sign this crap all the time. And what's worse, they think they've "retained" the right to self-publish their stuff. They think that they can negotiate their own deals on some things, and not on others, and that on the self-published books, they won't have to pay their agent a dime.

Even worse, every writer I know who has signed an agreement like this has done so *without consulting an attorney*. An attorney would eat these agreements for breakfast. A good attorney would advise a client to renegotiate this agreement at worst and not sign it *ever* at best.

These things are awful.

And yet, writers think they're doing well.

Indie writers will have just secured "representation" on every single thing they wrote, whether they thought they had or not. And note that this agreement goes *backwards* in time. So if you published indie since 2012, and signed with the agent in 2016, the agent is now grabbing for the right to stick his hand in your wallet on the 2012-2015 works as well.

People! Can I say this any clearer? *Stay away from agents.* Sell your work yourself. Hire an attorney to negotiate the deal.

You don't know how to sell your work to traditional markets yourself. That's probably good. Because right now, you don't want to. The contracts are *terrible*. The treatment is *terrible*. The benefits are *terrible*.

There's almost no upside to selling traditionally on novels right now.

When I first published Chapter 15 as a blog post, a number of readers asked me how to sell books traditionally without an agent. I'm not going to blog about that at all anymore, because I think it's a bad idea. There are older blogs on my website from years ago that mention it. Look there. Nothing has changed on how to *sell* to traditional publishers. However, what's changed are the contracts. They've gotten *worse*.

Better yet, if you want to follow that path, find someone else to advise you. I *won't* help you.

But, as I say to my students, you are responsible for your own career. If you want to get published traditionally, go ahead.

But consider these chapters beware chapters and act accordingly.

And seriously, whatever you do—traditional or indie—please don't hire an agent.

17

AGENTS AND AUDITS

Even after all of the things I wrote in the previous chapters, you *still* want an agent. Okay. That's your issue. But, I'll do my best to help you here.

Let's talk about auditing your agent.

I spent weeks Googling this topic, talking with other writers, looking up case law (ouch!), and trying to jog my memory, and have come up with nothing.

When I put "literary agent" and "audit" into search engines from Google to Duckduckgo.com, I get thousands—and I do mean thousands —of hits. These hits always involve literary agents auditing publishers (or threatening to) on behalf of writers.

When I put "literary agent" and "lawsuit" into search engines, I mostly get links to the Martha Grimes case of a few years ago, although I also found some very scary things, most of them already adjudicated cases on FindLaw.

I have yet to see anything about an author auditing her agent.

And why not? After all, literary agents handle writers' money. In fact, the agent gets the money first and funnels it to the writer, even though it's the writer's money. You'd think that *someone* would have audited an agent, just to make sure the books are being well-kept.

Well...there are so many problems here that I can barely begin to examine them.

First of all, no one has the right to go into another business and demand to see their books, even if that business owes that person money. There are only two ways you can audit the books of a business that owes you money. The first way is contractual. The second is for cause.

Let's deal with the contracts first. Agents proudly mention on their websites that they routinely force publishers to include audit clauses, and that the agents themselves will then "audit" the royalty statements to make sure they're accurate.

However, I have never ever ever ever seen an agency agreement that allows the writer the same rights that the agent negotiated on the writer's behalf with the publisher. The writer does *not* have the right to audit a literary agent, *even though most agents get* all *of the writer's money from the publishing house.* Those agents then cut a check—15% for the agent, and 85% for the writer.

Theoretically.

Think about this for a moment. The agent gets all the money and all the paperwork associated with that money. This almost always is part of the contractual agreement the writer has with the agent. As we saw in Chapters 17 and 18, the agent has the publisher slip in an "agency clause" into the publishing contract which essentially says that the agent will receive the money and that receipt will mark the end of the publisher's obligation under that agreement.

Now remember this: Literary agents aren't bonded or licensed or certified. They do not have an organization with teeth that can fine them or sue them or disbar them if they behave improperly. Nor are they publicly traded corporations, like some parent companies of publishing houses, so there's no way to audit on behalf of the share-holders or any other reason.

In other words, the only one watching the store—the only one with the *right* to watch the store—is the agent herself. My friend J. Steven York has made his cat into a literary agent to show how ridiculously easy it is to become a literary agent. The cat has her own website, and even though she calls herself "Bad Agent Sydney," satire-challenged writers have—quite seriously—written to her and asked for representation.

Most writers never vet their agent. They don't check with the local Better Business Bureau or the state attorney general to see if someone has filed complaints against the agent. They don't run a credit check to see if the agent can handle her own money, let alone theirs.

I know of so many agent stories about financial mismanagement, most of them because the agent was a sole proprietor and used client funds to pay personal rent or, in the case of one very famous agent, to buy cocaine.

Most agency agreements between the writer and the agent are so one-sided in the agent's favor that they terrify me. Of course, you can write your own agreement with an agent, and if you do, make sure it has an audit clause. You might even want to base that audit clause on the one for publishers that agents so happily tout on their blogs.

So, you have an agent, and no contractual way allowing an audit. How, then, can you audit your agent? You can only audit if a court determines that you have cause.

Cause is a dicey thing. You need to have enough evidence that financial mismanagement is going on that you can get a court order to hire a forensic accountant to go in and examine another business's books. In other words, you need proof.

If someone is deliberately stealing from you *and is good at it*, you won't have proof. You might have suspicions, but you'll never have proof.

I had suspicions for years that one of the agencies I used to work with had a problem with its foreign rights department. Years before I hired this agency, which I will call Boutique Agency, I had hired a sole proprietor agent, whom I will call Solo Agent.

Solo Agent embezzled from his clients routinely. When a client caught him and sued, that client had to sign a confidentiality agreement to get a settlement. This is one of the many reasons that I never found any reference to audits of Solo Agent in my Google searches, even though those audits happened and the court cases got settled. (Makes me wonder how many other agents insisted on—and got—confidentiality agreements in exchange for a settlement instead of a lawsuit.)

Solo Agent embezzled with foreign contracts. He never let his clients see the contracts, claiming they weren't in English (which is not true: The contracts are always translated into the language of the writer). I'm convinced he underpaid the foreign advances, and he claimed those books never ever earned out. I'm sure he pocketed the extra advance and the royalties, but I can't prove it in my case, since I didn't sue him.

How do I know this then? Well, people close to me sued Solo Agent and got the settlement. And others have—well, not exactly broken their confidentiality agreements, but have let me know that going with Solo Agent as an agent isn't a good idea because of something to do with foreign rights. Oh, and when I switched agents years later, all of my foreign editions with the same companies that had published previous editions paid me higher advances, and royalties after those advances earned out. One foreign publisher told me that I had always earned out for his company. *Always.* Even when Solo Agent was my agent.

Anyway, long story short, I'm very sensitive about my foreign payments because of Solo Agent. So when I became a client of Boutique Agency, I watched my payments like a hawk. Fast-forward several years. I fired Boutique Agency (for reasons unrelated to money). And suddenly, my foreign royalties from the Boutique Agency started to look weird.

They got paid late, or not at all. In my series novels, the foreign publishers would pay royalties on Books 2 and 4 but not on Books 1 and 3. Sometimes those royalties would show up *years* later.

I complained, but no longer had clout. The money still funneled through that agency because I hadn't gone through the nightmare of segregating funds. I had dozens of books which would have had to go through that process.

Instead, I simply made sure my rights reverted on those books as soon as possible, something that benefitted me years later when indie publishing started. Only I got my rights reverted to easily (and cheaply) get Boutique Agency off my back.

Foreign money still trickled in weirdly and inexplicably. But it wasn't foreign money that gave me the *obvious* cause. It was tie-in novels.

A lot of writers wrote tie-ins in those years, and often for the same editor at the same franchise in the same publishing company. The royalties statements would come bundled and packaged from that publishing company. You'd have to read those statements closely to realize that TV Franchise Novel: The Awakening was a different novel from Movie Franchise Novel: The Awakening.

The Boutique Agency started to send me royalty statements for other writers who had written similarly titled books. I complained and mentioned it to Boutique Agency. Nothing happened.

And then I got the super large payment that made my eyebrows go up.

I always read my royalty statements. Always.

And as I examined that royalty statement for that really big check, I saw another royalty statement attached. A royalty statement for a completely separate writer, whose novel had a similar title. A royalty statement for said writer, who deserved all but about $5 of the money that had been sent to me.

Fortunately, I had not deposited that check because, among other things, Boutique Agency had stopped getting my company name right, so the check needed to go into an account I kept open only because of Boutique Agency's incompetence.

I photocopied everything, then sent Boutique Agency a scathing letter, reminding them that they had fiduciary responsibility to me, and they had violated it.

Said fiduciary responsibility, by the way, comes from agency law. Please remember that I am not an attorney and I don't play one on TV. But a literary agent fits into the broad category of agents—like real estate agents—who exist under the law, and they are subject to a general thing called agency law.

The obligations that an agent—any agent, from a real estate agent to a literary agent—has to the principal (that's you) under agency law include:

1. **To act within the confines of the law**
2. **To act with reasonable care**
3. **To maintain loyalty to the principal**
4. **To disclose any material information to the principal**

Some of these terms, such as acting with "reasonable care" are legal terms in and of themselves and have specific meanings. There are a lot of other things that are involved in this side of the relationship, some of which you can find in the definition of fiduciary duties in the Free Law Library[1] online.

One of the many responsibilities is privacy between the agent and the client. Just by sending me the other client's royalty statements, the Boutique Agency was in breach of general agency law. But sending me another client's money, well, that was an obvious breach and one that would have easily given me enough cause to get a judge to grant me the right to audit the Boutique Agency's books.

It's expensive to hire forensic accountants, even with the court's permission. I was ready, though. Before I went to court, however, I decided to give Boutique Agency one last chance. I wrote a letter, citing all of the breaches, demanding a full accounting of my books, and reminding them of their fiduciary responsibilities to me.

The Boutique Agency not only terminated the remaining parts of our relationship *the next day*, they willingly wrote to all of my publishers *that week*, informing them to send me 85% of what was owed, and to cut a separate check for 15% for the agency. (This is called splitting checks).

Except the Boutique Agency's foreign agent balked at doing her part. She refused to contact the foreign publishers. She thought my request "insulting." I had to write a series of letters to get action there. Finally, I told Boutique Agency to stop worrying about writing those letters to my foreign publishers; I would do it myself. And guess what? Two days later, I got copies of letters sent to all of my foreign publishers.

Occasionally, I muse as to why Boutique Agency's foreign rights person didn't want to write those letters and wonder if I should have simply gone to court. I probably wouldn't have made much money on this (if any), but I could have blogged about the whole experience, and it might have caused a major upheaval.

You see, some really well known *New York Times* bestsellers—with series and movie franchises and all kinds of foreign rights—funnel all their money through Boutique Agency. Hundreds of millions of dollars flow through that place. At best, Boutique Agency's accounting department sucks. At worst, someone(s) at Boutique Agency has[ve] very sticky fingers.

By the way, because I'm a completest, let me add this: In a fiduciary relationship, you (the principal) have obligations as well. They are, generally speaking:

1. **pay the agent**
2. **reimburse the agent for reasonable expenses**

Nowhere does it say that you must let the agent get the money and disburse it to you. In fact, it's really, really, really rare outside of publishing for someone who is called an agent to get the money in his own account, and then disburse it to the client.

For example, when you sell your house, your real estate agent does not get the check for the house, put it in his account, take his commission, and give the rest to you. If you have an insurance claim that pays out, the money does not go to your individual agent first for her to remove her commission and then give the remainder to you. You get your check separately, usually in the mail, from your insurance company. If the check has to be hand-delivered, it is not a check from your insurance agent minus his fees, but a check from the insurance company itself, drawn from the corporate account that it has for this very kind of payout.

Writers are so used to the literary agent system that we don't question it at all. And yet, when Dean and I showed an attorney friend who specializes in corporate law (not intellectual property) a book contract, he freaked out. Not just at the jargon—he admitted he didn't understand that—but at the agent clause. He thought it was a joke. He couldn't believe how agents got paid. Or rather that writers, who had not checked an agent's *financial* credentials, let that agent handle their funds.

In hindsight, I don't understand it either. Yet I did it several times with different agents and different agencies. I could claim youthful ignorance—I got my first agent at the age of 28—but I had already been a business reporter for years, and I knew about all kinds of scams. I just didn't even consider how rife the agent/author relationship was for mismanagement until…well, until I encountered Solo Agent. Even then, Solo Agent didn't stop me from hiring the Boutique Agency without vetting them. I vetted later agents, but didn't ask for split payments, even though I should have.

And so should you.

If you have an agent, you should make sure that your payments get split. If the publishing company refuses to do that, then have the money come to you directly and *you* live up to your side of the fiduciary relationship: Pay your agent the moment the big check arrives.

If your agent balks at that—if he doesn't trust you to pay him his 15%—then why should you trust him to pay you 85%?

If you don't have an agent and believe you need one, then make sure you have an agent agreement that *you* draw up, not the agent. And in that agreement (which you need to draw up with the help of an IP attorney), add an audit clause so that you can audit the agent.

A lot of you indie writers believe you need an agent to sell foreign rights (you don't) or movie rights (you don't) or other subsidiary rights (you don't), so you hire someone to handle your books when you and an intellectual property attorney could do so much better on your own.

Think long and hard before you hire an agent to handle your work for you. The business model no longer works in today's new publishing environment so most agents are moving to dicey practices that, in fact, violate the fiduciary duties listed above.

Investigate anyone you hire, but before you do, question the assumption that you need to use a 20th century model (the agent) for a 21st century business.

If you think you need an agent, then research the hell out of the person you hire. Ask to check the firm's credit, get recommendations, and write your own agent agreement with an audit clause. Split payments or have payments come directly to you.

Just because a firm is "reputable" doesn't mean it can handle its books. That Boutique Agency has one of the best reputations in the business—and no, I won't tell you who it is. I'm telling you to be cautious no matter who you hire to handle your business affairs.

This is a writer beware situation, and a very serious one.

You don't want to be in the position where you believe you know that someone is mismanaging your funds, but you can't prove it. You don't want to get to the stage where you actually have cause, because that means something horrible has broken down somewhere.

You want the money you're owed—all of it—to come to you. You want your business relationships to remain aboveboard and honest.

Do your homework, take care of yourself, and make sure you're never in a position where you need to audit anyone because you suspect something is wrong.

Remember, you're responsible for your own career. If you sign a bad contract based on bad advice, you took that advice. If an agent whom you haven't vetted embezzles from you, then realize that you made it easier to scam you.

If you want a long career in the writing business, do three things:

Be smart. Respect yourself, and your business.

Be tough. Demand good terms from the people you work with. Then *enforce* those terms.

Be strong. Walk away from bad deals. Good ones will come your way.

If you do those three things, you'll have a career that lasts longer than a few years. You'll be a professional, published writer for the rest of your working life.

18

AGENTS AND ESTATES

When I initially wrote Chapter 14 on Prince's lack of a will as a blog post, some people (who apparently never read my blog before) asked me if agents should handle a writer's estate.

No, agents should not.

Before I even get to the issues below, let me tell you this: Many literary agencies are small businesses, just like your writing business is. Many agents have prepared no better for their deaths than Prince did for his. Think about that, before you decide to hire an agent for anything, let alone for managing an estate.

I wrote some of this long before Prince died, and I'd been waiting for the right moment to share it. Prince's death provided me with the right moment. So, here goes:

It took forever to get my husband to convince our good friend Bill Trojan to have a will. Bill had one of the most amazing collections of collectables I have ever seen. He had also been single and frugal for the twenty-five years I'd known him. He owned his house outright.

Dean constantly nagged Bill about writing a will. And Bill would always respond, "What do I care about what'll happen to my stuff after I die? *I'll be dead.*"

As I've aged, I understand where Bill was coming from. I have a lot of stuff, more than I can fathom, particularly considering I moved to Oregon nearly 30 years ago with Dean, my cat Buglet, and most of my possessions stuffed into a LeCar. I did ship 20 boxes of books, but that was it. Not even enough for a small U-Haul trailer, let alone a van.

Now, I have several buildings-worth of things although, to be fair, much of it came courtesy of Dean (a major collector) and Bill, who bequeathed part of his collection to Dean and me (maybe as revenge for all the nagging).

Yes, Bill ended up with a will, thank heavens. He bequeathed a goodly portion of his cash to a major charity in his hometown, all of his art and his pulps (and there was a lot of both) to another friend, and the rest of it to me and Dean. Bill also made some promises that he hadn't put into a revised will, and Dean (as executor) made sure those promises were upheld as well. The comic book collection went to a comic book collector, and some more cash, plus the television and other electronics (and valuables), to one of Bill's neighbors.

Dean was one of the best executors I've ever seen. He was ethical, aboveboard, and he went the extra mile—so much so that it hurt his health.

Dean is rare, and I'm not saying that because I'm his wife.

I'm saying that because I've been dealing with estates for the past few years.

Full disclaimer: I wrote this chapter concurrently with the events I mention here, but I did not publish the blog post until some point later. When you read this, you'll have no idea how long ago I had these experiences or which estates I'm referring to. Because my estate work will continue after I finish this blog, and I'm sure I'll have other stories to tell, probably hidden in that same "future blogs" file for some future date.

(Bloggy time travel. Who knew?)

Anyway, these estates I'm dealing with belong to writers. As many of you know, I've been working a series of reprint anthologies aimed at reviving the history of the science fiction field. Because I want to reprint stories published as early as the 1930s and 1940s, I am almost by definition, dealing with estates.

I'm also doing anthologies that mix new and reprint fiction, which also leads me to estates.

Before I started these projects, I had only a tangential interaction with writers' estates. When Ralph Vicinanza who was a major (unmarried) agent died suddenly, his entire estate went to his sister, a clueless woman who had no idea how to run a business, let alone a literary agency.

Behind the scenes, I did a lot of hand-holding with heirs to estates handled by that agency. These heirs were brilliant people, many of whom had grown up around Grandpa the Writer or Mommy the Writer, but never learned the business of writing. The heirs often made their own money at super high-powered careers of their own, but they were lost when it came to publishing.

Since Mommy the Writer was famous and quite prolific, the estates were as hard to wrap your arms around as Bill's estate had been. Tens of thousands if not hundreds of thousands of tiny pieces needed to be categorized, valued, and traced.

It was daunting work. Impossible, really, for someone who already had a major career, children, and a life of their own.

So, if you had asked me five years ago what you the writer should do when it came to who should handle your estate, I would have told you this:

1. Choose someone to manage the literary part of your estate who has an interest in publishing, particularly the publishing business.
2. Make sure that person gets a percentage of what she does to manage the literary estate.
3. If you don't have any heirs, pick a charity to receive the money from your estate, and then designate a representative to handle the management of the estate. Make sure the charity receives enough money so that if the estate is mismanaged (and they often are), the charity will complain and a new representative will be appointed.
4. ~~If you don't have any heirs or you don't have any smart heirs, and the charity you've chosen is outside of the publishing~~

~~industry, then get a literary agency that has a long list of literary estates to handle your estate after your death.~~

You'll note that I have put a line through point four. I do so because some of you will ignore the rest of this post and think that I am advising you to hire an agent to handle your estate.

Yes, I used to give that advice.

And—God as my witness—I was so wrong that I'm embarrassed by it.

Another disclaimer: As I worked on these projects, I encountered two agents who represented their estate clients exceedingly well.

One, an agent of longstanding, handled several clients at one time, was a good negotiator for them, was friendly, got me information, and didn't make me feel like I was bothering that agent by even making contact. (You think I'm kidding; I'm not.) For the sake of simplicity, I'm going to call this agent The Good Agent.

I'd been warned about the other agent. I'd been told that agent was a hard negotiator, that agent always raised the price, and that agent was difficult to work with.

Turned out, that agent was easy to work with, as long as I expected a tough negotiator. I went in with a lower offer than I would have otherwise, the agent negotiated to the top of my pay scale, and we were done.

From then on, everything went like clockwork. That agent was probably the most professional person I worked with in all my dealings. I was relieved by that.

On the estate side, I have now worked with a lot of agents, many of them Big Name Agents. The Big Name Agents who handled multimillion dollar clients as well as estates all assigned the estate matters to assistants.

The assistants were so incredibly clueless that I actually felt sorry for them. The assistants didn't know who I was (not a big deal to me), didn't know the names of the various companies I was working with (some of which they should have known), did not understand the contract terms and asked *me* about them—which you should never ever ever do in a negotiation.

If you're negotiating, you shouldn't let the other party know the depth of your ignorance. Seriously. Think that through for a minute. These assistants have bosses. They're the Big Name Agent, hired (in theory) for the prestige and for the Agent's experience in all matters. And the Big Name Agent did not use that prestige or that experience in these negotiations. The Big Name Agent was too busy to be bothered – for a client.

This is quite disturbing to me.

The worst thing I encountered from these agencies, though, was that no one gave a shit about the estate or the writer. Seriously.

Again, **a disclaimer:** The Good Agent discussed the stories with me, knew exactly where the stories had been previously published, and *had read them.* Not only that, the agent *liked* them.

Without consulting a computer file or taking a break to look anything up, the Good Agent knew where those stories were previously published and also knew whether or not an electronic file of those stories existed. That detail will become important in a minute.

But let me also add that in working with more than two dozen agents, the Good Agent is *an exception,* a big major exception.

So here are the problems I ran into.

—Most of these agents had no copy of the story. They told me to get the story from wherever. If I asked for an electronic file, they cavalierly told me there wasn't one, and I should scan it myself. They often didn't even recommend a place to scan it from.

I found several of these stories online, reprinted in online publications, and I copied from those free online publications rather than scan. I hired a copy editor to go over the document I made and compare it to a collection of Famous Dead Author's stories. I always took a collection that had come out when Famous Dead Author was still alive, figuring Famous Dead Author had proofed that collection.

In one case, my copy editor found so many discrepancies that she said it took her a very long time to make sure the files matched.

Frankly, it's not my job to make sure I have the right version of the story in my anthology. It's the author's job to make sure the story is the right version. If the author is dead, then the estate should make sure the anthologist has the right story.

Only the Good Agent had estate-approved versions of the stories I requested. In fact, the Good Agent mentioned in email that one of the stories had been approved by the estate down to the very last comma. Yay! That was what I wanted.

—Several agents didn't handle the rights to the short stories of their Famous Dead Authors. The agents had farmed out the rights to places like permissions companies. Permissions companies used to specialize in coordinating permissions through publishing houses, not working for agents. Yet somehow, through some convoluted process, those companies ended up handling the rights for Famous Dead Author's short stories (but not the novels).

I found this several times. Most of these outside non-agent companies treated me—a person who wanted to license a story—like mud on their shoes.

In one notable case, the man handling the permissions was a complete and utter asshole. He did not respond to my emails. He did not return my phone calls.

(Please note that some agents were that rude as well. It took a lot of persistence to reach them.)

Finally, late one Friday afternoon, I called the permissions company after having made several other phone calls. I didn't expect anyone in the East Coast office. I just figured I'd leave another message.

At this point, I wasn't even sure that the permissions department had received my emails or logged my calls.

I reached this man. He was exceptionally rude from the start, which I figured had something to do with it being late in the day on Friday. I told him I wanted the story for my anthology.

He told me that we would never come to terms. Then he told me he hadn't gotten my email, even though from the sentence he had uttered earlier, it was clear he had. He knew what my terms were before I had verbally reiterated them.

He told me that my anthology was not worth his time. Clueless me, I'm still thinking this guy is having a bad day. I said, "Surely we can negotiate something here. I think this story is important to this anthology."

He then quoted me a price which was exactly half my advance for the entire anthology. Thinking we were negotiating in good faith, I said that the price for the story was high and that I was prepared to offer one-eighth the price he had listed. I figured he'd come back with one-quarter, and we'd be happy.

He then told me *again* that we couldn't come to terms and said, "because, as I said, the price for this story is…" and he gave me a *brand new number*, *double* the price he had initially listed.

Realize that I take concurrent notes when I'm on the phone with anyone I'm doing business with. I had already written down the first amount.

I said, "That's double what you had just quoted me."

He said, "Keep pushing me, and I'll double it again."

I was shocked and breathless. I had never encountered this before. I said, "Your client belongs in this anthology. Surely we can come to terms if we negotiate in good faith."

"I don't think we can negotiate in good faith here," he said, "and it wouldn't be any good for my author to be in your *genre* anthology."

"Your author is a genre author," I said. "You might want to think about that."

And then I hung up, because I was about to launch into a tirade.

I bent over, furious, and thought about pounding something into submission. Instead—fortunately—I decided to write to an editor acquaintance who had included this author in an anthology recently, and ask for the correct way to approach this super-dooper asshole in permissions.

The editor acquaintance wrote back a 3,000-word screed against this asshole, said that the editor had put up with the asshole's nonsense to get the author in the anthology.

Much as I love the author, I wasn't willing to put up with the bullying, so that author—to date—has not been in any of my anthologies, much as I love the author's work.

I have contacted the agent on the estate and told this story. The agent has promised me this will get resolved. To date, I have no idea if the agent has solved the problem. Frankly, I know the agent. I doubt the problem will ever be solved.

—Agents (and these other representatives) are rude and dismissive.

The super-dooper asshole wasn't the only creature of his type that I have encountered in this process. He was just the worst.

I've had a lot of representatives—agents, their assistants, and these permissions people—be exceptionally rude to me when I bothered them with a request.

Realize here that I'm offering *money*. I want to give Famous Dead Author visibility. The visibility will keep Famous Dead Author in the discussion, will introduce Famous Dead Author to new readers, and will end up selling more copies of Famous Dead Author's already in-print works.

I'm actually doing work the estate would—or should—support. But the estate itself doesn't get contacted, and the intermediaries are dismissive at best.

—The representatives hired by some of the estates did not know who controlled the rights to the story I wanted.

Again, I'm not kidding.

Here's a situation I encountered over and over again. After much searching, I finally found out who handled the estate. Searching often meant asking my editor friends, or the writers organization for that genre, or writing to someone on Famous Dead Author's website. Often, all of those people would point me to the wrong representative.

One representative got pissed at me for contacting someone else in the office, even though three separate people (and a website) identified that other agent as the agent of record.

So…I finally find the agent of record. In theory. I ask for permission to license the story for the anthology or the project I'm working on. (Sometimes I was dealing with nonfiction.) The agent of record would seek approval from the estate. And then….

I swear to God I'd find myself in the twilight zone. Agent of record would tell me that the estate wants to do this deal, but I needed to contact some permissions company instead of the agent. I would contact the permissions company which would negotiate with me, then tell me I had to talk to some other representative from some other company. That representative would send me to yet *another* representative who…wait for it…

Would send me back to the agent of record.

In one case, all of those representatives represented a separate piece of the single short story. One represented English language print rights, another French print rights, another electronic rights.

Realize that I encountered this several times.

One instance was for an author whose estate spent years in litigation as various heirs argued over it. The heirs ended up splitting the estate into little bits. I don't know if the reason I had trouble with that story was because of the heirs or because of the settlement or because of some other reason.

But the other estates this happened on? They should've been straightforward, and they weren't. A lot of different companies had their fingers in this little short story pie.

I have no friggin' idea what kind of shit-ass contracts *someone* signed after Famous Dead Author left the planet, but I can guarantee you that no one was paying attention to contract terms when they did so to set up these arrangements.

I can also tell you that no representative seemed to care about how stupidly baroque all of this was. And I'll wager you cash money that no one has ever told the estate what the hell is really going on.

—Agent doesn't care and/or doesn't know that Famous Dead Author's works are all out of print and unavailable. Yeah, I can't believe it either, but when I mentioned it to a few of the agents about their client estates, the agents were shocked to realize that nothing had been in print for years.

I could go on. I haven't even touched the surface of some of the stupidity I've been dealing with. It's appalling.

Would this be better if the estate had hired a literary lawyer to handle all of its business dealings? I don't know. Lawyers have varying degrees of competency.

But at least lawyers are licensed and subject to regulations that govern how they conduct their business. If they fail at their business, there's actual consequences for those actions.

I'm guessing—and I have to say guessing because I don't know—that a lawyer handling the estate's business would be a hell of a lot better than any agent or agency. Or permissions company or publishing company.

One thing I can say with complete certainty is that the estate should hire a dedicated person (not an heir) to keep track of all the rights and permissions, handle the licensing, and make sure that the situations I listed above don't happen.

That person should be paid by the estate. That person should probably get a salary plus bonuses if that person keeps works in print and makes money for the estate.

How does such a thing work?

I don't know.

Should you as a writer care about this for your estate? If you want your work to live beyond you, you should.

Because...refer back to the case of super-dooper asshole. The Famous Dead Author in question there is one of the most important authors of the 20th century in a particular genre. One of the greats.

And I've opted to not reprint any of Famous Dead Author's stories until super-dooper asshole no longer handles the rights—as if super-dooper asshole would even deal with me, which he has proven that he will not.

I am not the only editor to make that decision. In fact, several other editors in that genre have made the same decision. I only know of two editors who are willing to take on super-dooper asshole to include that particular Famous Dead Author in their anthologies. God knows how much money it's costing the estate, and worse, God knows how many other authors are being shorted so that super-dooper asshole can feel like he won some imaginary negotiation game.

I hate to tell you this: You will die one day. If you're lucky, you will leave a strong fiction legacy.

If you want that legacy to survive, you have to plan the future of your estate. You have to put it into hands as ethical and competent as Dean's were when he handled our friend Bill's estate.

If your attitude is the same as Bill's was initially—*what do I care? I'll be dead*—then make no plans. Or figure your agent will handle it. Or someone will deal with it.

Your legacy will die, like that Famous Dead Author's legacy is dying.

All that work you've done to write art so you can be read 100 years from now will die with you.

I hope to hell this chapter scared you.

Because dealing with incompetent assistants and venal assholes has scared the hell out of me.

And I thought I couldn't be surprised by anything in publishing any more.

I was wrong.

19

MY AGENT WILL NEGOTIATE

Imagine this scenario:

You're a divorce attorney with more than thirty years of experience. You charge hundreds of dollars per hour for your expertise. You have what seems to be a relatively easy divorce on your hands. After all, the client has told you that he and his soon-to-be ex-wife agree on the terms. They simply need you and her attorney to hammer out the details.

It'll take a few hours, but not much more than that.

So, not a lot of money for your law firm, but enough to cover your time.

You head to the conference room where you agreed to meet the wife's attorney. And, instead of the named partner whom the wife claims is her attorney, you find a fresh-faced twenty-one year-old with a stack of papers and a laptop in front of her.

Newly graduated from college with an English degree, this twenty-one year old got a job as a coffee-fetching receptionist to the Big Name Lawyer. The twenty-one year-old has never even sniffed at law school. She graduated from college with her BA in May. This is August.

You ask where Big Name Lawyer is, only to be told that he's on vacation and unreachable for the next two weeks. He has asked the twenty-one-year-old to handle this very simple case for him.

The scenario has to stop here because, in the real world of attorneys, what Big Name Lawyer has done would get him called before the bar and, depending on his clout, either disbarred or reprimanded severely. There would be serious and public consequences for sending a young person with *absolutely no legal experience* and no guidance to represent a client in a legal matter.

In the world of literary agents, however, such things are *common*.

In fact, I dealt with a similar scenario on one of the anthology projects worked on. (I ran into lesser versions of this a total of eleven times in the year after I experienced the events described below.)

Anyway, what happened was this: Super Big Name agent, the name on the door of the agency, went on a month-long vacation after I contacted him requesting permission to reprint a short story. He left the negotiations in the hands of his brand-new assistant, a young woman who had just graduated from college with—you guessed it—an English degree.

To her credit, the young woman was conscientious and did her very best. I would hire her in a heartbeat—as a *receptionist*, or maybe, in data entry, or as a file clerk, with the hope that she might learn how to be a professional something or other someday. She was sincere and hard-working.

She tried hard to negotiate a contract she did not understand *at all*. She asked *me*, the person on the other side of the desk from her, the person *on the opposite side*, why the contract I had sent (a standard short story contract with a freelance editor) was only one page long, instead of the 25 pages like all the other contracts she saw from the same publishing house.

I had to explain to her that she was looking at *book* contracts from a publisher. I was a freelancer and as such, *I* had the 25-page long contract with the publisher. I was simply contracting for the reprint rights to one short story. Me. Just me. And if the project went south from the book publisher, *I* could take the contents and move to another publisher.

I cringed as I sent that email, wondering if I would have to explain the word "freelance." But, good English major that she was, our recent college graduate knew how to look up words in the dictionary, and she understood "freelance." She didn't understand any of the rest of it, although she gamely tried to negotiate the contract—asking for all the wrong things, for the wrong reasons, and, if she had prevailed, hurting Big Name agent's client substantially.

Fortunately for her, I had run out of patience about two weeks into Big Name agent's vacation and copied him on an email that I sent to her, an email that included the entire unbelievably stupid thread.

Note that Big Name Agent isn't a lawyer either, and has no right to negotiate a contract for anyone. He too is practicing law without a license. Me, I was representing *myself*, so I could get away with handling the negotiations on my own. (Just like I could in court, if I were stupid enough to try. And also note that a lawyer looked over the short story contract before I ever started using it.)

Big Name Agent immediately took over the negotiations—or, rather, sent a curt letter to both me and the assistant saying everything was just fine. If he had actually been doing his job, he could have fine-tuned the contract. At least five other parties in the same anthology had done so— all of them *authors representing themselves*.

Because, you see, I issued a contract that was good for both parties, but the contract did favor me. Because I *issued* it. I was perfectly willing to negotiate a few points—and did, but only if asked.

In other words, Big Name Agent did a terrible job all by his little lonesome, even if you take the recent college graduate out of the picture.

Realize that the client had no idea this was going on. (My next step, if the Big Name Agent hadn't responded, would have been to send a third email copying the writer as well as the Big Name Agent.) The client *still* doesn't know. Maybe if I ever see the client in person, and I feel comfortable discussing it, I'll mention something.

Or not.

Because it's not my job to say anything. It's none of my business.

But here's the reality of the situation:

Famous Writer hires Big Name Agent for his so-called expertise, to handle all aspects of Famous Writer's career. Famous Writer believes

Big Name Agent will do a fantastic job at all times, keeping Famous Writer's interests in mind.

Instead, Big Name Agent sends a *recent college graduate with no knowledge of the business at all* to represent Famous Writer in a *legal* matter.

It's against the law in all fifty states to practice law without a license. So not only is Big Name Agent breaking the law, not only is Famous Writer getting cheated by Big Name Agent (with a bait-and-switch), but Big Name Agent is asking a young naïve recent college graduate to break the law in order to do her job. And I'll wager she has no idea she did anything illegal when she negotiated with me on behalf of the agency's client.

I felt for the recent college graduate. I really did.

I thought Famous Writer was unbelievably dumb to have an agent handle a short story. (Big Name Agent's cut would have been barely in three figures.)

I have known Big Name Agent for over two decades now, since he began his career with another agency. I thought he was a stupid asshole back then. I think he's a more polished version of the same stupid asshole now.

Yeah, yeah, those of you with agents are thinking, *That would never happen to me.* I'm pretty sure it has happened to you. Big Name Agent was training his assistant just like he had been trained thirty-some years ago. I know agent after agent after agent who dump their assistants on small tasks that aren't "worth" the agent's time. Often those small tasks include contract negotiation for "small" (meaning "not lucrative") projects.

But you writers with agents, you're sure, you're *positive* this has never happened to you.

So, let me ask you:

How do you know? Do you know who does the actual negotiations of your contracts with your publishers? Have you *asked* your agent?

Who handles his business while he's on vacation? What *does* his assistant actually do?

Does your agent negotiate your contracts or does the agency have a legal department filled with *lawyers*? (Most don't. They have a legal department filled with assistants who are ordered to call the [single] lawyer on retainer only when necessary.)

Some time ago, I wrote a post on something else that mentioned in passing that I would never ever ever recommend that a new writer hire an agent any more. Many traditionally published writers shared the post, but disagreed with me on agents.

And every single traditionally published writer said this: *I can't sell my book without my agent. No editor will look at a book without an agent.*

Or the 2016 variation:

I can't sell foreign rights without my agent. No foreign publisher will look at a book if it's not presented by an agent.

Neither of these things are true.

But pretend they are true. So, do this, traditionally published writers. Hire an agent to *sell* your book. Pay that damn agent a flat fee for doing so, not 15% for the life of the copyright. Then hire a *lawyer* to negotiate the contract. A lawyer who *specializes* in intellectual property.

Because the traditional publishing house has lawyers draft the contract you're negotiating. The traditional publishing house has lawyers *negotiate* the contract with your agent. Those lawyers work for an international conglomerate. Those lawyers draft and negotiate book contracts and auxiliary rights contracts *every day*. Those lawyers *specialize* in getting the best deal for their employer, the international conglomerate. *Not* for the publishing arm. For the *conglomerate*. The entire big huge company.

You, traditionally published writer, have *an English major* at your side. Yes, that English major might have 25 years in the business, but he's still *an English major* with *zero* legal training.

Zero.

Your agent, the English major, is going up against experienced corporate lawyers who know that changing one word in a contract— one *word*—can change the meaning of the entire contract. I mentioned that to one Big Name Agent a few months ago, and she laughed at me.

That's a myth, she said.

I just about fell out of my chair. And because I couldn't believe she actually believed that, let alone spoke that phrase aloud, I said, *So you have an attorney handle your contract negotiations, right?*

Oh, she said, *we have one on retainer. I don't use his services that often. Once the boilerplate is negotiated, there isn't much more for him to do.*

This woman handles millions of dollars in client book deals. *And she knows almost as little as our friend, the recent college graduate.*

Have I put the fear of agents into you yet?

There is no reason to hire an agent to represent your work in 2016. None. No reason at all.

Not even to sell your book. Because you can do it. And then you can hire a lawyer, who will charge you a flat one-time *fee,* not 15% for the life of the copyright, to *legally* negotiate your contract for you.

Get your head out of the sand.

If you listen to me about nothing else, hear this: Hire a lawyer to handle all your legal negotiations.

Hire a *lawyer.*

Just like you would if you were heading to court.

Because you might someday. Lots of writers do. They go up against their publishers. I know of three writers who contacted me about their court cases in the past six months. None of those cases made the publishing news outlets. And that doesn't count all the writers who *threaten* a suit against their publishers.

Hire a *lawyer.*

Stop thinking agents will save you.

Learn the publishing business as it is in 2016—not as it was in 1986.

Because you're getting screwed if you don't learn how to be a 21st century business person.

And the sad thing is this: Like Famous Writer, you have no freakin' idea what's going on with your career.

None.

ATTORNEYS

I have to berate writers to get an attorney. Writers are terrified of attorneys. Writers think attorneys are expensive and impossible to work with. Writers think hiring an attorney will harm them.

Writers are wrong. —From Chapter 20

20

HOW TO HIRE AN ATTORNEY

Throughout this entire book, I've told you to hire an attorney to handle your contract negotiations instead of hiring an agent. This advice should apply to all your legal needs when it comes to writing. Even though agents say they'll "manage" your career, they really won't. They'll give advice they're not qualified to give—as in legal advice for contracts when they're not a lawyer or in how to write a novel when they've never written anything—and then they'll take 15% for the life of the project.

Here's the funny thing, though. I have to berate writers to get an attorney. Writers are *terrified* of attorneys. Writers think attorneys are expensive and impossible to work with. Writers think hiring an attorney will harm them.

Writers are wrong.

Agents cost the writer money. 15% over the life of a project can run into the tens of thousands if not the millions of dollars if things take off. *Attorneys* bill until the job is over, and most jobs the writer hires the attorney for will only take a few hours. That's a few hundred, maybe a few thousand, dollars *at most*.

But writers have this image of attorneys as assholes and bullies. I know a lot of assholes and bullies, only a handful of whom are attorneys. Attorneys are trained to be direct and to the point. They learn how to ask the right questions to get the right answers.

Writers look at agents as caretakers, nice people who will handle their business and make them feel good about themselves.

Here's the thing, folks: People who gravitate to professions that involve sales are very personable. They're good at reading others, and great at making a potential client feel good about themselves.

Attorneys don't have to be charming or personable. They get more than enough work without charming someone into believing that they have the secret handshake.

Here are the important differences between agents and attorneys.

1. Attorneys are *regulated*. Agents aren't.
2. Attorneys, as officers of the court, have to follow rules of behavior. Agents don't.
3. Attorneys are licensed. Agents aren't.
4. Attorneys charge by the job (hourly or flat fee). Agents charge a percentage for the lifetime of the project.
5. Attorneys have *years* of training in the law. Agents have none.
6. Some of that attorney training includes training in negotiation. Agents get no training in negotiation.

I can go on, but I won't.

Let me get rid of another myth.

You hire an attorney for *one job*. Whatever that job is. Maybe it's negotiating an option agreement out of Hollywood. Maybe it's drafting a contract for your new business.

I've hired attorneys to handle wills. I've hired an attorney to handle a divorce. I've hired an attorney to read a legal document I did not understand and have him explain it to me—not negotiate it, not change it—just *explain* it.

If you weren't really satisfied with the work your attorney did on that one job, then don't hire the attorney for the *next* job. You also have a lot of recourses if you feel you've been harmed by that attorney's behavior—from never hiring that attorney again to contacting the local bar.

You can have an attorney that handles most of your business matters for *years* or you can hire an attorney for a single negotiation. My excellent divorce attorney is not the same person I hired to help with a will, and they are not the people I contacted to explain that legal document.

Because here's the thing:

Attorneys come in different types.

The law is large and complicated. It differs in each country. It differs based on type of case—criminal, civil—and ways those cases are handled—litigation, contracts. You don't hire an attorney who only handles maritime law cases to negotiate your book contract. That attorney would be as at sea with the book contract as you are. (Okay, yes, I punned. So sue me. Using a lawyer…)

Anyway, lawyers have different specialties. In some states, confusingly, the lawyer can't claim to have a specialty. That lawyer has "an interest in" a certain type of law. The lawyer will tell you that they don't handle a certain kind of case, and then they will refer you to another lawyer. Don't worry. Referrals happen a lot.

Better, though, if you enter the right ballpark from the start. So as you begin your search, realize that many lawyers—particularly small town lawyers—are generalists. They handle a whole bunch of cases, from criminal law to corporate law.

For your business—your *writing* business—you'll want a good attorney who can help you on the local level with the best way to set up your business for the state you live in. There are corporate considerations (corporations cost money to create and maintain), tax considerations, and many other rules and regulations. Local business attorneys know these things.

But for your contracts and copyrights, you want an intellectual property attorney or a literary lawyer. If you're dealing with movie companies, you'll want someone who has successfully negotiated with studio lawyers, but is not necessarily a studio lawyer. Just someone who is familiar with the tricks Hollywood lawyers play.

Realize that even attorneys with specialties have limitations. Make sure, for example, that the intellectual property attorney you hire understands *copyright* as well as *trademark*. It would be nice if your intellectual property attorney understands the publishing industry. You might also want help figuring out if you should trademark your super-dooper main character from your mystery novel. Then you might want someone who has an experience with trademarks.

You see?

And yes, I know I just overwhelmed you.

But realize this as well: Attorneys will *tell you* if they lack the expertise to deal with something. They don't want the learning curve any more than you want them to learn on your dime. Attorneys will refer you to the person who can best do that particular job, hoping you will come back and hire the referring attorney when you need their expertise.

What you need right now are names of literary lawyers. I don't have many names, and I wouldn't commit to them in this blog even if I did. But the writer Laura Resnick keeps a list of literary lawyers on her writer's resources page[1]. She updates that list when she hears something, good or bad, about an attorney. Her website is Lauraresnick.com. Look under the writer's resources section.

Also, there is an organization called Volunteer Lawyers for the Arts, which is available in some states. The St. Louis Chapter lists the states where VLA exists on the Get Help page of their website[2]. Their site is vlaa.org.

If you need to hire a different kind of attorney, say, a business attorney, ExpertLaw.com has a page of suggestions on how to find that attorney[3].

In her book, *Self-Publisher's Legal Handbook*, Helen Sedwick has a section on hiring attorneys. She's focusing on attorneys for possible litigation, but her advice holds. The chapter is also online on her blog, which you can find on her website, helensedwick.com.[4]

Sedwick and I agree on the most important thing you need in an attorney. That's *experience*. When I knew I needed to get a divorce, I called a good friend of mine and asked her who the best family law attorney was in the State of Wisconsin. She gave me a name. Then I asked another friend the same question. He gave me the same name.

Then I researched the attorney. I checked with the state bar to make sure that no one had filed any complaints against her. I did some other due diligence.

This was all in the 1980s, when researching was hard. Some of this stuff is on the internet now, and you can find it easily.

If you have a choice between a *cheap* brand-new attorney two years out of law school, who has hung out his own shingle and runs his own single-person firm, and an *expensive* attorney with thirty years of experience in copyrights and contracts, for Godssake, hire the expensive attorney. Not because of her rates, but because of her experience. A simple task will take her fifteen minutes. It might take the brand-new attorney three days to find the relevant case law, and he still might not get it right.

Since you're hiring an attorney for expertise, make sure they actually *have* expertise, and not just a few semesters of contract law at a mediocre law school.

If possible, sit down with the attorney before hiring them. Before you set up the meeting, however, clarify whether or not you will be charged for that initial hour.

Most attorneys will talk to you as a prospective client for fifteen minutes to an hour for free. A few of the attorneys at big firms will charge a reduced rate or a one-time fee for that meeting. Pay the money. See if you're compatible with this person.

Sedwick says this[5]:

> *...avoid bullies. Also avoid gladiators with something to prove to the world. (Not on your nickel, please.) Be wary of attorneys who brag too much about their own achievements or who assure you your case is a "slam dunk."*

One other thing she recommends is this: Find out if the attorney you're talking to is the attorney who will actually handle your case. In some multiperson law firms, easier cases go to the associates. They're still attorneys, but with less experience and/or less clout.

You might not need clout on this particular case, and might be fine with the associate. But you need to *meet* that associate if they're going to handle your case. If you like the Big Name Lawyer, and hate the associate who'll be handling your business, *don't hire* that law firm.

It's pretty simple.

You can talk to several lawyers before hiring any one of them for a single case. When Dean and I had to deal with our friend Bill's estate, we talked to two different lawyers before settling on the attorney who ended up handling the whole thing. That's not unusual.

Writers often say that they are going to hire an agent because they can't afford an attorney. Y'know, the old *for want of a nail* thing.

Yes, many attorneys require payment *before* they start working for you. However, that payment is a retainer, which goes toward paying your bill. If you don't use the full retainer, then the attorney will refund the remaining portion when your business is concluded.

It works like this. Attorney A charges $50 per hour. You have a meeting with her about what you want to hire her for, and she asks for a retainer. Some attorneys ask for a retainer of 10% of the overall guestimated costs of the job, some ask for a specific retainer. Let's say that Attorney A asks for a $500 retainer.

That means you get ten hours of her services on this particular job before you pay another dime.

She needs to detail out the expenses—which you agree upon beforehand—and she will give you a detailed accounting of the time she spent. Good attorneys detail their time to the minute. (There's software for that now.)

An attorney you don't want to hire again will give you a bill that says 10 hours @$50, and that's all it says.

(Agents, by the way, don't have to detail out how they work for you. They can lie and say they have when they have not.)

Most attorneys charge by the hour, although some attorneys will have flat fee services. Some do a hybrid of these things—a flat-fee service for, say, a minor contract review, and an hourly billing for any negotiations or something that isn't boilerplate.

Find out *before* you hire.

You can minimize your costs as well.

Most people hire an attorney and then go to the attorney and ask what the attorney needs. The attorney then spends the first hour or two grilling the client on what the client *wants* before ever figuring out what they all need to get the job done.

The best thing you can do when you decide to hire an attorney is be organized. You need to figure out beforehand what, exactly, you're hiring the attorney for.

You can't just tell an attorney you want career management. Remember, an attorney does a specific job for you. That might be to negotiate a traditional book contract or to help you develop a contract.

If you only have a vague notion of what you need, that's better than most folks who go into a law office. Write down the vague notion, plus have a list of questions *ahead of time* for the attorney.

During the meeting, write down the attorney's answers. Don't rely on your memory.

The more specific you can be, the less money the attorney will cost you. The attorney will know exactly what you want, rather than doing hours of work flailing about *figuring out* what you want.

Once you've settled on what you want the attorney to do, tell the attorney how much money you have budgeted for the job. The attorney will tell you if that's too much or too little. If the attorney says the costs will be significantly more than what you can afford, find out if you can make do with less from the attorney or if there's work you can do.

In the case of my long-ago divorce, I was broke. I made $8,000 that year, which is about $16,000 in today's dollars. I managed to move to Oregon, start a new business, and pay off some of my ex-husband's old debts. The best family law attorney in the State of Wisconsin charged me a $500 retainer ($1000 in today's dollars), and I paid her right away, forgoing other important things to do so.

She managed to handle my entire divorce, long distance, over several months. She charged me another $1000 ($2000 in today's dollars), but she knew I couldn't pay it right away. So we worked out a payment plan, which I stuck to for the two years it took to pay her off.

Apparently, my payment plan with her was not unusual. She handled a lot of divorces from people who had meager incomes, and she worked with all of us to get the right payment.

She was honest with me in our first and only meeting about the cost of the divorce, and because she was one of the best attorneys in the state, she did her job in record time. Her estimate was $1,000 higher than what she actually ended up charging me.

She knew my budget and my situation. She also knew that I couldn't afford a protracted divorce procedure. All of that factored into what we ended up doing in that particular case.

In the case of the attorney who reviewed a contract for me and Dean, the attorney read the contract (a hefty document), and then contacted us. He said that to explain the contract in great detail would take double what we had already paid. He was willing to do so, but didn't think we needed it. His advice? Don't sign the contract, and walk away from the company.

We did.

But we could have opted to pay the money and understand all parts of the contract. We could also have hired him to negotiate that contract and improve it.

We decided against it.

But the attorney presented us with a choice. He also acknowledged the budget and the possible avenues.

The decision on what to do, however, was *ours*—mine and Dean's.

That's how attorneys work.

When I blogged this contract series, someone asked what happens if you don't like an attorney that you hired. It's pretty simple: You never hire that attorney again.

If you dislike the job they're doing in the *middle* of the job, you fire the attorney. Sedwick tells you how to part ways with an attorney in her piece. Nolo.com has a great long piece, titled "What To Do When You're Mad at Your Lawyer," on how to fire your attorney[6].

Here's one excerpt:

It's your absolute right to fire your lawyer at any time for any reason. Give it serious consideration if you're convinced the lawyer is doing a bad job or if your relationship with the lawyer has become intolerable.

The Nolo piece has explanations of what to do in a variety of circumstances, and how to proceed if you believe you ended up with a bad apple.

If you end up with a bad agent, you probably signed a contract that entitles the agent to 15% of your earnings *even after you fired them.*

If you fire your attorney, they have to stop charging you *immediately*. You're done paying them the moment you settle the final bill.

Think of 15% of every project the incompetent agent touched paid for *years* and compare it to the few hundred dollars for an attorney, and no more contact *ever*. Which do you prefer? I know which one I prefer.

I'm going to say it again: Lawyers are good people. They're smart, ethical, and helpful. Stop being afraid of them. They can help you so much more than any agent can.

Become a real business person. Hire the right people for the right job. If you need someone to explain a legal document, hire an attorney. If you need to know how to set up your corporation, hire an attorney. If you need to get out of a bad contract, hire an attorney.

Be proactive. Take charge of your business and your career. Yes, you might be afraid of attorneys. Have you actually met one? Have you sat down with one? Or do you get all of your opinions about lawyers from Shakespeare and television?

Whether traditionally published, hybrid, or indie published, writers are all running a small business.

To run a business, you need access to a good attorney and a good accountant. These are people you pay by the job. You might end up having a long-term relationship with them—we've had our accountant for 20 years now—but you might not.

No one is going to take care of you. But you can hire good advice on a per-job basis. An attorney is one of those people who can give you good advice.

When you have the right people for the right job, you'll be surprised at how much smoother your business will run.

A FEW IMPORTANT CLOSING THOUGHTS

I don't see it as my job to talk you out of anything. My job is to inform you. —
From Chapter 23

21

THUGS, LAWYERS, AND WRITERS

Here's the best and worst thing about writers:

We have fantastic imaginations. Those imaginations serve us well when we write books and stories. Those imaginations often fail us when we enter the business world.

What do I mean?

It's rare to find a writer with a Pollyanna view of the world. Most writers are better at gloom and doom than they are at unremitting optimism.

Writers also have an inflated sense of self—we couldn't do our jobs otherwise—and a weirdly introverted need to be the center of attention. If we screw up, we feel like the entire world knows—and the entire world will react.

Badly.

For reasons I don't understand, writers also want rules. They want to know how to write, what to write, and what to do when they're finished writing. They cobble bits and pieces of information from blog posts to Mrs. Hanson's Fourth Grade English class, and come up with some convoluted set of rules that they believe every writer could and would follow.

And, more so than in almost any other profession I've encountered, most writers are ethical to the point of self-harm. For example, in the United States, we have an annual homework assignment—our federal and state tax returns. Convoluted laws and all kinds of regulation allow for deductibles and legal ways to move income from the taxable side of the equation to the not-taxable side of the equation.

Writers often won't use those deductibles and regulations that favor them, preferring to pay the full tax burden. Why? They believe that everyone should pay their fair share. That's all well and good, if a bit illogical. Because anyone with those kinds of ethics who wants to do Good Works is better off hanging onto their money and donating it to charities of their choice. Besides, even with the deductions, most people will end up paying some form of tax.

Of course, who am I to talk? Because the U.S. Tax Code allows deductions for charitable donations, and I refuse to take those. Why? Because I believe that I shouldn't be rewarded for giving to a charity; the gift is reward enough. (I never take the free prizes either for the same reason.)

So writers are all weird in their own little ways.

But the writerly weirdness causes conflict with our careers and our businesses, in part because we are (as a group) imaginative, rule-bound, pessimistic, ethical, and the center of our own small universes.

We bring all of those things into the realm of contracts.

Be honest with yourself: What do you imagine will happen to you if you don't follow your book contract to the letter?

Many of you imagine the Worst Case Scenario. What is that? You don't know, because it's never happened to you or your friends or your friends' friends. Writers tend not to discuss what happens when they don't follow their contracts to the letter.

But most writers *imagine* they know. They imagine those thugs from the old Warner Brothers cartoons showing up at their doorstep, doing bad Jimmy Cagney impressions, and threatening them with everything from bodily harm to loss of their home to—I don't know.

You dirty rat, see, I know you ain't been followin' your contract, see, and I'm here ta set ya straight, see...

Or maybe the villain you envision in your imagination is more refined, more of a Hollywood executive type—a *You'll never work in this town again*—kind of threat.

Yeah, I'll spread the word, kid, and no one'll ever buy your books again. They'll know what kind of trouble you are, and I'll make sure of it. You're screwed, buddy. You're just plain screwed.

Or maybe…I don't know…a lightning bolt will strike you dead because you didn't follow the rules to the letter. I'm really not sure because, I'm sorry to admit, my imagination fails me at this point.

I've spent too much time with lawyers, businesspeople, and sales executives. To them, the entire world is negotiable.

Recently, I found myself explaining writers to lawyers. Lawyers know that contracts are not written in stone. They're rarely written in blood. All contracts can be changed, modified, muted, and defanged with enough effort. Sometimes that effort requires a judge and a courtroom.

Often that effort is as simple as a letter of notification, saying quite clearly that one party to the contract no longer wants to follow one particular clause in the contract. The other party may simply accept that notification, or the other party might protest. Either way, a dialogue has been opened and the contract might end up being renegotiated.

However, lawyers—all lawyers I've met anyway—say something when discussing contracts that confounds most writers. Lawyers use the word "ignore" a lot.

Here's how the conversation goes:

Kris: [flailing about, describing in great and horrid detail how upset she is about a contract clause that is ridiculous, probably unenforceable, and most likely will not stand up in court.]

Lawyer Friend: I don't think that clause is legal.

Kris: But writers will follow it anyway.

Lawyer Friend: Tell them to ignore the clause and see what happens.

Kris: Writers would never do that.

Lawyer Friend: Why not? People ignore unenforceable clauses in contracts all the time.

Kris: Writers just won't. They follow rules.

Lawyer Friend: What's the worst that could happen?

Kris: I don't know. You tell me.

Lawyer Friend: [shrugs] They'll end up in court. Might be good for everyone involved, so that there's clarity on that clause.

Lawyers aren't afraid of thugs and goons and cartoon characters that go bump in the night. They're not afraid of someone who plays the Big Dog and says, *You'll never work in this town again.* Lawyers generally say, *Well, let's see.*

Lawyers know there's usually a solution—and it's often as simple as standing up and saying to the person on the other side of the contract, *I'm not playing your silly game. No. I'm not doing it. Now, what are you going to do?*

Often, the person on the other side backs down. If not, the negotiation has started, and there's many many many emails and letters exchanged before someone takes the nuclear option of going to court.

You don't believe me? Then look at The Passive Voice's discussion of one of my non-compete chapters, back when it was a blog. The Passive Guy, a lawyer, wrote [emphasis mine][1]:

> So can an author **simply ignore** the non-compete provisions in a publishing agreement that includes a provision saying New York law applies to the interpretation of the contract and any litigation on the subject will take place in New York?
>
> PG says that any author who wanted to do so and was prepared to pay for a court fight in New York City would probably be doing a favor for a lot of authors. If the Author's Guild wanted to do something that really benefited a great many trad-pubbed authors, it would fund such litigation.
>
> Unfortunately for the general state of justice, not a lot of authors are likely to be interested in becoming a test case to determine the status of author/publisher non-compete agreements under New York law.

Here's the bottom line, people. I know a bunch of you are stuck in contracts you don't like. Publishers are reinterpreting contracts in whole new ways, ways that they never looked at in the past.

The big shift is that publishers no longer see themselves as manufacturers and distributers of *books.* They're running a rights management business, which means taking advantage of the full copyright on a property, instead of licensing a tiny part of that copyright.

Publishers are changing their definition of terms in a contract, without informing the writers. Other businesses do the same. Hollywood has done it since time immemorial. The Writers Guild strike in 2007-2008[2] started because studios assumed they had the right to license (and not pay royalties for) digital rights to existing properties. The Writers Guild wanted those rights accounted for separately. It got ugly, but the Guild prevailed—thank heavens for screenwriters. Because those rights turned into a real cash cow. Streaming, anyone?

Writers—because of their imaginations, their unwillingness to learn business, their silly willingness to believe their agents (untrained in the law) instead of hiring lawyers—will let themselves get stuck in a bad situation over and over and over again. I have no idea how many of you have non-compete clauses that you follow when you shouldn't. Or how many of you are afraid to renegotiate your out-of-print clauses. Or how many of you are afraid to challenge your publishers' right to publish an ebook *at all*.

Or how many of you are being forced to work with an erratic employee of the publishing house or the game company. Sometimes I suck it up, knowing the contract is short-term. (I'm doing that right now with a particularly annoying idiot, counting the days until the agreement between us is done.)

Sometimes, though, I go directly to the person I'm in business with —the president or vice president of *the company*—the person with actual clout, and demand a different employee to work with. I've blogged about this in the past[3]. You need to respect yourself.

If you're stuck, get unstuck, whatever that means. First you have to figure out what has you stuck. Then you need to figure out a solution. If you can't do that on your own—if you don't know what's possible—then hire a lawyer. Because a lawyer will be able to look at your contract and tell you what your options are.

The lawyer might mutter the word "ignore." Or the lawyer might advise you to write a letter. Or the lawyer might discuss an addendum or a contract renegotiation.

All of these things are possible—

If you take your imagination out of the game. If you stop making things up and start acting like a person in control of her business.

Yep, it's scary.

But I can guarantee that no thugs will come to your door.

And, maybe, just maybe, you'll get unstuck.

Maybe, just maybe, you'll end up with a career.

Instead of wishing you had one.

22

A VERY SHORT COURSE IN NEGOTIATION

Before you dive into contract negotiations with anyone, go forth and read a book on negotiation. Yes, I know, the word "negotiation" isn't a pretty one.

In fact, if your response to my last two sentences was either to cringe or to say blithely, "I have people for that," realize that I am talking to you in particular. You folks, with your head in the sand. Yeah, you. Stand up for a minute. I know negotiation scares you. It scares all of us. I'm not telling you to do the actual face-to-face stuff yourself. But I am telling you that you must guide these negotiations, either behind the scenes with your "people" or via email or whatever cover of darkness you need to complete this messy job.

There are a lot of good books on negotiation, but I would be remiss if I didn't tell you about mine. It's a section of my *Freelancer's Survival Guide* called *How to Negotiate Anything*. You can read that section online for free on my blog[1] or you can order the section as a stand-alone book (in trade or ebook), or as part of the gigantic *Freelancer's Guide* itself which has a trade paper edition as well as an ebook edition.

Here are the salient points from that section of the guide. (If you want explanation of any of those items, look at the books I recommended or the relevant chapters on my blog.)

First, the rules of negotiation:

1. **Know What You Want.**
2. **Ask.**
3. **Be Prepared to Walk Away.**
4. **Stay Calm.**
5. **Never Reveal Your Entire Hand.**
6. **Don't Flip-Flop.**

Second, the rules of contract negotiation:

1. **Expect to Negotiate a Contract.**
2. **Imagine How the Terms of the Contract Will Impact You Over the Lifetime of the Contract.**
3. **Focus on What You Want.**
4. **Make Sure You Have an Equitable Way to Terminate the Contract.**
5. **Make Sure You Know How You'll Get Paid or How You Will Make Payments.**
6. **Control as Much of the Contract as Possible.**
7. **Once Both Parties Sign, Negotiation is Over.**

In the past, most writers did not think of any of these things, trusting their advisors to help them through the difficulties of negotiation. But with things in such flux, our advisors often have less information about the changes in publishing than we do. So we need to make decisions on our own.

A sidebar: I have always felt that writers should be actively involved in their careers. When I started teaching professional writers how to make breakthroughs in their careers, I wanted to put up a sign that said, *No Whining*. But that really doesn't work. Instead, my husband Dean Wesley Smith and I came up with a sign that reflects our philosophy:

You Are Responsible for Your Own Career.

You signed the contract. Your agent didn't sign it. Your attorney didn't sign it. You did. Your agent or your attorney might have given you advice, but you took that advice. You took that deal, finalized that negotiation, worked with that company. If you got screwed, then it's your responsibility to make sure it never happens again. If you had incredible success, then congratulations. That success came from your actions as well.

Okay. That's all. (That's a lot, said in a few words.)

Go forth. Negotiate.

And maybe, just maybe, have fun.

23

MYTHBUSTING

When I blogged about contracts and dealbreakers, I lost some of my indie readers, who waited for me to finish the series before I returned to the regular blog. Those readers believe they will never sign the kind of contract I'm dealing with. They also believe that they're protected because they're in business for themselves.

In some respects, they are protected. They don't have agents trying to scam them, along with publishers trying to grab their rights.

Or are these readers protected? You see, many terms of service have rights grabs buried inside the boilerplate—y'know, that stuff you just click through to use someone's service.

Sometimes, other people will call the service on their bad TOS, and the service will change the TOS—for *future* agreements. But those changes aren't always retroactive. If you signed on years ago, when the terms were at their worst, those old terms might still apply to you.

As with all contracts and agreements, it varies from person to person, item to item, contract to contract, and company to company.

Yes, you have to keep track of all of that. *You*. So start learning this stuff.

Thanks to another writer's bad situation, I am able to cite an existing multimillion dollar book contract. I did so in Appendix 1: A Real Book

Contract, however, just in case the contract itself vanishes from the internet.

That contract handily proved every point I was trying to make with this book. Publishers *are* grabbing rights; agents are *worse*.

And yet, if you scan through the comments throughout the series on the blog itself, you'll see writers who still want that traditional publishing deal. *Even though they now know (and admit) that they will get screwed.*

I can't help those people. You can't help those people. Don't even try.

But a lot of you did listen, and are listening, and will use the information in this book. Thank you for picking it up and thanks to all of those who helped along the way.

To wrap up, I'm going to address the indie/hybrid writers among us.

I know many of you think you'll never see these contracts.

I also know many of you still believe some outdated myths.

I'm going to address a few of those myths here.

Agent Myths

Myth: You need an agent to sell your books overseas.

Here's the thing, folks. Any agent you sign with to sell your foreign rights will have all of the bad contract practices I listed in this book. And that agent might (will) insert the same kind of rights-grab language that exists in the contract in Appendix 1. On top of all that, your agent in your home country will partner with an agent in the foreign country, so you'll have *two* agents grabbing at your money (which is almost untraceable) and at your rights.

Run away. Run.

Besides, folks. Those of you who want an agent to sell your foreign rights have no idea how an agent actually *sells* those rights. If they *sell* the rights.

All the agent does is compile a new releases list (usually three times a year) and send it to all the foreign rights agents they partner with. Yes, if you're one of the big bestsellers, the agent will handsell your book to the foreign rights agent, but usually in that case, foreign publishers will come calling *anyway*.

Some agents actually go to overseas book fairs, and talk to foreign rights publishers. The agent pitches *their agency* and then hands the publisher a list of available works.

That's *all*.

The agent does *no work*. Either they farm out the work to another (foreign) agent. Or they answer the phone or an email. *Nothing more.*

Finally, agents embezzle from their clients a lot. And the area where the most embezzlement occurs is foreign rights. If your book earns royalties, how will you know? Most writers don't track their foreign book's royalty statements. (Heck, most writers don't track their royalty statements, period.) And if you signed a contract as bad as the one in the Appendix, your publisher(s) don't have to give you an accurate royalty statement ever. Go read that contract[1] if you doubt me.

The Solution: You can handle your foreign rights yourself, faster, better, and without losing any copyright or having someone embezzle from you. This world is very small now. You can contact foreign publishers directly.

If those publishers publish English language books in translation, they have people on staff who can read English language emails. Learn how to submit stories and novels to them. A good first step to learning this is the area on award-winning writer Douglas Smith's website smithwriter.com that provides a tutorial in foreign short story markets[2]. If you build a following in a foreign short story market, eventually book publishers in that market will take an interest in your work.

You will also learn the names of translators who might be willing to work with you to translate your work and allow you to indie publish it. But you know what you will need in that circumstance? You'll need a contract between you and the translator. Heh. Wow. Guess you'll need to learn more about rights and contracts then.

Even if you only make one traditional foreign sale per year, you will probably earn more than you would ever earn if you hired an agent, *even if the agent sold a book for you overseas.*

One other point: In 2016, your English-language book will have a worldwide release only if you publish it yourself. Get out of Kindle

Select, people, and go wide. Use Kobo, which is growing dramatically. Realize that iBooks has fingers all over the world.

Sure, you might only sell one or two titles to a particular country, but you don't know if one of those titles sold to an editor at a foreign publishing house who is checking out this English-language book a friend recommended. And if the editor likes your book, then guess what? She'll contact you *via email* about how to acquire the translation rights for that book for her company. Make sure you have a contact form on your website. (You have a website, right?)

Myth: You need an agent to sell your books to big traditional markets.

No, you don't. You just have to learn how to do it, and as I have said over and over again, I am not going to teach you how to do it.

These contracts and rights deals through traditional publishers are *awful*, people. They will control your careers and your works. If you want writing to remain a hobby, get a traditional book deal.

If you want a career, stay away from traditional book publishers.

Besides, traditional book publishers are *actively* cutting their book lines right now. They're drowning. The numbers I heard from Random Penguin/Randy Penguin/whatever they're calling themselves in the summer of 2016 are this: They're cutting their titles from 900 to 250.

Think there's room for your book in those 250 slots? Um, no. Writers I know who have been cut this past year include a large number of *New York Times* bestsellers. Only those writers weren't mega bestsellers.

That 250 is for Big Guns and people who "write" novelty books, like the Kardashians. Not for you.

But go ahead. Bang your head against that wall. Break through and have leaches and hangers-on destroy your career. If you don't understand what's so bad about all of the contract terms discussed in this book, and you don't want to learn, then you've figured out what kind of life you want to live—and it certainly ain't the life of a professional writer.

Traditional Publishers Do It Better

Myth: Traditional publishers will get my book into bookstores.

Really? Where? What bookstores? Small independents? Barnes & Noble? Amazon?

Oh, wait. You mean *paper* books, right? Yeah. Okay. Still, I ask you. Where? What bookstores? What are you talking about? Do you think it's still 1999?

Truth: Most books are sold *online* these days. That includes *paper* books. If you publish your own books, you can get them into Amazon easily, Barnes & Noble (not as easily), and independent bookstores (if you understand things like Indie-Bound).

Here's the thing: Even if a traditional publisher publishes your book in paper, no bookstore is obligated to take that book or to put it on the shelf. What indie writers learn when they take print-only deals is this: The traditional publisher is no more able to sell print books than the writer was.

And on top of it, the writer loses much of the copyright on their book. In fact, the writer often loses everything in that traditional deal, including and not limited to, money. The writer will also lose control of her next projects, usually due to noncompetes buried in the *boilerplate*.

If the writer went through an agent, the writer will lose even more. See the clause in Chapter 16 "Agent Agreements" in which the agent demanded that the writer have every self-published book approved by the *agent* before the book goes live. Realize that the agency who has that clause in its contract *is as famous as William Morris* (which negotiated the contract in the Appendix).

As many indies have learned in the last seven years, paper-only deals are *terrible* for the writer. Stay away from them. They're as bad as a regular publishing deal *because they **are** a regular publishing deal.*

Myth: Traditional publishers can promote a work better than an indie writer can.

Truth: Take a look at the contract cited in the Appendix. The only party in that contract who is *obligated* to promote a book *is the writer*. The publisher can opt out of promotion at any point.

And that's if the publisher actually knew how to promote books. Sure, publishers have deep pockets, but they don't know how to invest in effective advertising or how to *sell* books *to readers*. Not bookstores. *Readers*.

As this world has changed, publishers have changed their marketing strategies not one bit. If you don't understand this, pick up my book *Discoverability* and/or look at the free blog posts on my website[3]. (But realize those blogs were published out of order.)

Once again, for an empty promise *not backed up in the contract*, a writer will lose control of her intellectual property.

And she'll lose the ability to participate in all of the various ways that books actually *do* sell to readers.

For example, in September, I had books in three different Storybundles. Those bundles sell thousands of copies. Most bundlers, like Storybundle, do not work with mainstream publishers—in part because of contractual issues. I've curated a few bundles with some traditionally published writers who farmed the work to their agents, and guess what? None of us (me or the bundlers who experienced this) will *ever* do that again.

Opportunities lost, folks.

No traditional publisher will let you put your book in a 99-cent ebook bundle with other writers on, say, Amazon, not even for a limited time. Because that means the traditional publisher would have to partner with its competitors. The traditional publisher won't allow it for a $50 ebook bundle either. Not happening.

Nor will most traditional publishers bundle the books in your series together. The traditional publishers publish *once* and then move on to the next book. Any promotions, any rejiggering of the book itself, *will not happen*.

I know, I know. You will make your own decision regardless of what I say. And then you'll write to me as *two separate people* did in August, saying that they had made a mistake, and could I help them learn how to indie publish after all.

If there's anything left to indie publish. If you haven't sold control of all of your books to a major corporation, maybe I'll be able to help you.

I'm pretty much done with contracts and dealbreakers. Other indie bloggers are quitting because they don't like the dirty tricks coming out of traditional publishing and they can't seem to talk their readers out of making bad deals.

I don't see it as my job to talk you out of anything. My job is to inform you.

I've done that with this book. I am going to list a few points that you should have gotten out of this book.

Point The First: Always hire a lawyer to advise you on legal matters concerning your writing *business*.

Point The Second: Make sure you have a contract that governs every relationship you have in your business, from the editors you hire to the co-writers you work with.

Point The Third: Learn how to negotiate. (Always do your negotiations via email.)

Point The Fourth: Learn copyright law.

Point The Fifth: Learn copyright law.

Point The Sixth: Hire a lawyer already!

Okay, I'm repeating myself. So I'm going to leave you with a movie recommendation. Watch *Begin Again*, with Mark Ruffalo and Keira Knightly. Watch *through* the credits. (And yes, Ruffalo's character is an utter *asshole* in the first half hour. Stick with it. You'll understand.)

Realize that the music industry is way ahead of the publishing industry in rights and music publishing and everything else.

If you don't want to watch the movie, then at least check out the endnote and follow the link to the scene[4]. It's from the end of the film, so if you plan to watch the movie, don't watch this clip.

There. I have done what I can.

You are now on your own.

Good luck.

APPENDIX 1

A REAL BOOK CONTRACT

Under normal circumstances, I would have reconfigured the blog post titled "A Real Book Contract" as Chapter 13 of this book. But I'm not sure how long the links cited here will last. I am not reprinting the contract here. In order to understand what's written below, you need to go to this link online http://media.publishersmarketplace.com/wp-content/uploads/2016/08/SethGrahameSmithlawsuit.pdf and read the contract there.

I hope that it remains up, so that you can all see what I'm talking about in this book is very, very real.

A month after I posted this blog, the court case in question was dismissed with prejudice. What I found on PacerMonitor was this[1]:

PLEASE TAKE NOTICE that Plaintiff, HACHETTE BOOK GROUP, INC., pursuant to Rule 41(a)(1)(A)(i) of the Federal Rules of Civil Procedure, hereby dismisses this action with prejudice against the defendant(s) Baby Gorilla Inc., Seth Grahame-Smith.

What that exactly means, I don't know. As I've said before, I'm not a lawyer. I will probably dig into the filing later, but it's not relevant to this post, so I'm not going to modify anything here.

The fact that the case is dismissed, however, simply reaffirms my decision to put this post at the end of the book. The links I'm providing to the contract might vanish at any moment. You might have to Google the case to see what I'm discussing in this post.

And here's the post, with only a few modifications from its initial appearance.

One of my readers forwarded me an article from *Locus Online*[2] about Hachette suing one of their bestselling authors. It seems that for some reason, Seth Grahame-Smith did not turn in the second book of his contract with Grand Central for the follow-up book after *Abraham Lincoln: Vampire Hunter*. After two extensions of his deadline, and a threat from Grand Central, Grahame-Smith turned in something that Grand Central found terribly unacceptable. They claim he appropriated a 120-year-old manuscript as part of the book.

Considering Grahame-Smith also wrote *Pride and Prejudice and Zombies*, a book substantially based on a 203-year-old novel, I kinda had a yeah-so? reaction to the 120-year-old manuscript thing. So I went and read the lawsuit, and realized a few things.

First, the deal was made in 2010, before a lot of the major changes in the traditional publishing industry occurred. The handwriting was on the wall but back then this *Pride and Prejudice and Zombies* thing was *hot*, so Grand Central ponied up a four-million-dollar advance, paid in $500,000 chunks.

Grahame-Smith received at least $1.5 million of those chunks, maybe as much as $2.5 million before the relationship soured.

Grand Central's parent company Hachette is suing Grahame-Smith for $500,000, the advance on that second book of this contract.

Figure this: The publisher believes it's better to sue the author than it is to leave that $500,000 outstanding. There are several reasons that Hachette could have made the decision to file suit.

For example, the time has long passed for the second property to ever earn what the first properties did.

If you read the contract closely, you'll see that there is some time-is-of-the-essence stuff buried in it, although that phrase is not used. The Delivery clause (p.5 of the contract) is unbelievably specific, and that has to be because of the timeliness of the property. (We'll get to the contract in a minute.)

By 2016, it's really clear that Hachette will lose money on this second book. Better to file suit and ask for the $500,000 *plus interest* than it is to pay out an additional $1.5 million owed through the contract. Legal fees won't equal that amount, even if the case makes it to court.

The case is a pretty standard breach-of-contract suit, and from my glance, it looks winnable for Hachette. Even if it's not, the contract will be canceled, and Hachette won't owe Grahame-Smith another dime.

It's pretty much guaranteed that Hachette wouldn't have accepted a manuscript from Grahame-Smith for any reason in 2016. Hachette was looking at a major financial loss on the second book in this contract.

Expect more of these kinds of suits in the future. If the writers who got huge advances do not meet their obligations with the publishers, the publishers will cut their losses and run as fast as they possibly can.

But what does this suit have to do with the contracts/dealbreakers series?

This:

For the first time, I can share with you a *complete* publishing contract. Go to the link at the top of this section, and scroll down to the contract itself. (The contract starts on page 9.) Try to read it.

Have you done so? Good.

Because I'm going to tell you a few things.

1. This is an *agent*-negotiated contract. However, the agency that negotiated the contract is William Morris. I can tell you from experience that William Morris has lawyers *on staff*. In theory, those lawyers advise the agents. So, in theory, William Morris had lawyers who talked to Grand Central's lawyers while negotiating this contract.

2. I don't care what entity negotiated for the writer. Whoever the hell it was did a piss-poor job. I have had better contracts for novels paying me $10,000 than this multimillion-dollar contract. I have to admit: I'm shocked by this contract. It's a

midlist writer contract (for a writer with no clout) dressed in million-dollar clothing.

I scanned, but I didn't see anything I would expect in a multimillion dollar contract. No escalators. No protections for the writer. Low royalty rates. Bad discount clauses.

Half the stuff I listed as dealbreakers in this book are *better* than many of the terms in this contract.

Plus there are some wrinkles here that I have never seen before. In the Termination Clause (page 17), for example, the writer must notify the publisher if motion picture or television rights options (or full-on licenses) exist.

I have *never* seen that. It means the publisher expected these books to get optioned for film, and that in such an instance, termination might end up being impossible.

And then...and then...oh, my God, and then!

The agent clause (p. 19-20). It is the *worst* agent clause I have ever seen. Worse than the ones I warned you about in the Agent section. It has this lovely addition, which is new to me:

The provisions of this paragraph 25 shall survive the expiration of this Agreement and are specifically included for the benefit of the Agent which is hereby named as a third-party beneficiary.

Wow. Just—wow. Go to my website, read the original agent clause post that I wrote (which became Chapter 15) and read the comments[3]. See what the *lawyers* who responded said about the duties of agents and how these clauses are most likely illegal.

From one of the lawyers answering a question on the post: "Yes [the agent clause] is illegal. (1) "Agent" is a legal term for someone empowered to act on behalf of another person. (2) A conflict of interest occurs when a person acting as an agent benefits from the transaction. If a lawyer did this, the lawyer would be [disciplined]...."

So, here's today's homework assignment.

Read this full traditional publishing contract. *Print the contract out first*, and see if you understand it.

Then realize that this contract isn't the worst I've seen, and it certainly isn't the best. It's a really crappy multimillion dollar contract—the author should have received protection from his representatives, but we all know how good that representation is.

Then realize that traditional publishing is not really giving these big advances any more. The big-advance books aren't earning out. Which is why Hachette is cutting its losses here.

So your chance of getting this kind of advance is pretty slim. And even if you do, did you notice the lovely clause about promotion?

*The Publisher shall have the sole discretion to determine what, **if any**, promotional services the Publisher may perform for the **work**...*

(I added the bold for emphasis here and below.)

That's clause 8(d) (p.14) and while there are other clauses that apply to promotion, the operative phrase here is "if any." It means all those other clauses are wasted typing. If the publisher doesn't want to promote these books, *the publisher doesn't have to.* Ever.

Those of you who believe you need a traditional publisher to make a go of your writing career need to understand that I have seen that clause in almost *every single* traditional publishing contract I've seen over the last ten years.

Unless the writer actively negotiated a marketing plan for their book with the publisher, appended that plan to the contract, *and deleted that if-any clause,* the publisher doesn't have to do *anything* to promote any book.

Why would a publisher do that, you ask. You got me. But publishers really don't want to be obligated to promote the properties they've purchased.

If you want to be traditionally published, and you do not understand this contract, then you have a lot of learning to do. You need to understand all the clauses here.

And you also need to understand that only two of the three parties to this contract will benefit from it. The first party to benefit is the publisher. If these books had been successful—and the first one was—the publisher didn't have to do much of anything to rake in the dough.

In fact, there's another scary clause that favors the publisher in this contract, a clause that I had never seen before. The royalty statements *don't have to be accurate.* It says so right in the contract. It uses a phrase I've never seen in *any* contract before.

It says:

*The Publisher shall render semi-annual statements of "**estimated net sales**" and net licensing revenues...*

"Estimated net sales." That's new to me. The Publisher then defines "estimated net sales" as "sales less actual returns and less a reasonable reserve against returns of the Work..."

"Reasonable reserve" is not defined, and if the author wants to know what the publisher actually is withholding, the writer has to ask, in writing, for that information. The writer also has the right to audit the publisher—at the writer's expense, of course.

Oh, and—there's no cap on returns, and no time limit on the reserve.

I had the misfortune of mis-negotiating a reserve on returns twenty years ago on a work-for-hire project. I still get royalty statements—on a book published in 1995—in which *reserve against returns* continue to be withheld. Even now! Twenty-one years later.

You don't think a publisher would do that on a book that they paid millions for? Think again.

The other entity that benefits from this contract is the agent. Who is specifically named as a third-party beneficiary of this contract. Who is agent, according to the agent clause, for *the duration of the copyright.*

What does the writer get?

Four million dollars, paid in seven installments...provided the writer lives up to the terms of the contract which, apparently, Grahame-Smith did not do. For some reason, he failed to fulfill the second half of this contract. So even if he wasn't sued by his publisher, he wouldn't have received the full four million.

He made, at most, two and a half million, minus agent fees and commissions, spread out over *years.*

And he wouldn't have seen another dime on these projects, because they were jointly accounted (meaning one book could earn out and the other wouldn't, so the publisher could apply all the earnings of the first book to the unearned balance of the second), and then there's that crappy royalty statement thing, and then, and then, and then…

Folks, this is why I'm asking you over and over again why you would ever want a traditional book contract. Traditional print-only contracts (you indie writers) are just like this with the ebook stuff removed.

And to the indies who want to hire an agent to handle your foreign rights, look at the agent clause. The publisher stuff here is bad, but the agent clause is ever so much worse.

Please, do your homework this week, and *read* this contract. Print it out. Try to understand it. Realize that all of the clauses work together to form a whole contract, that's binding on the author.

Learn from this free information that has come from another writer's bad situation.

This is how writers learn their business.

You have an opportunity here to avoid the mistakes I made, the mistakes that Grahame-Smith made. You have the opportunity to learn how—pain-free—to take control of your own careers.

Do so.

APPENDIX 2

The Copyright Handbook by Stephen Fishman, Nolo Press, 2014 (or the most current version).

Discoverability by Kristine Kathryn Rusch, WMG Publishing, 2014.

How to Negotiate Anything by Kristine Kathryn Rusch, WMG Publishing, 2010.

The Nine Worst Provisions in Your Publishing Contract by David P. Vandagriff, OW Press, 2016. (Amazon ebook only)

Self-Publisher's Legal Handbook by Helen Sedwick, Ten Gallon Press, 2014.

NOTES

Introduction

1. http://www.publishersmarketplace.com/
2. http://legal-dictionary.thefreedictionary.com/agency

1. Contract Basics

1. http://www.lawhandbook.org.au/07_01_02_elements_of_a_contract/
2. http://www.nolo.com/legal-encyclopedia/contracts-basics-33367.html
3. http://www.businessdictionary.com/definition/contract.html

3. Understanding Copyright

1. http://helensedwick.com/11-things-every-writer-should-know-about-copyrights/
2. http://www.mbbp.com/news/know-your-copyrights
3. http://www.nolo.com/legal-encyclopedia/copyright-basics-faq-29079.html
4. http://www.copyright.gov/help/faq/
5. https://www.law.cornell.edu/uscode/text/17
6. http://www.michaelgeist.ca/
7. http://www.deanwesleysmith.com/killing-the-top-ten-sacred-cows-of-publishing-8-you-cant-make-a-living-with-your-fiction/

4. The Option Clause

1. http://www.thepassivevoice.com/2016/04/know-your-rights/
2. http://www.rotlaw.com/legal-library/what-is-good-faith/

6. The Non-Compete Clause 2

1. http://fortune.com/2016/06/22/jimmy-johns-non-compete-agreements/
2. http://www.terikanefield.com/About-Teri.html

7. The Grant of Rights Clause

1. http://www.zackcompany.com/zack-blog/entry/whats-driving-self-publishing-qcompany-policyq

9. Rights Reversion

1. http://kriswrites.com/2011/04/20/the-business-rusch-royalty-statements-update/
2. http://kriswrites.com/2012/08/15/the-business-rusch-a-tale-of-two-royalty-statements/
3. http://dearauthor.com/features/reclaiming-your-copyright-after-thirty-five-years/
4. https://libraries.mit.edu/news/reclaiming-copyright-2/14404/
5. http://www.copyright.gov/docs/203.html

10. Discount Abuse

1. http://kriswrites.com/business-rusch-publishing-articles/discoverability-series/
2. https://www.authorsguild.org/industry-advocacy/end-the-discount-double-cross/
3. http://publishingperspectives.com/2016/06/conference-publishing-rights/#.V_rWeIVs7Jz

11. Moral Rights and Editing Clauses

1. http://kriswrites.com/2016/03/09/business-musings-the-copyedit-from-heck/

12. Other Evil Clauses

1. http://accrispin.blogspot.com/2016/07/how-publishers-abuse-termination-fees.html
2. https://www.buzzfeed.com/josephbernstein/heres-all-the-data-pokemon-go-is-collecting-from-your-phone?bffbmain&ref=bffbmain&utm_term=.ueJjgxpPk#.mtqZ0pjrN
3. http://publishlawyer.com/the-net-revenue-royalty-clause/

13. Sneaky Money Grabs

1. http://www.geekwire.com/2016/team-publishing-startup-booktrope-shutting-y-combinator-grad-cites-revenue-shortfall/
2. http://the-digital-reader.com/2016/06/01/the-sudden-demise-of-booktrope-is-forcing-authors-to-become-publishers/
3. http://web.archive.org/web/20150322162636/http://booktrope.com/bt-media/booktrope-author-agreement.pdf
4. http://kriswrites.com/2011/08/17/the-business-rusch-common-sense-and-the-writer/
5. https://medium.com/@upgradestory/author-seeks-publisher-a-not-so-happy-ending-481d7aeb753f#.1jsztg2ja
6. http://web.archive.org/web/20150322162856/http://booktrope.com/bt-media/booktrope-sample-cta.pdf
7. http://www.geekwire.com/2016/team-publishing-startup-booktrope-shutting-y-combinator-grad-cites-revenue-shortfall/

8. http://web.archive.org/web/20150322162636/http://booktrope.com/bt-media/booktrope-author-agreement.pdf
9. https://medium.com/@upgradestory/author-seeks-publisher-a-not-so-happy-ending-481d7aeb753f#.x652n2yg5

14. Prince, Estates, and The Future

1. http://www.thepassivevoice.com/2016/04/know-your-rights/
2. http://bigstory.ap.org/article/b7bcc90e42904f679c07158bf5e851a3/who-will-step-forward-claim-princes-millions
3. *Michael Jackson, Inc: The Rise, Fall, and Rebirth of a Billion-Dollar Empire* by Zach O'Malley Greenberg, Atria Books, 2014, p.225.
4. http://www.startribune.com/judge-orders-bremer-trust-to-handle-prince-s-estate/377313121/
5. http://www.forbes.com/sites/janetnovack/2016/04/25/could-prince-estate-end-up-following-michael-jacksons-into-tax-court/#73f291114bbb
6. http://www.newsweek.com/what-will-become-princes-vault-unreleased-songs-453113
7. http://journal.neilgaiman.com/2006/10/important-and-pass-it-on.html

15. The Agent Clause

1. http://www.sfscope.com/2011/05/ralph-vicinanza-literary-agency-closing/
2. http://www.thepassivevoice.com/2012/03/agent-loses-a-suit-against-an-author-for-commissions/
3. https://janefriedman.com/i-left-my-agent/
4. http://clairecook.com/resources/writing/

16. Agent Agreements

1. http://www.thepassivevoice.com/2012/03/agent-loses-a-suit-against-an-author-for-commissions/

17. Agents and Audits

1. http://legal-dictionary.thefreedictionary.com/fiduciary+duty

20. How to Hire an Attorney

1. http://www.lauraresnick.com/writers-resources/#literary-lawyers
2. http://vlaa.org/get-help/other-vlas/
3. http://www.expertlaw.com/library/consumer/howtohire.html
4. http://helensedwick.com/how-to-hire-an-attorney/
5. http://helensedwick.com/how-to-hire-an-attorney/

6. http://www.nolo.com/legal-encyclopedia/problems-with-lawyer-tips-strategies-29925.html

21. Thugs, Lawyers, and Writers

1. http://www.thepassivevoice.com/2016/06/an-important-notice-on-the-non-compete-clause/
2. https://en.wikipedia.org/wiki/2007%E2%80%9308_Writers_Guild_of_America_strike
3. http://kriswrites.com/2011/10/26/the-business-rusch-believe-in-yourself/

22. A Very Short Course in Negotiation

1. http://kriswrites.com/2009/12/03/freelancers-survival-guide-negotiation-part-one/

23. Mythbusting

1. http://media.publishersmarketplace.com/wp-content/uploads/2016/08/SethGrahameSmithlawsuit.pdf
2. http://www.smithwriter.com/FML_article
3. http://kriswrites.com/business-rusch-publishing-articles/discoverability-series/
4. https://youtu.be/Ko2zvfubJ3c

Appendix 1

1. https://www.pacermonitor.com/public/case/18999528/
   Hachette_Book_Group,_Inc_v_GrahameSmith_et_al
2. http://www.locusmag.com/News/2016/08/hachette-sues-seth-grahame-smith/
3. http://kriswrites.com/2016/08/10/business-musings-the-agent-clause-contracts-dealbreakers/#comments

DEAN WESLEY SMITH

The Magic Bakery

COPYRIGHT IN THE MODERN
WORLD OF FICTION PUBLISHING

A WMG WRITER'S GUIDE

INTRODUCTION

Indie writers make great money these days with their small and medium-sized businesses. Some make millions, while at the same time others sell few books.

The writers selling few copies tend to look for reasons why they are not selling. I could spend a lot of time listing all the reasons writers find for a book not selling, but almost always the reason is a very simple business reason.

Inventory.

And a complete failure to understand what they are selling.

But that seemingly simple answer has a vast universe of issues around it. And understanding inventory in publishing takes an understanding of copyright.

So for this book, I am going to extend the metaphor of a Magic Bakery far past its breaking point. Over the years, as I have used this metaphor to help people understand how the business of publishing works, the metaphor seems to help.

And it helps writers understand copyright, the very thing that generates the sales and the money for the business.

So here goes.

Let's open the door to the Magic Bakery, let the wonderful smells of baking bread and fresh doughnuts flow around us. Ignore the racks of cookies sitting in one case and the counter full of wonderful cakes with chocolate frostings.

Head right for the vast cases in the center of the bakery full of pies of all types. All cut and ready to be served either whole or by the slice.

Welcome to your writing business.

The Back Room

Back behind the main counter, beyond that swinging door, is where the magic really occurs.

Flower and flavoring and fresh fruit. Then add sugar and other ingredients and it all comes together in a certain way to create a pie.

A magic pie.

Skill is involved to make the pie, to have it look right, smell right, and most importantly, taste right to the customer.

Years of practiced skill.

Yup, I'm talking about your creation of story. Novel or short story, doesn't matter.

Just like a pie, you take things from the world and combine them in your own unique way to create a wonderful product, a story, for your customers.

Some stories are similar to one another as in a series. Others are as different as a chocolate cream pie would be to a Dutch apple pie. But the customers don't much care.

Sure, each customer has a favorite. Some like the chocolate cream, others go for cherry. But if you have a regular, a true fan, they will try most everything eventually.

A Few Things This Book Will Cover

So in this book, as each chapter goes on, I will talk about opening your bakery when you are still learning how to bake. (Yes, you should, to answer that basic question right off.)

You are learning how to make your pies look like a pie and have a unique taste that customers will return for over and over. That takes time and work. Learning any skill does.

Also, this book will deal some with how the presentation to the customers in your bakery is critical as well.

And how to even get your customers to the front door of your bakery and then what do you do when they walk through the door to help the customer stay, buy, and return later.

All critical aspects to any business.

Real bakeries or magic. Hardware stores or bookstores.

All businesses worry about those exact problems.

But mostly this book will talk about the magic in the pie itself.

You see, just one element of your magic pie is that when you remove a piece, if you do it correctly, that piece can make you money with a customer and yet the pie will remain whole.

The piece of pie that just made you money magically is back in the pie and ready to sell again.

A magic pie.

And that is only one small aspect of the magic.

So stay with me for some chapters here as I extend this metaphor to the extreme in order to help you understand the value, the importance, and the magic of copyright in your writing.

And also help you understand some real reasons why your work isn't selling many copies in this new, crowded world.

You might not like the reasons. But at least you will know how to fix the problems.

And by the end of this book you will know how to have a bakery where lines of customers form out the door to buy your wonderful work.

That is what this book is all about.

Onward.

1

Digging down into all the vast areas of how writers sell books and the business of selling fiction, I figured the best way to start this would be on the surface, explaining some real logical, but forgotten (by writers), business concepts.

So an example: A young writer (not in age, but in experience) writes and finishes a first novel. And somehow manages to avoid all the traps of rewriting and letting a peer workshop kill the book. Fantastic!

This is a real event and once published should be celebrated. First novels are important to every writer. Get copies out to family, tell friends where the book can be bought, and then go back to writing the next book.

But sadly, the book sells almost no copies. A few to family and friends and nothing else. No one is reading it. And this is the problem of the new world of indie publishing.

Discouragement for no logical reason. You wrote a book your first readers like, why isn't it selling? And pretty soon the young writer is so discouraged they quit.

Now there are lots of reasons that first novel might not be selling, actually. But the main one concerns the Magic Bakery. And basic business.

SOME HISTORY FIRST

In the old days of traditional publishing only, over ten years ago now as I write this, there was only one path into publishing a book and getting it to readers to buy.

The path was simple: You somehow, through some form, got the book to an editor. This took time and often lots of rejections. Years and years of time.

So the advice back then was to mail the book to someone (editor, agent, subway rat who knew someone who could buy the book for a publisher) and then go back to writing the next book.

This process often took so long and was filled with so many rejections, a writer either quit (most) or kept writing and got better. My first sold novel was my third written novel. And my fourth written novel never saw the light of day.

The time it took allowed writers with drive to improve skills and keep writing. The system forced it.

NOW THE NEW WORLD

There is no system. No one forces a writer to wait to get a book out to readers and no writer should wait. That old system of gatekeepers was too stupid for words.

But now the young writer puts the book out there and there are no sales.

What could be wrong? Why doesn't the book sell?

Clearing out some basic reasons first...

... Your cover sucks and looks like a beginner did it or the art.

... Your sales blurb is so long, so full of plot, and so passive it puts readers to sleep.

... Your opening is so thin, so full of action with no depth, no one would buy it.

... You don't know genre and put the book on the wrong shelf in the electronic stores.

But sure, you might have those things wrong, you fix them, and your book still won't sell.

Why not?

The Magic Bakery is why not.

A PERSONAL STORY FIRST

In early 1977 I decided I wanted to start a used bookstore while I was going to college for a degree in architecture. And not an antiquarian bookstore, but a type of bookstore I had seen starting up in California when I was a golf professional. Basically a paperback exchange.

This was a fairly new concept in 1977 and it sounded like fun. But I had one major issue. I had maybe 400 books I wanted to part with in my collection. So the idea was sort of just a pipe dream until one day I was going up the escalator into my bank when I saw a small For Rent sign on a big metal door at the top of five stairs at the top of the escalator.

You turned right to go into the bank, the stairs went up to the left and to this big metal fire door. I went through the big door into a small lobby. An attorney had a large office ahead, a doctor to the left, and down a dark hallway was the For Rent sign.

An office smaller than most kid's bedrooms. $75 per month. I was hooked.

My wife-at-the-time wanted nothing to do with the idea of starting a business. She was working on her masters. So I promised her I would keep the spending under $200 to start it. I rented the place for $100 for a month counting the deposit, bought about $50 in old pine lumber and built shelves to fill the place. Every wall and in the middle of the small room as well. I bought a used desk for $10 and then took up my 400 books. They looked really, really sad.

Almost the entire store was empty. Pathetic didn't begin to describe it.

So I told my wife-at-the-time I needed to go buy some books and headed out that weekend to find books around the Pacific Northwest. I managed to bring home another thousand paperbacks.

I spent more than $200, but not part of our household funds. I had been playing on blackjack teams in Vegas for a number of years before I met my-then-wife and never told her I had money in cutout paperbacks in my book collections that I had been using to pay for college. The rule about my books was that if they were in a bag, no one touched them. No one bothered to ask me how I could get through college without a loan and only worked a few nights tending bar and driving a school bus. Her parents paid for her expenses.

(I finally told her a few years ago. She is still a friend.)

So I took three hundred out of my own "college fund" and bought the books. They still looked very sad in the room full of empty shelves.

I hung out a sign. No one came at first. Nothing to come for.

So I kept searching for more books, garage sales, you name it, and slowly people started to find the little store down the hall. And I had enough books by that point to sell them or trade them something.

Eventually I grew out of that room, took over the big lawyer's office and then a year later moved the store into its own building down on the street. All while finishing my masters in architecture and then starting law school.

Magic Bakery

The young writer has their one finished book. It is up for sale and no one is buying. Covers, blurbs, opening, and self problem fixed.

No one is buying the book.

Why not?

Imagine you are a customer and you see this great sign for a bakery. Makes your mouth water at the idea of getting something.

You go in. The bell on the door jingles and around you are massive empty shelves and display cases.

All empty except for up near the cash register is this one pie.

If you were the customer, what would you do? Be honest...

You would turn around and walk out, of course. No way are you going to buy from a bakery that only has one product sitting there all alone.

There is no magic to this concept. It is just a logical customer reaction.

You have no product yet.

But that can be fixed...

Now if you stay writing, creating, you will slowly fill the shelves and display cases.

And since in the Magic Bakery nothing spoils, eventually the shelves and the cases will be full. And as you do get more product, some people will stay and buy.

I have over 300 different products in my magic bakery. And many of the products are in different forms.

You know the business concept at play: Selection and flavors. Things to bring the customers to the register to buy.

This concept is not so magic. It is just logical business.

So if you are discouraged about your first or third novel not selling what you hoped, just think of that big empty bakery and go back to writing. Given enough time, you will fill it.

Or at least get enough product in the bakery so that people will start buying as they did in my little bookstore.

2

So what makes this bakery so magic anyway? Copyright, that's what.

As the *Copyright Handbook* says, "Copyright is the legal device that provides the creator of a work of art or literature, or a work that conveys information or idea, the right to control how the work is used."

So what is so magic about that? All countries in the world have copyright protections in one form or another. As of the writing of this chapter, almost all countries in the world have signed onto one copyright convention or another, agreeing to the basic aspects of copyright protections.

In fact, here in the States, copyright protection was written into the Constitution right from the beginning, it is that important.

But what makes it magic? Actually just one phrase in that definition I gave you is the source of the magic.

"... the right to control how the work is used."

SPOILED COPYRIGHT

Spoiled copyright is a concept that is flat hard to imagine now in this modern world of electronic shelves. As I said in the last chapter, that pie you have sitting there in your shop will never spoil.

Copyright never spoils.

And since we are using a pie as a metaphor for copyright, imagine baking a pie and it will taste just as good five years later as it did on the day you baked it.

Or 70 years later. Or 100 years later if you live for another 30 years after the baking.

This idea that copyright never spoils is almost impossible for writers coming out of traditional publishing to wrap minds around. It took me some time I must admit.

Traditional publishing companies (for decades) used the produce model for books. They treated books like fruit. Not kidding.

The publishers would set a time the book would appear. Then the book would appear and within a set time the book would "spoil" in the eyes of the publisher and bookstores and be pulled and returned to the publisher for credit. For all intents and purposes, that book was dead.

Rotten fruit. Very few books survived that fate. Very, very few.

The reality was that the copyright was just fine. It actually hadn't spoiled. Just the publishers thought of it as dead.

And so did the authors.

And even if an author got the rights back from the company, chances are the book never saw the light of day again.

Writers who got books reverted still had the right to control the use of the book, sure, but the belief was that the copyright had spoiled and the book or story was done. Used up. Rotted fruit.

Then along comes this new world and electronic shelves with unlimited space. And suddenly all those dead and spoiled books took on a new life.

The magic of copyright never spoiling.

A book that only had four weeks on the shelf 20 years ago now had a chance to find a new audience who weren't even born the first time the book appeared.

My first novel came out in 1989. So basically anyone under 35 would not have read that book unless they found it in a used bookstore. Now that first novel is back out and earning me money for the first time in almost 30 years. And finding new readers who might enjoy it.

It is in this new world that the hard fact of a copyright never spoiling actually started to become a reality to many writers.

It also, after about six or seven years, started to dawn on the major publishers as well, which is why they now buy all rights for the entire life of a copyright. They now understand as well that copyright has value over long periods of time and won't spoil. (They haven't figured out what to do with the rights they are keeping, but they have figured out enough to keep them.)

The magic in the copyright-filled pie now rules. But like with any good magic, you have to know how to unleash the spell. I will get to that.

FIRST SALE AND ELECTRONIC LICENSE

Right now, before I go any farther here in chapter two, I had better get everyone on the same page with a few more basics.

Copyright is the protection of the expression. So when you sell a paper copy of the book, you transfer no copyright. Copyright can only be transferred by a written agreement. You are basically selling a block of paper. Nothing more.

That physical book, that pile of paper, exists and the new owner of the book can sell the block of paper itself. But they have no right to take any of the words from the book and use them.

None. They bought the paper, not the words on the paper.

This is called the First Sale Doctrine and it applies mostly only to paper books.

So in Magic Bakery terms, when a customer in the Magic Bakery buys a piece of your pie (paperback piece), the piece remains in the pie even though the customer gets to enjoy the taste of the pie and walk out of the store with a pile of paper. The piece never leaves the pie.

Magic. An ever-replenishing inventory. Wish I would have had that with my bookstore.

Now we have the new electronic books. So you have the slice of your pie called "Electronic Rights" up on Amazon.

Basically what you have done is rented from the big Amazon Mall some space to include your Magic Bakery inside their mall.

You also have your Magic Bakery in the Kobo Mall, the B&N Mall, and so on.

When a customer comes through your door and wants a piece of pie in electronic form, they can enjoy it, but they have bought nothing. They have licensed the right to read it only.

Nothing more.

They cannot trade or sell that electronic copy. They own nothing and in fact, you never sold them anything, you licensed to the reader the right to read the work.

Nothing more. **First Sales does not apply to electronic copies.**

So either selling paper copies to a reader or licensing electronic copy to a reader, your pie remains whole sitting in your Magic Bakery.

So over a month's time you sell or license 100 pieces of that pie. The pie has not changed or diminished or spoiled in any fashion.

Every store on the planet wishes for magic inventory like that. Only writers and artists and other copyright holders have it.

WHY ONLY A PIECE?

This is now where the real fun and magic starts to happen.

Why didn't I say that a person buying the paper book didn't buy the entire pie?

Because the entire pie is not just paperback rights. Or electronic licensing rights. Or audio rights.

Say you write a novel. The novel is the pie. The copyright is what you license from the pie, the pieces of the pie, basically.

Each area of the pie is a different right. One small slice is paperback rights, one small slice is hardback rights, one small slice is electronic, one small slice is audio, and on and on.

You never sell the entire pie.

Now going to traditional publishers, they want to buy the entire pie and put your magic in their store. And writers are doing that all the time, allowing their magic pie to leave their bakery.

Visualize it this way: Some person from New York publishing in a suit walks into your Magic Bakery and flops some small amount of money on the counter. You say sure and they take your magic pie and turn and leave your store, leaving that spot on the counter forever empty. FOREVER EMPTY. They walk your magic pie down the mall to their massive anchor store and put your pie in their Magic Bakery.

You have now sold inventory to a store that is competing with your store.

And you will never get that pie back.

In real world terms, this is "all rights for the life of the copyright" contracts. If you see that in your contract for anything, RUN!!

In coming chapters will be a ton more about this problem. And a lot more about how you can divide up the pie, make more money from each slice, and never lose control.

And remember, every story you finish, every novel, every article (including this Magic Bakery book I am writing right now here in front of you) is a new pie. Another product to have in my display cases and on my shelves when a customer comes through the door of my Magic Bakery.

And the larger the store you have, the more product you have, the more customers and the more money you make if you keep the floors swept, the glass on the display cases clean, and a smile on your face.

Frighteningly enough, it really does work that way.

3

How do you slice a magic pie? The answer is simply as many ways as you want.

The wonderful thing about copyright is that you can license any part of it. And you can name the part and dictate the terms and define the shape of the part.

I know this is difficult to imagine. And the pie analogy sort of falls apart because pie is a physical thing that can only be sliced in so many ways.

But image the pie is solid and you have a saw that can slice off a piece so thin you can barely see the slice under a microscope.

Yup, you can do that with a magic pie.

Honest.

A few broad examples...

Say you were approached by a publisher in a small country you had to go to Google to find on the map. The publisher wanted to translate and print your book only in that country's language. And only in hard-back with dust jacket. And only five hundred copies. And only for one year.

You figure out where the country is at and say sure. The contract comes and you get your saw and slice off a tiny, tiny thin license. Translation rights into (country's language only) for hardback only for a run of 500 copies only for only a year.

In a year that tiny, tiny slice will reappear back in the magic pie of copyright for that novel and you can sell it again.

Or say you have a novel headed into a game or movie. You have retained all toy rights. So a manufacture of resin busts comes to you and wants to license the right to make busts of your characters in a limited edition run of one thousand copies signed by the artist.

Out comes the saw and you slice off a tiny, tiny thin license for resin character busts for a limited one thousand copies. And you sell the plush license to the characters to another company and the action figures of the characters to another company and so on and so on.

All limited-time licenses because you understand copyright and contracts.

My wife, Kristine Kathryn Rusch, on her blog, did most of a year about publishing contracts and there is now a book out of those blogs. That is all basic stuff, but you have to know the basics before you can learn how to use the saw to cut tiny, tiny thin pieces.

And you cannot do that if you have allowed the magic pie to leave your control, your Magic Bakery.

Some Horror Stories from the Magic Bakery

These are about magic pies leaving your bakery.

First off, agents, especially book and Hollywood agents, are not your friends, folks. Avoid at all costs. All horror stories start and end with the word "agent."

I am not kidding.

Here is a real-life Magic Bakery horror story. Agent sold a writer's novel series to Hollywood. The writer was uninformed about how copyright really worked and the agent was either a crook or stupid or didn't realize what he was doing. Take your pick.

The contract the writer signed sold (not licensed) the Hollywood studio rights to the books in the series. What the writer didn't know about what his agent told him to sign was that it also gave away all control of his characters.

And Hollywood didn't want him writing any more of those characters since they controlled them. Writer lost in the court. He signed the contract.

In other words, what the writer did was stand behind the counter of his Magic Bakery and watch the Hollywood agent carry his magic pie out of the door and take it to another store to make money for someone else.

Another real story.

Remember a writer by the name of Clancy? Wrote this novel called *The Hunt for Red October* that became a major bestseller and a movie. It had a character in it called Jack Ryan.

Clancy stood behind his counter and watched the magic pie leave his bakery for $500 total. Someone else sliced up the pie as they wanted and the pie became a bestselling book and then a movie. Eventually Clancy sued for the right to even use Jack Ryan as a character again in another book.

They settled and he had to pay to use his own character.

Why? Because he let the magic pie that was *The Hunt for Red October* leave his store to make someone else money.

I bet I could come up with another 20 of these horror stories just off the top of my head. After 40 years in this business I have heard so many of them it makes me sick.

Staying with the Analogy

You have a recipe for a wonderful magic pie. You go to all the work to create that pie and use special ingredients that make that pie special.

Then not only do you sell the magic pie you created and let it leave your business, you sell the recipe to the pie as well and all the ingredients. And you sell the right to ever make anything similar to it again.

Why would anyone do that?

I ask myself that every day because it happens 100s, if not 1,000s of times every day in Magic Bakeries all over the world.

Writers do not know what they have, do not understand the value of the golden goose that is the story or novel they created.

So they sell their magic pie for all rights for the life of the copyright to a major publisher. Movie rights, toy rights, translation rights, video, audio, electronic, paper, and on and on. All making someone else money.

And even worse, the writers often sign a contract saying they will not go back and make more magic pies without permission from the buyer of the last magic pie.

Might as well shut that Magic Bakery down. It is finished.

Go to any convention and watch the young writers flocking to agents, listen to the discussions about how to break into traditional publishing.

Then as you listen, realize what they are working so hard to do is make sure their magic pie leaves their Magic Bakery.

Summary Statement

Never ever let your entire magic pie out of your control.

License slices only and then for a limited time only.

Nothing more.

And slice the pieces you do license very, very thin. As thin as you can.

And then keep making new magic pies to fill the shelves.

4

I started off chapter three with a question and an answer: "How do you slice a magic pie? The answer is simply as many ways as you want."

But first you have to have a magic pie to slice.

You have to have copyright to license. And that is the rub, the place where so many writers flat run into a massive wall. It takes time and a lot of practice and knocking down personal demons to produce new stories and novels regularly.

Anyone can do it for a short time. A year. Maybe two. But then with just a few cases in their Magic Bakery half full and the rest of the bakery still empty, the writer fades away.

The magic pies don't spoil as I talked about earlier, but they sure gather dust. No one comes through the door and no one keeps up the bakery.

When the writer stops caring about their own business, the business dies. It is called quitting and it is the only way to fail in this modern world of publishing.

Now I understand how hard this is. Clearly understand. And this problem of looking at empty shelves almost got me as well.

So a personal story...

As Kris and I moved from traditional publishing to indie publishing,

I got the statement from young writers over and over how easy I had it because I already had work.

Well, I knew how to tell stories, sure. And I had sold millions of books and had made my living in publishing since 1988. Sure.

But the indie world made me into a flat beginner. So when some young writer with three or four or five novels said that I had this huge advantage over them, I just nodded and said nothing.

The only real advantage I had was that I was a better storyteller.

You see, the dirty truth was I had no books. Well, I actually had two, one was my first published novel I had the rights back to and one was a thriller I had written and then tossed in a drawer. And I had a ton of short stories.

For almost all of my career, I was a media writer and a ghost writer. I wrote over one hundred novels under pen names or media books and I didn't own a one of them. I had baked the magic pie in someone else's bakery.

So I had nothing but the short stories and I didn't feel I wanted to bring the thriller or the first novel out right off the bat.

I felt I needed to fill my Magic Bakery.

It felt impossible, I must admit.

I would stand in that Magic Bakery and stare at all the empty shelves and wonder how in the world at my age I would ever fill them. In other words, I had to start my writing career completely over in my 60s.

So with two novel pies sitting in the back room and my bakery almost completely empty except for some shelves of short story pies to one side, I started to work in 2011. All of the shelves were cleaned and polished and just waiting for me to fill them.

Waiting for me to get baking.

I did some more short stories to get started and then lost most of a year to a personal friend's death and estate.

By the time I got back to writing, it was almost 2013. And again I did more short stories to try to get going.

Then in the summer of 2013 I decided I really needed to get baking. I was tired of staring at all the empty shelves.

So I started up *Smith's Monthly,* which needed a novel, four short stories, and a serial every month. And I had to write it all. Every word of a monthly seventy thousand word magazine.

I wrote like crazy that summer to get a few novel pies on the shelf and the first issue came out in October 2013. I am a little behind at the moment here in 2017 as I write this, but I expect to be caught up by October 2017 with the 4th full year without missing a month. And then I plan to start into the fifth year.

Imagine in October a wall of my Magic Bakery will be full of forty-eight magic pies with the sign over the wall *Smith's Monthly* pies.

After four years I now have pies of different sorts filling my bakery.

These nonfiction books taken from blog posts.

The short stories have all been published standalone and a slice of each novel was taken and licensed to WMG to publish standalone.

And I combined slices of the short stories to be in collections and so on. Not counting short stories, last year alone I did twenty-six major books. The year before over thirty. This year will again be over thirty.

I went from having a mostly empty bakery to a decent inventory in my Magic Bakery in four years.

Over a hundred major products and hundreds of short stories.

And the customers are coming, even though I have done very little, if any advertising.

Seems people like the taste of a Cold Poker Gang pie or a Seeders Universe pie or a Poker Boy pie.

This Takes Time

There are a number of hot, young (in numbers of books) gurus out there at this moment preaching how to sell more books by this or that advertising device. Some of the advice is pretty good. And WMG is following some of it in moderation.

But almost without fail, these "experts" have an almost empty Magic Bakery. They have gotten very, very good at driving customers into their empty store, but have forgotten the reason to have the store in the first place.

Think folks. You might, through some advertising hype or another, go into a store you have never visited. We all do. Standard business stuff. But if you walked into the store with only a few things on the shelves, would you make it a point of going back?

Nope.

In our north Pop Culture Collectables store, we have over 20,000 books and 100,000 comics, toys, cars, games, and collectables of all sorts. It fills four large rooms and when someone comes in they are always surprised at how much we have and they always take time to explore all four rooms.

And they often buy something they didn't even know they wanted.

If they came through the door and we had two collectable cars, an old toy, five used paperbacks, and six used comics in the four rooms, think anyone would bother to stay? Or come back?

Nope.

It has taken us over a year now to get the store as full as it is. And we had all the inventory in the warehouse. It took a year to get it all out and priced.

Things take time.

As writers, we must create our own inventory. And that flat takes time.

But it will never happen if you don't start.

And it will never happen if you quit.

How to Even Start?

First—As I suggest in a number of classes, do an inventory of your Magic Bakery.

Everything. Every article that might be combined into a book, every short story, every novel.

Everything that you own copyright on and have created. Even stuff still in the back room you are too afraid to bring out and put on a shelf.

Second—See if there is any way to create new products with that inventory? You know, take a small slice from five short stories and combine it into a collection. Things like that.

Or get your work up on BundleRabbit so people can ask for the bundling slice of your pies. And so on and so on.

Third—Figure out your hours. How much time do you spend

writing each week creating new product? What is stopping you from getting some of the work in the back room out to the shelves?

In other words, find your demons. Check Heinlein's Five Rules and be honest about which rule you are falling down on.

Fourth—Make a five-year and ten-year plan. Expect it to take time to fill your shelves of your Magic Bakery.

Early on, make your focus not on getting customers through the door to be disappointed, but on making your Magic Bakery a place where people will want to return over and over when they do find it.

When you start thinking of your writing as a business and a retail store, it really is amazing how clear some basics about writing become.

I knew this four plus years ago when I started filling my shelves. And I do not plan on slowing down because my bakery really is magic. I have as much room as I need to expand when my inventory starts filling the shelves.

And I plan on doing a lot of expanding over the next 10 years.

5

I get a lot of questions about pen names and if writers should use pen names in this modern world of publishing.

So let me use the Magic Bakery to explain my answer to that question.

Now understand, the reason for this book about the Magic Bakery is to help writers understand copyright and the magic power of copyright in this world.

But the metaphor of the bakery can help in business logic as well.

And in sales.

And in promotions. For example, understanding the power of free is clearly illustrated in the Magic Bakery and I will get to that in a later chapter.

But for this chapter, I want to focus on Pen Names.

The New World

In the old world, we had to go down the mall and open up brand new stores and try to fill them every time we started a new pen name.

One store for every pen name.

So most of the time the pen name stores just looked empty and the readers, even if they liked something, had little else to buy.

In this new world, you keep all books under one name.

Think about it. When a customer walks into one of our Pop Culture Collectable stores here on the coast, they see toys, antique jewelry, games, comics, books, cookie jars, clocks, cars, and a bunch more.

We have all the sections in different parts of the store.

So you have a Magic Bakery. A customer walks through the door.

To the right, filling a wall, are all the science fiction pies and cakes. Straight ahead are the romance cakes and rolls, to the left, the mystery pies and snacks.

Then off to one side is the young adult section.

And on all the displays in the middle of the floor are all the short story pies, cakes, rolls, and such.

All are clearly marked so there is no confusion, the descriptions on each shelf clear as to the flavors of the pies.

The customer doesn't have to go to five half-empty stores to find all of your work. They found it all in one store, under one name.

Being Clear

There is no reason at all in this new world of reader-controlled publishing to use a pen name. Keep everything under one name and display that name in bright letters on the outside of your store.

Brand your store to that one name so readers can find everything you do.

They may not like the taste of your mystery blood pies, but they love your romance sweet pies.

Let the readers decide. Give them something to shop for.

Sure, with our stories, we could open a comic store, a toy car store, a collectible card store, a clock store, an antique toy store. Sure.

But it was easier to keep it all in one large store and put it all under one name.

Do the same with your writing.

One name, one Magic Bakery.

6

I get questions all the time about free. Should an author put up their book for free? How about their first book in a series? Does leaving something up for free forever work?

Interestingly enough, The Magic Bakery works perfectly to illustrate the answer to these questions so writers can decide for themselves.

All I'm going to be talking about in this chapter is basic, standard-retail sales practices. I won't tell you one thing new in the world. You can see some of these practices working every day from grocery stores to music stores.

But explaining these practices to authors who do not understand basic sales of retail has been an issue. And thus extreme myths have built up around the use of free in book sales.

And it seems everyone has an opinion, often not based on anything but "It worked for me for a little bit."

So using the Magic Bakery, let me show you some of the simple ways that free can be an effective sales tool for your products.

And some of the really boneheaded ways to use free that will hurt your business.

Copyright in Free

One quick point here in this book focused on mostly understanding copyright. When you give a story or book away for free, you do not lose the copyright protection on that work in any way.

My Basic Rule of Thumb About Free

Nothing ever sits on a bookstore shelf, real-wood shelf or electronic shelf, for free.

It is a very simple rule and when I say that to someone they automatically think I am against free. I am not. I am against using free in a poor business way. I use free all the time to help sales, as does WMG Publishing.

So now to the Magic Bakery to illustrate why this rule works for me and for others.

First, a simple positive way to use free.

A customer comes into your bakery. You have a wall of about 20 pies that are your novels, some are grouped together because they are series pies. All are priced. You may have a reduced price on a few first pies, but all are priced in a reasonable and fair manner.

You have a large counter in the middle of the room of short story pies, smaller and at a lower price than the larger pies on the wall.

You have specials you are running around the cash register.

And there, beside the specials, near the cash register, on top of a glass counter, you have a plate of bite-sized pieces of your latest creation for readers to sample.

The sign under that plate says, "Take one."

You have maybe a dozen pieces on the plate with small plastic forks and when those pieces of pie are gone, you take the plate to the back to wash. The idea is to get customers, for free, sampling your work so they will buy.

This form of use of free is standard in almost every form of store. You see this a lot in grocery stores. And in bakeries.

For authors, we do this as sample chapters in the back of another book.

Or free short stories for a week on a web site. And so on. Lots of ways to give limited, small samples in this modern world.

The key in sales are LIMITED and SHORT TERM.

Keep free short term and limited and never put it on a bookshelf anywhere.

Now the wrong way to use free.

A customer walks through your door and you have a wall of 20 pies in glass cases, all the smaller short story pies in a case in the center, and some specials near the cash register.

And there on your wall are three pies that say, "Free."

And a bunch of short stories that are "Free."

The customer can take an entire pie for free or buy one. As a customer, what would you do? Duh. You take the free pie and leave.

(Or you question the value of any of the pies and leave without anything.)

And, because of copyright, the pie is still sitting there after someone takes it for free. Magic Bakery, remember? So more and more people start hearing you are giving away free pies in your Magic Bakery.

And pretty soon your customers start to change. The only people who come through the door are people who only want the free stuff. They would never buy something under any circumstances, but you are giving your pies away for free, so they take one.

Pretty soon there would be lines out the door to get your free pies and you would make nothing. The free takers would crowd out and devalue the pies you are trying to sell.

That is the wrong use of free for any reason you may want to make up to justify it.

Now discounting is another topic. There are ways to discount first books in a series to entice buyers into getting into a series. This is also a common practice in most stores, actually.

A Personal Example

I live in a small town that has a huge discount mall. Now all smart shoppers know that the big chains mark up the prices before lowering them for the discount stores. Makes the "discount" price look better to those looking for deals.

Now I use the mall as a place to walk on rainy days. And at times, I go into stores to look around. The stores have their "discount" racks clear to the back. The discount racks are what is left of the normal merchandise that hasn't sold and they are just trying to clear.

But to get to that actually discounted stuff, I have to walk through their entire store. And every-so-often, that sales trick gets me and I see something I don't mind paying full price for.

That is a standard retail trick of discounting to get a customer in to buy other stuff.

But not one place in any of those stores is there a free item. Why not? Because they are all businesses, that's why not.

Writers need to learn how to act and think like regular business people.

So How to Use Free in Your Bakery?

A one-day give-away of one of your pies. Only for a very limited time and only for a very limited number.

I try not to laugh in writer's faces who tell me they have "sold" 20,000 books and when I ask, they actually gave away that many books.

Free is not a sale.

Free is free. A sale is when you make something from the exchange. So follow basic retail practices. If you are going to give something away for free, do it for a short time and a limited number.

And then make it special.

And again, never put it on a shelf of any bookstore.

Once again, over the years, I have tried not to laugh when writers go on about how to game Amazon's system and get their book there for free. I have laughed many times, but not in the writer's faces, luckily.

You ever wonder why you have to game the smartest business on the planet at the moment to get something on their shelves for free? Oh, let me think— They don't make any money.

Yet they are a business. You are taking up their shelf space with something that makes them no money.

You walk into our Pop Culture Collectable stores here in town and there isn't one thing on the shelves for free. So do we give things away at times? Sure. Free comic book day once a year. Things like that. Promotions that are limited and short term to bring customers into the store to buy other things.

Limited and short term.

There is no reason at all for us to go to the time and energy to get inventory and then put it on our shelves for free. No reason for any business to do that.

And certainly no reason for you to do that in your Magic Bakery.

Just imagine walking into a pie shop and there is a wall of pies that all look great, and five or six of them say, "Free" under it. Try to imagine that.

If you can't imagine that, good. But if you want to start learning how to use free correctly, then start looking around at other businesses outside of electronic books and see what they do with free.

In the business and sales world, free is a powerful, powerful tool if used correctly and for the right reasons.

Make sure your Magic Bakery is a place someone can come to buy your wonderful work. And that free is used in ways (not on the shelves of your bakery) to entice buyers into your bakery.

Free is short time, limited supply, and never on the major book-store shelves.

Simple Magic Bakery rules-of-thumb that are nothing more than standard retail business practices.

7

I knew I was going to need to talk about this topic in a chapter and honestly, have dreaded it. Writers, especially newer writers have no understanding of the value of their own work and how others value it.

So with that problem in mind, I am going to try to add a level of understanding of value of copyright to this book. For most of you, I will fail at this, but at least I can say I tried right here in Chapter Seven.

I'm calling this chapter "Perceived Value" of the inventory in the Magic Bakery.

I cannot even begin to count the hundreds and hundreds of times I have heard a new writer say, "I'm new so I should give my stuff away or sell it for only 99 cents."

I will not get into a pricing discussion here. There are lots of other places out there in the vast world of the inner-tubes to shout about your price being better or worse than another price. Go to it.

I am talking about "Perceived Value."

The Dollar Store

Here in the US, there are numbers of chains of stores known for selling things at one dollar. To make sure I was correct in my perceived value of the goods in the Dollar Store, I stopped by the one here on the coast a few days ago.

Lots of small toys, all cheap. Lots of household stuff you could get for a buck in any supermarket.

Everything that was either normally a buck in another store or some cheap knockoff. The entire store.

Now, if I had gone in there looking for a fine bottle of wine, I would have been very disappointed. But I went in there knowing I would be finding exactly what I found. Cheap stuff worth less than a buck.

My "Perceived Value" of that store was right on. I went in expecting cheap and I got cheap. Both in price and quality of the goods.

Let me repeat that: **I got cheap price and a cheap quality of the goods.**

And I was not surprised.

So I log onto a website for a writer I do not know. (Most writers, both experienced and new. I have no way of knowing the difference. And neither do readers.) And I see nothing but free and 99 cent books. What do I expect?

I expect a cheap and lower level of goods.

And since I like to be entertained and only have so much reading time, I will go find another author. Yes, I will pay more. But my two hours of reading won't be wasted.

Quality wine vs. a buck bottle of whine. Sorry, I like a good wine.

Readers are no different. (Sure, there are the only buy cheap or free reader and they sometimes find something worth reading. I got that. Not my customer.)

The Discount Mall Principle

Perceived value is a major art form in discount malls. We have a massive discount mall here and all of the stores in that mall show the original price on every item and then the discount price and the sale price and then for today only take off another 25% if you can stand on one leg and snort.

But that original price is right there on the tag. You can get a $200 coat for today only if you snort loud enough for $49.99. The customer has a perceived value of the coat at $200. Wow, what a deal and they grab it.

Also top brand-name stores are in the mall. Nike for example. Just by walking in that door the customer knows of the perceived value of a Nike shoe.

The Magic Bakery Value

Since you own your Magic Bakery and create all the product, you have the freedom to set your own prices. A logical way to do that is to figure out what other books in your genre are selling for. Then look at what Amazon suggests is a sweet spot.

In other words, toss out all your emotions about the lack of value of your work and do the research to figure out what is a good price range for your genre.

It really is very simple. And then, if you have the price stated clearly, you can do those special one-day sales to see how well your customers can snort.

You set the perceived value of your work.

Do not set it with emotions and fear and self-loathing.

Pretty sure self-loathing is not a principle in business pricing economics. (Except for young writers in fiction. Since new writers gained this control, they have taken self-loathing of their own work into the gutter of pricing. Stop now. Just stop.)

The New Traditional Model of Perceived Value

Here is where things get tough and I will not turn one person's head, but I have to talk about it.

Intellectual property (IP) is what makes up all the pies and cakes in your bakery. Everyone got that?

IP has a value. (Yeah, Dean, we know, we know.)

But alas, you do not know at what level.

Ever wonder why over the last ten years traditional publishing contracts have gone to all-rights for the life of the copyright?

Ever wonder why it is almost impossible now to get books back from traditional publishers once you have sold all rights?

Because IP has a value. Not just a sales value of possible income earned. An accounting value to major corporations.

There are many, many companies now that are buying IP and have no intent of ever marketing it or publishing it or making it into a movie. They simply want the IP.

Yes, your IP. (Your pie, your cake.)

I'll bet you didn't know that there are a ton of major companies out there with the only job, the only reason they exist, is to value IP for other companies.

Don't believe me? Simply Google "IP Valuation" and then do some reading.

THIS PRACTICE HAS ONLY BEEN AROUND FOR A DECADE OR TWO. Yeah, about the time traditional publishers stopped putting in even decent claw-back clauses for your rights and bought everything.

They bought your entire magic pie and they took it out of your store and they know how to value it. They do not care if anything is ever made. They need the value for their bottom lines in the accounting.

Your pie adds value to the big corporation base.

At the moment there are four or five ways that are basic ways that these valuation companies value your IP. But a couple of the sites said there are over 25 other alternative methods.

Trust me, traditional publishing, after grabbing your IP for next to nothing, leaving your bakery with your pie, know all the tricks of making your IP far, far more valuable to their bottom line than what they actually paid.

There is even one method called "Relief from Royalty" that allows the valuation to be made up in case they needed to sell the movie rights, or the translation rights, or whatever. And assuming all those rights did sell in this made-up "arms-length" scenario, that would be the value of your IP.

And did you know one major thing about IP??? It is a property and thus can, under certain circumstances, be depreciated by the corporation.

So they buy your IP for $5,000 because they promised you a movie. They now own it.

They value it under one of the many ways of valuation far, far higher than what they paid and get some major valuation company to sign off on it.

Then they start depreciating it to get the tax deductions on other money coming in. Only one minor way.

Another method is the "Venture Capital Method" which is a name for what I try to get writers to understand about the value of their copyright over the 70 years past death. This method basically values the possible future cash flow OVER THE ASSETS LIFE. And there is no adjustment to any probability of success. Just a wild guess as to what it might make over its lifetime. Yup.

Your wonderful pie is nothing more than an accounting trick.

(If you want to read one good article about this on the IP Watchdog site, it is here. But do the Google search. It will blow you away.)

Summary

—Never sell all rights. Never let your pie leave your bakery for any reason or any amount of money.

—Research and learn the common indie prices for your books, both paper and electronic. (Ignore traditional publishing prices, as you have just figured out, they sort of don't much care any more.)

—Grow a sense of self-worth that your writing has value. Then treat it as it has value.

How your readers perceive your work is everything in this new world. Start making sure they don't think of your stuff as cheap plastic doomed for the Dollar Store.

Doors to the Bakery

Any business must have a way to get into the business.

For example, at our North collectable store here in town you can enter through an interior staircase and climb, or climb an exterior staircase. Both methods take some work for customers and we also have a special entrance in the back that comes in without stairs.

Three entrances. We have the store full of enough cool stuff, we hope it is worth the customer's climb.

So how do readers, publishers, and others get into your bakery to buy your magic pies?

The fun of Magic Bakeries, there are many actual doors.

Far more doors, actually, than you have products in the bakery.

Yeah, a Magic Bakery is a strange place, but it is magical after all.

An example: Say you have written one short story only and published it.

The magic pie that is that short story is sitting on the shelf all by itself. Your bakery is empty and no customers are really going to stop by, even if they happen to find your one story somewhere.

So at that moment in time, your bakery only has a few dozen doors and nothing to hold customers when they arrive.

Why that many doors? Because you have been smart and put the story out wide, meaning Amazon, B&N, Kobo, D2D and so on through all the places D2D and Smashwords distribute to. (I'll talk about paper below.)

So for the sake of simple, say that your one story is for sale at a dozen places.

One story times a dozen places is a dozen ways someone can find your story and thus enter your Magic Bakery.

Every Story is a Door into Your Work

This concept flies in the face of the old myths about writing slow, only doing a book a year or two. Sorry if you are still using one of those myths as an excuse to not sit and write much. You need to figure out how to change that.

Productivity is king in this modern world and the reason is simple. Every story or novel or collection you put out is a doorway to your Magic Bakery and all your other work.

So say I have 300 different products out there in one form or another. (I have more.) Each product is sold wide. So I have about 3,600 doors into my bakery that readers can come through at any moment. Or movie folks or gaming offers or overseas publishers.

Those doors are all over the world, folks.

This is the basic concept of discoverability in this Magic Bakery metaphor.

The more work you have out for sale, the more readers can discover all of your work.

Other Doors?

There are hundreds and hundreds of ways to get readers through one of your doors. Again, your Magic Bakery must have product, be clean, and well lit, meaning people can see what flavor of magic pie they want to try.

An example of one great way is to sell a short story to a magazine or anthology. The door is your story in that book or magazine, which will be different when you publish the story out wide later on.

For example, you sell a story to *Asimov's* and it is printed in their magazine. They get to about a hundred thousand readers through their varied means. That door is now open into your bakery because readers there can enjoy your story and follow your name through the door into your other work.

Bundles are another great door that opens and closes. For example, as I write this, I have novels in two great bundles. Now both novels are out there wide in electronic and paper. But for three weeks, each novel in each bundle will have a new door that readers can follow to my Magic Bakery and all my other work.

There are many, many other ways. From Bookbub to Facebook promotions to Amazon ads to giving a story away on your blog every week and so on. So, so many ways and more being created every day.

But the basic premise is that any time you can set up a way for readers to find one of your stories, it creates a door into your bakery and all your other work.

Create Doors by Creating More Product

One of the most common questions I get is about collections. The question is always in a form like this: "If I have five of my short stories in a collection, should I also publish them stand-alone?"

My answer is always yes, of course. A collection is one door times all the places you have it for sale. For sake of the math, say 1 x 12 equals 12 doors.

If you put up the stories as stand-alone stories as well, you have created 60 more doors. So with stories in a collection and stand-alone, you would have at least 72 doors into your bakery.

That many more chances that a reader can discover your Magic Bakery and come in and sample more.

Take those 30 stories I wrote in April of 2017. I created 30 magic pies. Let's count the doors into my Magic Bakery I got from that month of having fun writing short fiction.

Each story will be published stand-alone. 30 x 12 = 360 doors.

Each will be put into a *Smith's Monthly* volume. About 8 volumes. 8 x 12 = 96 doors.

Each will be put in a five-story collection at some point. 6 collections. 6 x 12 = 72 doors.

So from writing 30 stories in 30 days and getting them out wide and in various forms, I created about 528 new entrance doors into my Magic Bakery. And who knows what the future of those 30 stories holds for even more doors.

That's why productivity is king in this new world. The more magic pies, the more doors into your bakery.

Now for Some Real Magic

The magic pie (your story) never leaves your bakery. Yet at the same time, that story exists out in all those places for readers to sample and find the door back to where that magic pie lives and all your other work lives.

Through the magic of copyright, your magic pie can be on the shelf in your store, completely in your control, while also being available for someone to license and read in electronic form all over the world.

So that is pretty nifty magic all by itself. It is the basis for the modern Magic Bakery.

But there is more. **The magic of paper copies.**

A paper copy of your book gets printed and sold. One reader found the door to your work. All great.

But that paper copy, **not the place it was sold**, but the paper copy itself, remains a door to your store as well.

How is that?

Say the book was read and then was donated to a library and sold there. So now that paper copy opened the door to your bakery for another reader.

This can't happen with electronic licenses. One sale, one customer. But not paper.

Say the book ends up in a used bookstore, the most magical place of all for opening doors to writer's Magic Bakeries. And someone finds it, takes it home, likes it and opens a door into your bakery.

Then trades the book back in or gives it to a library or to a friend.

So you have your work for sale on Amazon and a few other places in paper. Each place is a door to your bakery times the number of books you have in print.

But watch the number of sales each month in print, because each sale is a potential new door into your work for a reader or numbers of new readers at some point.

This concept has always been around, just never talked much about in the old traditional days. Writers back then only had one door and that was to sell the story to a publisher. And Magic Bakeries are pretty much non-existent when you sell all rights to traditional publishers.

But now paper copies can be a massive tool in bringing in loyal customers to your Magic Bakery because every paper book sold becomes a possible number of future doors.

The New World of Discoverability (I mean doors)

The thinking is simple: The more product you have in your Magic Bakery, the more possible doors there are out there for someone to find your work.

But you can see why I have always shouted about the silliness of being exclusive anywhere. It limits your doors into your bakery. It really is that simple.

And the more doors you have, the more people can find your Magic Bakery with all your work sitting gleaming on the shelves.

And the more product in your place, the more doors and the more readers will shop around when they do find you.

So above I said I have about 3,600 doors plus into my bakery. That number was based on just electronic license.

But hundreds of my books are in print and selling and each time one books sells, I know for a fact that one copy that sold might be a future door to a brand new customer.

And that's why sometimes my Magic Bakery gets real crowded with customers. And for any shop owner, that is a fun thing to see.

9

Success and the Future

Now there are two words that almost every writer I have met can't fathom or even see when it comes to their own writing and business.

Now granted, some writers give those two words lip service, and in different workshops Kris and I work at getting writers to think ahead. It feels like walking into a brick wall.

Success and future planning when it comes to writing and a publishing business are just not possible for almost every writer to fathom.

And honestly, I understand that. My goal, for a very long time, was to make a living at my writing. I had NO concept what that meant other than the basics of "paying my bills" with my writing income that month.

Notice the thought is making a living, not a career. A living can happen for a year. And a ton of writers in this modern world of indie publishing can make a living for a year or two, as long as the hot-new-trend they stumbled into continues.

You see this a great deal in the writers in Kindle Select. (And three years from the time I write this writers will be asking me "What was

Kindle Select?") This book of blog posts will far, far outlast that blip in the publishing history.

These writers give no thought at all to building a career.

Let me give a quick definition that I use. "Making a Living" is a very short-term goal. "Building a Career" is the ability to make a living every year, year-after-year, over decades.

Everything I teach and everything in this book is aimed at helping writers build careers. If you want the most recent fad, go have fun. Bank the money is my suggestion.

So now, for this chapter, I am going to talk mostly about success.

Selling to Traditional Publishing

Got to deal with this first because to many beginning writers, simply selling to a major publisher is a success.

The sad writers who do this in 2017 (as I write this) are not giving one thought to the future or long-term career building. They are selling all rights to their books for a few thousand dollars and the pat on their heads that tells them that some English major in an office in New York really likes them.

Then for a short time a year or two later their books will be published overpriced, restricted in distribution, and with a great sense of "Is that all there is?"

Soon the book will be pushed to the back and forgotten, just an IP valuation on a corporate balance sheet. But wow is their family proud of them, but wonder why they are still working their day jobs.

To these writers success is measured by a sale to a single editor. That's it.

That's their definition of success. Sort of sad, huh?

And by signing the contract they make their future with those books very simple. They no longer own the books, so those books have no future.

Reality of Numbers

Publishing is a very large industry. Very large. And if you know how to manage your magic pies correctly, your work in publishing can extend into many other areas as well. Movies, television, games, to name just some obvious ones.

But writers tend to be focused on how to make an extra sale here, or give something away there, to gain more imaginary numbers on a mailing list. These writers make no plans and have no concept at all of what might happen when it comes to real success and real money.

One question we do in both the online monthly business class and a variation of it in the Strengths Business workshop, is what would happen if you knew suddenly that in three months 100,000 dollars would hit your account.

The answers are head-shaking because it is clear no writer we have asked that question to has thought ahead to that kind of small success. (And yes, that is a small success in publishing.)

And if you are thinking you would take that small success, I sure understand. But that also illustrates the problem. Your vision, your ability to see a future and real success, is very limited.

A good attorney friend of mine once said that he envied me with my job. He went to work, made great money, and then went home. All the money he could make in a day he made. To keep making money he had to go back to work the next day. But when I got up and went to writing, every day I had a chance of hitting a home run and making millions.

And sometimes that possibility was with a novel I wrote years before.

He saw the publishing profession so much better than most writers.

Sadly, there is nothing I can say to most here in this chapter to convince most anyone. Think about it. Even those who do make the huge money are always called "lucky" or "outliers" by those who can't imagine doing it themselves.

There is a vested interest in writers as a class to not think about real success or the future.

So What Do You Do to Get Ready for Success?

First, never sell your entire magic pie. For any reason to anyone.
Keep that magic pie, that copyright, firmly planted in your bakery.

That is the basic center of everything. Then your pie, as the future unfolds, can earn you money.

What else can you do?

—Start studying writers who are successful in careers. Not those flash writers chasing the most recent trend. Study writers who have been writing and selling and in a career in one form or another for decades. There are a lot of us.

—Start understanding business and money. Your Magic Bakery is a business. Start understanding things like cash streams, corporations, tax protections, and so on. For example, that 100,000 you get in suddenly. If you understand what I just said, you will keep it all. If you don't, you will pay over half of it to governments.

—Start learning how stories and novels get outside of publishing. What do you need to do? Learn that.

—Get your work into every market you can around the world and let it build. And keep writing what you love.

—Learn all the ways you can divide up your magic pies.

—Then be patient. You can't learn any of the above overnight, or even in a year.

You are a writer. Write the next book, the next story, the next blog post as I am doing here.

Then, as I am doing here, after you are finished, see how many ways you can turn slices of the pie you just created into cash streams.

Next chapter will be about thinking about the future. You know, that place beyond Christmas.

10

Beyond Next Year

As I said last chapter, it has been my observation that most writers never look more than a year out, if that. And that lack of being able to see five years and ten years and fifty years into the future causes all sorts of really bad decisions.

Now, I wish I could say I had been an exception to this in my first few decades or so in publishing. Nope. Kris was a bunch better at looking long term and making decisions based on that vision. But I wasn't. And wow did I make some boneheaded mistakes because of that lack of vision.

So now here I am trying to maybe help one or two people expand into the future their plans and hopes and focus.

The Magic Bakery

It is the future that really is important in a Magic Bakery. Let me try to explain why in just a couple simple points.

—Your copyright, your magic pie, will last and stay fresh for 70 years past your death (In the US, 50 years in other countries). At that 70 year mark your heirs will lose control over it, but that does not mean they still can't make money from it for another 70 years or longer.

—You have no idea what technology will be coming in the next century. No clue. (New ways to cut your magic pie.)

(Example: I wrote one of the very first electronic books Pocket Books ever published. The year was 2000 and trust me, even with electronic books being sort of in existence for a decade or more before that, I thought it stupid. Shows what I knew. Again, in those years I wasn't the best at seeing the future.)

—If you structure the business of your bakery correctly (a coming chapter), your business will not only make you a lot of money in your lifetime, but also survive you and thrive. But the business has to be set up for the future.

So Many Ways to Fail

Those three points above seem very simple and obvious, don't they? But wow can you fail in so many ways when you stand in your Magic Bakery, surrounded by all your magic pies, and have no sense of tomorrow.

Let me give you three major failure points.

—Sell your book to a major traditional publisher (or movie producer) for all rights for the term of the copyright. Pie vanishes from your bakery. Writers who do this give zero thought to the future of their business at all. To them their book has no value beyond the tiny pat on the head traditional publishers give them and a little bit of money. Or hope for a movie that won't get made.

—You don't learn business and sales, so your store sits there with few customers and eventually you drift away to do something else. Your pies never mold or grow old, but dust covers the shelves and paint peels off the front of your store and no one goes in. (This happens to 80-90% of all fiction writers, sadly.)

You all know this kind of thing. Your store becomes a "whatever-happened-to?" store. We have all walked down a mall, seen an empty spot and asked "Whatever happened to that place?" Imagine that was where your Magic Bakery was at and you get the sad idea of what happens when you quit.

—You don't understand how Intellectual Property (IP) works, so you make no preparation for the day something happens to you. So those 70 years plus that your Magic Bakery could remain open and flourishing and making your family or some charity money vanish when they dump your body in the ground.

All three of those major failure points are from lack of being able to deal with the future.

A Ticking Time Bomb

Remember a few chapters back I mentioned the new world of IP Valuation? Not your issue, right? Your stories only make a few hundred so they can't be worth much. Right?

Again, no thought to any future. Courts and estate probate judges are understanding IP valuation and are starting to apply different forms of evaluation. If you are making a nice bit of money from your stories and you have not set up the right structure to move your IP to your heirs, they could get hit with a tax bill upon your death that could destroy everything. Wouldn't that be a nice gift to leave your family?

Easily fixed if you think about the future at all. But alas, most writers don't.

And that leads to the next problem–

What Is Your Magic Bakery Worth?

Most newer writers and all traditionally published writers would say nothing. And the reason for that is that there are no pies on the shelves. The bakery is mostly empty.

Even if there were magic pies on those shelves, most writers would still say it wasn't worth much at all. Why? Because they can't see past a year or so.

Now I understand that moving forward, IP needs freshening at times to remain attractive to the current buyer. Not going to talk about that ongoing task. I know it all too well. So for this, I will assume you do that work, or have it done, or your estate will do it.

So if you can imagine that as a possibility, what might your bakery be worth?

For what amount would I sell all rights to all 300 of my magic pies, plus the bakery itself? What kind of future income do my 300 plus magic pies have possible?

And in three years that number will be past 400, and so on, not counting all the IP that will return to me under the 35 year rule starting in 2026.

Impossible to calculate. But fun to look at when you realize you really are creating something of value, even though it only sells five copies a year. It still has value.

Heinlein's Rule #2 states simply: Finish what you write.

When you finish a story, you have added value to your Magic Bakery. It really is that simple.

How to Learn to Think Forward

Sure, work to make money now. Work to sell your stuff now. But all the while, keep these basic things in mind.

—**Never allow your IP to leave your bakery.** You license slices, nothing more. For only the term needed and when the term is up that slice will magically appear back in your pie.

—**When discouraged, thinking of shutting the doors for good, do an inventory of your existing IP.** Then try to put a value on it, keeping in mind your lifetime and 70 years beyond. Imagine two or three things being made into movies, imagine others being games, still others being part of some unknown tech. Then write the next story or book and add even more value.

—**Learn Business.** Tons of great books for small businesses out there. Understand what a good year of growth might be. That will help with perspective instead of always listening to the latest fad from the latest hot guru of marketing and thinking you are not doing enough.

—**Learn Estates.** It will help you if you figure out a way to help your favorite family and/or charity with your business if you can get it large enough. In other words, write your fun stories for a larger purpose in the future.

—**Make It a Challenge.** You want to have the best bakery. The most successful. The larger, the nicer your bakery is, the more customers you will get, the more sales, the more value. But building the best bakery takes time. Growing any business takes time. Make it a challenge. Not something to be afraid of, but something to have fun with.

Summary

A wonderful thing about our Magic Bakeries: They really are magical.

Copyright is an amazing ingredient in our pies that allows us to build and run these wonderful places full of diverse products. And magically attract customers from all over the world.

Our magic pies can be enjoyed as a book, a movie, an audio file, in tons of different languages, and who knows what else is coming in the future. All without ever leaving our bakery.

Copyright also allows us the time to build these magical places.

You just have to know that the future is out there and first accept it, then plan for it.

11

Maintenance

This book, at its heart, has been about the business of fiction. And selling fiction. And the copyright associated with fiction.

Fact: So many writers ignore copyright and eventually go away. Long-term writers know copyright and know how to get every bit of money we can from copyright. That might be the most important element to why a long-term writer is a long-term writer and not a "what-ever-happened-to" writer.

Fact: So many writers equate the hours it took to write something with the value of the story. A short story can't have much value because it only took four hours to write it. That is the thinking. I hear that all the time with writers afraid to charge a fair value for their short stories. Head-shaking.

And those two "facts" cause extreme problems, both large and small. And where those two facts come into play the most is in the long-term maintenance of copyright.

How I Learned Value

Early on as a writer, I too equated the value of the time spent with the value of the story. Now understand, I considered myself expensive. I would never sell a story for under 5 cents per word and almost never did a media book for less than $20,000. Often a lot more and ghost novels even more than that.

And I could spend hours writing every day, so I was considered fast. And thus it didn't take me much time at all to earn that advance on a novel or the sale money from a short story. So in my head I had set some value for my work at the amount I could get out of it and that was related to the time I spent writing it.

One simple story fairly early in my career quickly proved to me how stupid that very short-sighted thinking was. The story was called "In the Shade of the Slowboat Man." I wrote it in under three hours while sitting facing Nina Kiriki Hoffman in a living room at a writer's retreat. It was one of three short stories I did in that day or so.

It was for a vampire anthology, but the editor bounced it because it was too "nice" for his anthology. So I was about to toss it in a drawer when Kris forced me to send it to Ed Ferman at F&SF and he bought it. And then it was on the final Nebula ballot that year and in the Nebula Awards Anthology as well. Cool. I made a little more than I expected from it. But my worldview as to value and time was still intact.

Until I got an offer for a radio play for the short story and they hired Kris to write the script. And suddenly that three-hour short story made us another $10,000 and was turned into a really great radio play.

And then the story got picked up for a number of reprint places and optioned once for a movie and I made money on all that. (I still think it would make a great movie.)

And then I ended up reprinting it in Smith's Monthly and also putting it up as a stand-alone for $2.99 in electronic and $4.99 in paper and it sells regularly every year for years now.

Three hours. One simple short story. Twenty-plus years after I wrote the short story, it is still earning me money, more money every year than I expected to get from it at first.

That was the first story that finally got me realizing the long-term value of copyright. I have other short stories now that I have made more money on. "Jukebox Gifts" as an example.

Those magic pies are very popular with the customers of my Magic Bakery.

Maintenance of the Magic Bakery

As I said last chapter, magic pies do not spoil.

But sadly, they can be forgotten. And often are.

Now at the ten-year mark of indie publishing, there are statistics coming out now about the large percentage of stories and books that sell no copies in a year. (This was always the case before, but no one talked about that.)

Think of all the billions of stories and novels now available to readers as a giant ocean. In this new world, the stories that sell are the ones on the surface of the giant ocean of fiction available to readers.

The ones that don't sell are far, far below the surface, down in the dark, impossible to find or sell.

Now when I started into indie publishing, I had over a hundred published traditional novels, over 60 of which were under this name. And everyone thought that I was lucky. Used to make me very angry when someone would say that because I knew the truth. I wasn't lucky. I considered someone starting fresh lucky. I had a massive wall in front of me to climb over.

When you clicked on my name on Amazon back then, all you saw was Star Trek, Men in Black, gaming novels and so on. Books I had been paid for and didn't make another dime on and did not own the magic Pie.

So when I started I put up in fairly quick order over 50 of my own short stories. When you clicked on Amazon, my highest short story was nine pages deep in the list of 50 plus pages of my novels and stories at that point.

Deep is the operative word there. My stories were way, way deep under the surface and impossible to see. Driven to the depths by my success in traditional publishing.

So I knew I only had one choice if I was going to make a career under this name in this modern world. I had to churn the surface of the ocean of books and do a lot of product and basically overwhelm the system. And I did. Not with any promotion tricks, but with simple production.

And it took me years.

Do those early stories I put up now sell? Very few of them, because I haven't spent the time and energy to bring them back to the surface. (I will. All planned, actually.)

They are magic pies, sitting on my shelves in my bakery, but I have turned the lights off on that corner of the bakery. No one can see the pies, so they don't buy any of them.

So maintenance of the inventory of the bakery is critical.

And difficult.

A Sample of Maintenance

Kris has figured out a way to keep the older stories and novels from sitting in a corner with the lights off. For the short stories, she puts up a free short story on her blog every week. She has been doing this for years and years.

The story is still for sale on all the wide markets, of course. Only free on her blog.

And when she puts the story up for free, often WMG puts a new cover on it if it is an older story, we redo the blurb, and so on. In other words, she brushes off the dust from the magic pie and puts a spotlight over the pie and makes it a weekly special in her bakery.

And the story not only is free, but people buy it that week and often the story will keep on selling at a decent pace for some time to come.

Value for Decades

Magic pies can last a very long time if you are smart with contracts and don't let the entire pie leave your bakery. The pies can last for at least 50 or 70 years past your death (depending on your country) and even after that they will still have value.

But they will not have much value if you do not maintain them.

Magic Bakeries are like any other retail store. The inventory must be kept clean, the lights on for customers to see the product, and the door unlocked for anyone to enter from anywhere in the world.

There must also be someone to run the business and keep the bills paid, even after you die.

But more than anything else, the inventory must be moved around at times, displays changed, standard sales techniques used.

And the value of each pie in your bakery can't be determined by either the year you created the pie or the time it took to create. Your customers will not care about any of that.

You, the owner of the Magic Bakery must believe in every pie. And if the lights over a pie start to flicker, change the bulb.

Summary

I'm surprised, but the Magic Bakery, as a metaphor for copyright and the fiction writing business, does not seem to stretch too far in any area. When I started this, I thought it would.

Some basics I hope you got from this book in one metaphor or another.

—Writers need to learn to think like real businesses.

—Writers need to learn to think like retail and wholesale businesses.

—Writers need to learn copyright so they understand the ingredients of each pie they are creating and how the magic works.

—And writers, lastly, need to give value to their own work. Both as it is created, the year after it was created, and a hundred years after it was created.

The ocean full of reading will not be decreasing. So it is up to each writer to keep their stories near the surface and readers and buyers coming into their Magic Bakeries.

Now this book, this magic pie will take its rightful place in my bakery. I hope you enjoyed it as much as I did writing it.

And if you did, I hope you will try another pie. After all, magic pies are not fattening.

EPILOGUE

A Comment Reminded Me of Something

As I said, I did this book in a series of blogs on my website. And there were some great comments along the way. One brought up this last short chapter.

I used to wonder what rights I could sell to my fiction. What exactly those rights were all called. I thought for the longest time there were rules and I just couldn't find the rules or the secret door to go through to discover where those rules were posted.

I think all of us feel that way early on because we don't understand the true nature of copyright when we start writing. In fact, most writers, even though they will spend years writing, don't have a clue what they are trying to sell or license. And won't spend one minute trying to learn it.

Let alone learn the real nature of copyright, the deep down nature of it. That takes time to really understand.

So the truth? There is no magic list of what you can and can't sell in your copyright. Or what the names are of those magical things you slice out of your copyright pie.

And there are certainly no rules.

NONE.

ZERO. ZIP. ZILCH.

It took me some time to realize that as well.

I wanted to know what exactly First Serial Rights meant and First Anthology Rights, or Non-exclusive Anthology Rights and so on and so on, not realizing those are just made-up terms for contracts to help two parties define exactly what is needed.

And the reason those terms are used regularly, if you actually look at the terms, is because they clearly define a way to slice a copyright pie.

In essence, what I am trying to say is this: To describe the piece of your copyright pie you are licensing to another person in a contract, **you can call it anything the two of you agree to that will be clear as to what is being licensed.**

Now I had a comment wishing I had put more "meat" in my *Magic Bakery* book. The person had hoped I would define all that stuff. Even if I had tried, I would be wrong for the very next contract you saw.

How can I define terms, put meat, as the comment said, in an article when the very question shows a lack of knowledge of copyright in contracts?

There is no meat past you learning copyright and understanding that you are free to define the slice of your pie in any way you see fit. **As long as you and the person on the other side of the contract agree to the definition or name you put on it.**

The Magic Bakery was an attempt at helping with some basic understanding of copyright and business in this new world of publishing. I put all the "meat" I could in it and still keep it at a basic level.

As a young writer, not understanding copyright, I would have been disappointed as well that the book didn't give the secret handshake and the location of where all those terms were hidden.

Ahh, well. I knew the danger of trying to do a book on copyright in a world where writers are flat determined to not learn it.

So let me start the list of "meat" for those of you still looking for the sacred scroll of terms locked in that hidden vault in a Chicago basement. Then maybe you will understand the vault really is empty.

Example: Take your most recent magic pie off the shelf and get out a sharp magic knife. Then cut out a very, very thin slice to license and in the contract for that slice you can call that license "First North American Refrigerator Magnet Rights."

You can and should reserve "First English Refrigerator Magnet Rights" in the contract because you never know about those companies in other parts of the world. (A different slice.)

Also hold back all "Refrigerator Magnet Translation Rights." (Yet another slice.)

And make sure you are clear in your terms in your contract that the right does not include "First North American Button Rights." (Yet another slice.)

And make sure you say that all other rights are reserved to the author so nothing leaves your magic pie by accident.

Those are all real rights, folks, and if you can't figure out what they are, just slowly say aloud the name of the slice. The words describe the slice of the pie you are licensing.

It really is that simple.

As I said numbers of times in different chapters, every pie can be sliced into thousands of slices, limited only by your imagination on how to limit a right and your understanding of the basic nature of copyright.

As one reader said, and gave me permission to repeat, there is a simple formula for all of this.

The DJ Formula...

Time position + territory + language + usage = rights

Time Position = First, Second, Third, etc.

Territory = hemisphere, country, state, moon, Mars, etc.

Language = English, French, Spanish, etc.

Usage = anything that displays text, images, such as radio, movies, books, plays, comics, buttons, tea towels, etc.

Use that formula anytime you are trying to figure out how to slice your magic pie. It will do wonders to help you through any confusion you might have.

Hope that helps some with adding "meat" into the book. Magic Meat I suppose.

And finally, the metaphor stretched too far and broke.

NEWSLETTER SIGN-UP

Be the first to know!

Please sign up for the Kristine Kathryn Rusch and Dean Wesley Smith newsletters, and receive exclusive content, keep up with the latest news, releases and so much more—even the occasional giveaway.

So, what are you waiting for?
To sign up for Kristine Kathryn Rusch's newsletter go to kristinekathrynrusch.com.
To sign up for Dean Wesley Smith's newsletter go to deanwesleysmith.com

But wait! There's more. Sign up for the WMG Publishing newsletter, too, and get the latest news and releases from all of the WMG authors and lines, including Kristine Grayson, Kris Nelscott, Dean Wesley Smith, *Fiction River: An Original Anthology Magazine*, *Smith's Monthly*, *Pulphouse Fiction Magazine* and so much more.

To sign up go to wmgpublishing.com.

ABOUT THE AUTHOR

KRISTINE KATHRYN RUSCH

New York Times bestselling author Kristine Kathryn Rusch writes in almost every genre. Generally, she uses her real name (Rusch) for most of her writing. Under that name, she publishes bestselling science fiction and fantasy, award-winning mysteries, acclaimed mainstream fiction, controversial nonfiction, and the occasional romance. Her novels have made bestseller lists around the world and her short fiction has appeared in eighteen best of the year collections. She has won more than twenty-five awards for her fiction, including the Hugo, *Le Prix Imaginales*, the *Asimov's* Readers Choice award, and the *Ellery Queen Mystery Magazine* Readers Choice Award.

Publications from *The Chicago Tribune* to *Booklist* have included her Kris Nelscott mystery novels in their top-ten-best mystery novels of the year. The Nelscott books have received nominations for almost every award in the mystery field, including the best novel Edgar Award, and the Shamus Award.

She writes goofy romance novels as award-winner Kristine Grayson.

She also edits. Beginning with work at the innovative publishing company, Pulphouse, followed by her award-winning tenure at *The Magazine of Fantasy & Science Fiction*, she took fifteen years off before returning to editing with the original anthology series *Fiction River*, published by WMG Publishing. She acts as series editor with her husband, writer Dean Wesley Smith.

To keep up with everything she does, go to kriswrites.com and sign up for her newsletter. To track her many pen names and series, see their individual websites (krisnelscott.com, kristinegrayson.com, retrievalartist.com, divingintothewreck.com, fictionriver.com, pulp-housemagazine.com).

ABOUT THE AUTHOR

DEAN WESLEY SMITH

Considered one of the most prolific writers working in modern fiction, *USA Today* bestselling writer Dean Wesley Smith published almost two hundred novels in forty years, and hundreds and hundreds of short stories across many genres.

At the moment he produces novels in several major series, including the time travel Thunder Mountain novels set in the Old West, the galaxy-spanning Seeders Universe series, the urban fantasy Ghost of a Chance series, a superhero series starring Poker Boy, and a mystery series featuring the retired detectives of the Cold Poker Gang.

His monthly magazine, *Smith's Monthly*, which consists of only his own fiction, premiered in October 2013 and offers readers more than 70,000 words per issue, including a new and original novel every month.

During his career, Dean also wrote a couple dozen *Star Trek* novels, the only two original *Men in Black* novels, Spider-Man and X-Men novels, plus novels set in gaming and television worlds. Writing with his wife Kristine Kathryn Rusch under the name Kathryn Wesley, he wrote the novel for the NBC miniseries The Tenth Kingdom and other books for *Hallmark Hall of Fam*e movies.

He wrote novels under dozens of pen names in the worlds of comic books and movies, including novelizations of almost a dozen films, from *The Final Fantasy* to *Steel* to *Rundown*.

Dean also worked as a fiction editor off and on, starting at Pulphouse Publishing, then at *VB Tech Journal*, then Pocket Books, and now at WMG Publishing, where he and Kristine Kathryn Rusch serve as series editors for the acclaimed *Fiction River* anthology series, which launched in 2013. In 2018, WMG Publishing Inc. launched the first issue of the reincarnated *Pulphouse Fiction Magazine,* with Dean reprising his role as editor.

For more information about Dean's books and ongoing projects, please visit his website at www.deanwesleysmith.com and sign up for his newsletter.

Printed in Great Britain
by Amazon